W9-CUW-982

# WHO DO YOU THINK YOU ARE?

## Discover The Purpose Of Your Life

### By Keith Leon

Relationship Specialist and Co-author of

*The Seven Steps to Successful Relationships*

### Foreword by Jack Canfield

Co-creator of *Chicken Soup for the Soul®* and author of *The Success*

*Principles: How to Get from Where You Are to Where You Want to Be* ™

**Babypie Publishing**
**Los Angeles, CA**

First Edition
10 9 8 7 6 5 4 3 2

Cover Design by Cathi Stevenson
**www.bookcoverexpress.com**

Interior Design by Rudy Milanovich

**Electronic Book ISBN: 0-9753668-0-7**
**Soft Cover Book ISBN: 0-9753668-1-5**

Babypie Publishing
Los Angeles, CA

*There are men and women who make the world better by being the kind of people they are. They have the gift of kindness or courage or loyalty or integrity. It really matters very little whether they are behind the wheel of a truck or running a business or bringing up a family. They teach the truth by living it.*

- James A. Garfield

# – Author's Suggestion –

Each person whom I selected to participate in this book is truly living his or her purpose. The stories and the wisdom being shared by these great teachers are rich, and in my opinion, are something to be considered, pondered and savored. My suggestion to you is that you read two or three stories at a time, then set the book down and really consider what you've read before moving on to the next story.

To support you in this, I have developed a Who Do You Think You Are? Action Guide – a downloadable companion to the book, which will help you to clarify what you learn from each of the stories and put your learning into action in your own life. To get your Action Guide, go to **www.Relationship-Masters.com**

# CONTENTS

# ACKNOWLEDGMENTS

I am grateful to the following people:

Jack Canfield. You are an incredible friend and mentor to me. Your work has touched my life in ways you can't even imagine. This project was built on a foundation of strength and courage developed using your processes and your suggestions. Your first *Chicken Soup* book literally saved my life. It pulled me out of the worst depression period I had ever experienced.

To the personal assistants of each participant, I give you thanks. For some of you it was a juggling act to squeeze in the interview for this book. Thank you on behalf of all the fans, seminar participants, readers or followers of the person you represent for all the work you do.

To the people who allowed me to interview them, and whose answers and stories appear in this book: it was an honor to meet each and every one of you and to ask you these three very important questions. I appreciate you creating time in your busy schedules to meet with me, and for opening your hearts and sharing your life discoveries with our readers. May you continue to live your purpose and inspire us with the wonderful work that you do.

To Yossi Ghinsberg, Mary Beth Cameron, Jimmy Wilson, Ona Brown and Lisa Nichols who allowed me to interview them, and whose stories do not appear in this book due to space constrictions and last minute editing.

Thank you to all my family and friends who supported me with love and encouragement through this project, as well as in my every day life. This world is a better place because you are in it.

Maura, your belief in this project and in me has stayed strong and true from the beginning. Thank you for coming up with the great title and for brainstorming with me until it felt like a "heart project." Thanks for the beautiful poem. You are powerful woman! Your relationship skills are top notch, and your ability to come up with seminar content is mind-boggling.

Timar, you are a Law of Attraction master! Your support and unwavering belief in me and this project has been incredible. I thank you for keeping me on track and focused on the end result. You are a gracious student, a wonderful teacher, and the best son a father could ever wish for.

Mom, you always told me that I could do "anything" I put my

mind to. Thanks for being supportive of my visions, goals and missions in life. Every dollar we *didn't* have was made up for with love. Your ability to continue through life with the hurdles you have had to jump has been inspirational. You are my Number One Fan, and no one can ever take that title away from you. I love you.

Dad and Sandi, your long lasting relationship inspires me. David, Melissa, Heidi, Rene; Aaron and Cheri, thanks for your well wishes and loving support.

The Di Gioia family, your support for Maura and me through the years (and especially the last year) is very much appreciated. Herb and Rita, I never could have dreamed up better in-laws than the two of you. It's a joy to spend time with you and I look forward to being able to do that again real soon. Diana, Dante, and David, thank you for welcoming me to your family with open arms and for "getting me." Mel, Larinda and Maria, thank you for supporting your partners so lovingly, and for being supportive of Maura and me, and the work we do.

To my mentors: Jack Canfield, Rev. Michael Beckwith, Jimmy Wilson, Mark Victor Hansen, David Schirmer, Bob Proctor, Chris and Janet Attwood, Harv Eker, John Gray, Byron Katie, John Kehoe, Phyllis and Colle Davis, Louise Hay, Christine Comaford-Lynch, Stu and Candace Semigran, Ester Hicks, Deepak Chopra, Ben Cuny and Dr. Russ Smith - thank you for being the gift of you, and for sharing your gifts and advice with me.

To the members of my mastermind group: Garry Moses, Joshua Jolley, Kris Carey, Leslie Gebhart and Mark Kliewer - I appreciate being part of such a loving and supportive group of people. Thanks for your support during the One Million Love Notes project and for brainstorming with me until this project immerged.

To my coaching clients: it is a pleasure to watch you realize your dreams, goals and aspirations. Know that the work *you have done* is what has created everything in your life. Thank you for allowing me to be part of your creation process. You rock!

To Mary Beth Cameron, your love and support during this project has been a blessing in my life.

Thanks to Danika Dinsmore and David Ross for editing this book for me. Finally, thanks to all of the assistants and participants in our seminars, workshops and concerts over the past few years. Thanks for sharing your time, talents, love, joy and support with Maura and me.

# FOREWORD

When Keith first told me about this book I knew he was really onto something. Keith is asking the questions we've all asked ourselves at one time or another. I meet tens of thousands of people each year, and one common theme among the people I meet and teach is self-discovery. They all want to know, "Why am I here?" and "What is my purpose?" I believe we can all benefit from asking ourselves these questions, because once we are clear on the answers, we can align all of our goals and activities with our life purpose, and, as a result, achieve a much greater sense of joy and fulfillment in our life.

Keith has spent many years searching for his answers, and even though he has become very clear on why *he's* here, he became captivated by the idea of asking these same questions to a wide variety of people who have had great success in their lives as well as people who are just starting out but who are clearly on a path and know their purpose. As a result of the diverse group of people Keith has interviewed, I know that many of them will speak directly to you and your life's path. They may help you refine your own understanding of what you have thought your purpose to be, or they may help you discover and define your life purpose for the very first time. There is a lot of wisdom in the pages of this book, as well as a lot of practical information for how to more fully understand and embrace your life purpose.

I've known Keith for some time now, and it's clear to me that his purpose is to deeply and positively touch the lives of anyone and everyone he comes into contact with. My first connection to Keith was through his music when he was performing at an event at which I was speaking. His songs inspired and uplifted me and led me to seek out a friendship with him. Over time I have come to learn that in addition to his music, Keith also lives his purpose through his dynamic speaking, training, coaching and writing and, probably most importantly, by being a living demonstration of the keys to relationship success that he teaches with his wife Maura.

I know you will enjoy reading this book as much as I did because it will inspire you to be all that you are capable of and it will provide you with practical tips on how to do that. Having worked with over one million people in workshops, seminars, training and coaching, I have come to know that you do have a specific purpose in this life, and if it hasn't already been revealed to you, this book will help. I'm quite sure that if you read the wisdom being imparted by the inspiring mentors in this book, and you go within and consider their words, you'll be much clearer about how to discover and manifest the purpose of your life.

Jack Canfield, co-creator of *Chicken Soup for the Soul*®
and author of *The Success Principles: How to Get
From Where You Are to Where You Want to Be*™

# INTRODUCTION

The way this book came into existence is a miracle in itself. My wife Maura and I had just experienced the biggest business failure of our lives. Maura chose to take a mourning period and I found myself at a crossroads: do I stay in the muck or move on? I chose to say "NEXT!" and move on as quickly as I could from the "failure" I had experienced.

One day I turned to my wife and said, "Give me the greatest book title I've ever heard, that's all I need is a good book title."

It took her all of a minute and a half. She looked at me and said, "Who Do You Think You Are?"

I was blown away. I thought it *was* the greatest book title I had ever heard. I asked Maura, "What would it be about?"

We brainstormed a bit and came up with an idea or two. We originally thought it would be a book of interviews with people who had gone from rags to riches, a book all about success and how those who are successful think and act.

I contacted one of the teachers from *The Secret* and asked to meet with him. He agreed to meet and we set a date. I then told my wife we had a meeting and we needed to complete our pitch on the book.

"What book?" she asked.

"*Who Do You Think You Are?*" I replied.

"That idea is half-baked," she said.

I responded, "Well then we'd better bake it and quick."

We met with this man, who has now become a mentor of ours, and spent a half-day with him. I am so grateful for that time, as this great teacher put my wife and me on a path of abundance. He helped us realize our self-worth, something we had been missing until then.

It wasn't long before I realized that this mentor wasn't going to have the time to collaborate on the project. In addition, the project didn't have enough "juice" for me the way it was, so, I went to prayer with it. I checked within myself and sat with the title until the purpose of the book came to me! I did what many wise mentors will tell you to do. I went inside for the answer I was searching for.

As I sat in silence waiting for the answer to my question, I remembered back to a time when I was searching for my life's purpose. I had spent many years asking *Who am I? What is my purpose?* I went from church to church, synagogue to mosque, looking for the answers. As a matter of fact, during this search I spent much time wishing I could sit in front of all the people I considered to be successful and clearly living their purpose so that I could ask them the three questions I ask in this book. I found myself thinking about all the people who are still searching for their *life's purpose*, and that's when I came up with the idea for this book.

I realized that I had been surrounding myself with these great teachers, had built relationships with many of them, and that I was now in a position where I could ask these questions for the people who are still searching. I thought about all the people who had seen *The Secret* and had heard the concepts presented perhaps for the first time, and how discovering their purpose may be exactly what they are looking to do.

Once I had the concept for the book in place, and it felt like the right project for the right reasons, I started to make some calls. I kept getting the same response when I asked each person if they would participate. "Yes" was the answer. I started calling it the YES Project, because no matter who I asked, "yes" was the answer. I knew I was really onto something great. I watched this list of great teachers form in front of my eyes, and my excitement grew more and more each day.

So whether you are searching for your purpose for the very first time, or you like rediscovering your purpose over and over again as you go through life, this is the book for you. I have done my best to include a diverse group of people, from all walks of life. I asked them all the same three questions. I have learned so much from the process of creating this book. I learned that I have the ability to pick up the phone and call anyone in this world with whom I want to speak. I learned that when you have the right project, for all the right reasons, the law of attraction will create a life experience even greater than you can imagine. I learned that all the participants have had an event, or series of events, that put him or her on a path to discovery, and it is truly my hope that this book will aid you in your discovery as well.

# ARE YOU HERE TO BE AN ENTREPRENEUR?

# Bob Proctor

*"I didn't believe I could change, but the more he talked to me, the more I believed he believed I could change, and I really believed in his belief in me."*

**Zig Ziglar may be the master motivator, Mark Victor Hansen and Jack Canfield of *Chicken Soup For the Soul*, the master storytellers; Anthony Robbins may be the guru of personal development, but Bob Proctor is the master thinker. When it comes to systematizing life, no one else can touch him. He is simply the best.**

**Bob Proctor is a direct link to the modern science of success stretching back to Andrew Carnegie the great financier and philanthropist. Carnegie's secrets inspired and enthused Napoleon Hill, whose book *Think and Grow Rich* in turn inspired a whole genre of success-philosophy books that now take up large sections of modern bookstores. Napoleon Hill, in turn passed the baton onto Earl Nightingale, who has since placed it in Bob Proctor's capable hands.**

**Proctor carries the message of these great teachers a step higher and explains in terms understood by tots and tycoons alike how a person goes about recognizing their potential and how to apply this effort in setting and achieving life goals. Featured in the blockbuster hit, *The Secret*, his extraordinary teaching ability has won him acclaim around the globe and has carried the Canadian-born personal development guru to the far reaches of the earth teaching people how to be more, do more and have more.**

**Find out more about Bob at: www.BobProctor.com**

## Who do you think you are?

Who am I? Well, that has changed over the years. It evolves because of awareness. I now see that we are God's highest form of creation. We're created in His image and we're here to do His work. Since God's the Creator and gave us creative faculties we should be creating, doing good work, always beyond what we're doing.

Jane Willhite, who runs PSI Seminars is a good friend of mine, and a number of years ago I went up to her ranch with Mark Meyerdirk and John Assaraf and we spent three days there. That's where I re-evaluated my purpose and my vision and I've let it guide me since then. The more I read 'My Purpose' and the more I look at it, the more I see wisdom in it. My purpose is to live and work in a prosperous environment that encourages productivity so that I may improve the service I render to my family, my company, my community, my nation and ultimately the world. My vision is to build a global organization dedicated to improving the quality of life worldwide. We create products and services at a profit, which is in harmony with the law of compensation. These products and services are created and marketed with like-minded people who share in our purpose.

Many years ago Karl Menninger said, 'environment's more important than heredity.' If we live and work in a prosperous environment that encourages productivity, that's going to stimulate our creative faculties and encourage us to keep improving on what we're doing. I believe that spirit is always for expansion and fuller expression, never for disintegration, and God operates by law and the laws are God's modus operandi. The more we understand the laws the better off we're going to be at keeping our life in harmony with those laws. So that's my stated purpose and I believe I'm on the right track because my results would indicate that.

I'm seventy-three and I've got as much energy as most people at twenty-three. I have attracted a phenomenal team of people in our company and I love what I do. I have a strong focus on money because I see it as an incredible creative instrument. I think money's used for two things. It's to help you be comfortable, and the more comfortable you are the more creative you can be. Beyond that, it's used to extend the service that you render beyond your own presence. Whatever I earn I invest back in what I do. I don't invest in real estate, stocks, bonds or anything like that. I'm not interested in creating great wealth, I'm interested in providing great service. What I earn goes back into the business and to what I do.

**What events or series of events lead to your discovery?**

Oddly enough, the first person who "reached me" asked me the same question as the one above: Who are you? I looked at him like he had fallen out of a tree and I said, "What do you mean, who am I? I'm Bob."

"You're not Bob," he said.

"Really, well who am I then?"

"Bob and Proctor are just two words," he said. "That's your name, it's not you."

I pointed to my body, "Well, okay, this is me."

"No, that's not you," he said. "That's your body. You've never heard anybody phone into work and say, 'Body's not coming in today; it's sick.' "

He really provoked me to think and it was possibly the first time in my life I really did think. He changed my life.

His name was Ray Stanford and he was a very ordinary guy. He's gone now. When I met him, he was moving houses...literally, he'd put them up on jacks and move them. He obviously saw something in me that I couldn't see in myself. He got me to sit down and really look at my results.

He put an 'R' on a sheet of paper and he said, "That represents results." He put two 'Hs' and a 'W' beside it and said, "That's happiness, health and wealth." Then he asked me if I thought he was a happy guy.

I said, "Yeah." I hadn't known him a long time, but he seemed pretty happy to me.

"Have you ever seen me when I was sick?"

"Uh, no."

"Have you ever seen me when I was broke?"

The guy always had money on him, so I said, "No."

"Well," he said, "you've got to be one of the most miserable people I've ever met. You're always broke, you're always complaining of a headache or backache or something. Why don't you change?"

I was earning $4,000 a year at the time and I owed $6,000. I could never see myself getting out of debt. I thought the only way to earn money was on my job. I was working at the fire department in a suburb of Toronto and I was stuck in a rut. I didn't believe I could change, but he did. The more he talked to me, the more I believed he believed I could change, and I really believed in his belief in me. He got me to read *Think and Grow Rich* and that's when my whole world started to change. That led me to Earl Nightingale's condensed narration of it and my income went up to $150,000 a year, then $175,000, then it went over a million.

I couldn't figure out what was happening. I was doing the right things but I didn't know what I was doing. I wasn't satisfied with the fact I had changed. I wanted to know why. According to my understanding, what was happening to me shouldn't have happened. I hadn't gone to school and I had no business experience. I realized that a lot of the things I'd been told weren't true. So I just kept studying and I've never stopped. That was in 1961. That was what led me to where I am today, studying the mind, the laws of the universe, and paradigms.

**If you could give advice to those who are still searching for their purpose in life, what would it be?**

I would tell them to do what I did. I've always had a coach or a mentor and it was always a person who had accomplished what I wanted to accomplish. I went to visit Earl Nightingale because I was so hooked on his stuff. I was living in Toronto and he was in Chicago. I scheduled a meeting with him for an hour and when I was leaving I asked him, "What's the real secret behind everything?"

He just looked at me and said, "You should find out what you love to do and then dedicate your life to it. The problem with most people is they never figure that out."

I got really excited because I knew what I wanted to do; I wanted to do what Earl was doing. I made up my mind when I left his office that that's what I would do. I ultimately ended up in an office right beside him because I wanted to work with him; then I got the benefit of working with his partner Lloyd Conant, too.

I've always had a tremendous coach or mentor. And because of Ray Stanford, I always did exactly what they told me whether I agreed with it or not. I would do it until I found out they were lying or it wouldn't work, but they never lied and it always worked. I realized that our paradigms are what mess us up. Our paradigms control our logic; they color our perception.

If you're getting advice from someone who has demonstrated, by results, that they've done what you want to do, even though the advice may seem illogical to you, you'll probably get to where you want to go.

I believe people should study a little bit every day. It should become habitual, like brushing your teeth, combing your hair, having a shower or getting dressed. Study the mind, the laws of the universe and paradigms. There's enough information on those subjects to keep a person studying forever. I've been doing that for going on fifty years and if I live for another fifty, I'll continue to do it. The rewards have been nothing short of amazing.

# Stewart Emery

*"I'm with Shakespeare, things are neither good nor bad but thinking makes them so."*

A wonderful storyteller with a great sense of humor, Stewart has appeared as a featured guest on television and radio talk shows (including the BBC and co–hosting a TV talk show about human sexuality in Los Angeles in the mid–70s). He has conducted coaching interviews with more than 12,000 people in the last three decades.

Through leading workshops and seminars, writing books, delivering keynotes, and making radio and television appearances, Stewart Emery has touched the lives of millions of people. He is also co-author of the international bestseller *Success Built to Last.*

Stewart lives in the San Francisco Bay area and served as the first CEO of *EST.* In 1975 Stewart Emery co–founded Actualizations, an international learning and development organization. In the late 70's he was selected by the national media as one of the ten most influential people in the Human Potential Movement.

Stewart Emery is Co–Founder (with Joan Emery) and President of Belvedere Consultants, a boutique–consulting firm located in the San Francisco Bay Area. Their passion is to support individuals and organizations turning talent into performance and enduring success. Core competencies include Cultural and Organizational Change Initiatives, Organizational Culture Assessments and 360 Feedback Initiatives, Executive Team Development, Leadership and Management Development, and Executive Coaching.

Find out more about Stewart Emery at: www.stewartemery.com

## Who do you think you are?

I'm not a big fan of these kinds of questions. I'm the kind of guy who would write a book titled: *If You Think You Know Who You Are - Buy This Book and Discover You're Somebody Else.* I don't ask myself this question. I've been meditating now for over 30 years and by persuasion, I am probably a Taoist or a Zen practitioner. I don't ask these kinds of questions and expect unpretentious answers. From what I've learned in our conversations with some of the world's most enduringly successful people, from Nobel Prize Laureates to billionaires, poets and artists, former US presidents and heads of state, together with people many of us have never heard of - people who are changing the world for the better - they don't ask themselves questions like this either.

If you ask them what they think it's all about, they've pretty much come to the conclusion that as you mature emotionally and mentally, you move from self-obsession and the expectation that life should serve you, to, as Senator John McCain told us, "being committed to a cause greater than oneself" and the realization that at the end of the day we are here to serve life.

**What events or series of events led to your discovery?**

The short story is that I was born to artist parents of very modest means. My father left after I was conceived and went off to serve in the Second World War. He was wounded and came back and passed away. Our home in the Blue Mountains of Australia was an isolated cabin constructed of gasoline cans filled with clay topped with a tin roof and basically without indoor plumbing. My father used to go there to paint watercolor landscapes. That's where I lived for the first 12 years of my life. Needless to say, it was pretty unpretentious.

I studied philosophy, psychology and economics at the University of Sydney. I taught design at the University of South Wales School of Architecture and along with a couple of very talented friends ran Honi Soit, the student newspaper of the University of Sydney.

I went from there to become highly successful in Australia as an advertising photographer and cinematographer and ultimately one of the creative directors of one of the largest ad agencies in the world. I was accountable for the look and feel of their television advertising and bringing it to creative acclaim. I woke up one day and realized I had solved the problem of being poor and had enough stuff to start my own world, but it hadn't made much difference as to how I felt on the inside. I still felt like the lonely little kid growing up in the Blue Mountains.

I had gotten to be pretty famous in a relatively small fishpond. Then one day I saw an issue of *Look Magazine,* edited by George Leonard, devoted to what was going on in California in the late 60s. By way of back story, in a meeting with Michael Murphy, (one of the cofounders of the Esalen Institute) Michael asked George what they should call this "happening" and George Leonard suggested that they could call it the "Human Potential Movement." The name stuck and the rest, as they say, is history.

I was, coincidentally at about the same time, leading what they call "T Groups" in Australia. I had a US-based client who invited me to the United States to do some work for them in San Francisco Bay Area. I came in 1971 for a couple of weeks and I'm still here. I kind of collided with what was happening in this human potential movement and ran into a brilliant fellow called Werner Erhard. We conducted a T group for Werner and his staff, which marked the beginning of EST. Many of the core ideas from the EST Training have become incorporated into a vast body of ongoing work many of us are engaged in today. These ideas include the work around belief systems, taking personal responsibility for the experience of our lives and creating outcomes that matter to us.

I'm a passionately curious man and the whole process of the emergence of human potential engaged my curiosity and awakened my passion. In Australia I had started reading from the works of Jiddu Krishnamurti, especially a little book called *Think On These Things*. San Francisco was where it was happening in those days and once I arrived I became swept away by the work. Today I'm still passionately curious about all that it means to be a human being. I am deeply moved when in the presence of human greatness and by our continuing work in support of human excellence. I think there's a lot of superficiality around the edges of "The Movement" these days, which I don't care for. I believe one has to go deep and a lot of people don't go deep, and that's a pity.

The majority of the wonderful woman and men you will meet in the pages of *Success Built To Last* described their lives as a serendipitous journey filled with unexpected wonders and riches beyond their early dreams. My life has been, and continues to be, like this. I am deeply grateful.

**If you could give advice to those who are still searching for their purpose in life, what would it be?**

I believe this is a very personal question. Purpose is an intensely personal choice. The flip answer is "it's whatever you want it to be." I am not an advocate of the theory that as part of the Grand Design for the Universe there's some unique purpose for each of us. I take the point of view, shared by a lot of extraordinarily accomplished people, that what we call meaning is a precious resource that lives within us that we can choose to invest in life—or not. I'm with Shakespeare, "things are neither good nor bad but thinking makes them so." This idea put into practice becomes an expression of personal accountability at the highest level.

We could re-phrase this to say, "nothing has meaning other than the meaning we give it." We do not live in the world; we live in our story about the world. We are the source responsible for the meaning our story has for us. If we change the meaning we change our life. That's one of the essential messages that we were giving to people in the EST Training and the Actualizations Workshop. Nothing has happened in the last thirty-five years that leads me to see this differently. How we invest our resource of meaning shapes our life and determines the quality of our experience and whether we are successful.

I've observed that people who are committed to a cause bigger than themselves, who are engaged in serving life rather than attempting to manipulate life into serving them, have richer, more satisfying, more enduringly successful lives. I don't assign spiritual causality to this reality. As a metaphor we could delve into the science of genetics and make a pretty good argument that genes are organized to choose cooperation over competition at any price because it's in the best interests of the gene's ability to do what genes do, which is replicate. So, what we have here is a kind of cooperative altruism at work in service of evolution. Whether this is cosmic design or serendipity, I do not know. For me, if it is serendipity, it is even more awe inspiring.

You have posed questions worthy of deep conversation that do not lend themselves to trivial answers. Organizations need to have a purpose, and I believe people need to become aware of what it is they are deeply passionate about, what it is they love to do—and then get really good at it. Our friends Janet and Chris Atwood have written a terrific book titled *The Passion Test*. I recommend that you to take the Passion Test for yourself. We noticed in *Success Built To Last* that successful people are unwilling to settle in life for doing something that they are not passionate about or don't love to do. And they get really good at doing what matters to them. Most people never learn how to become really good at anything—let alone something they love and that matters to them.

Enduringly successful people get really clear about what they are willing to invest meaning in, what matters to them, what they love to do, and then they develop a deliberate practice to get really good at it, and they go deep. They recruit people to their dream and they build organizations and networks capable of making a difference. Theirs is a chosen purpose. Is it also a pre-ordained purpose? Very few of the successful people I talk to see it this way. Meaning and purpose are things that they mindfully choose. They live with integrity to meaning. That is to say they manage their thoughts and actions in service of this meaning and their chosen purpose. In this way they live the fully accountable life.

May you choose wisely!

# Dave Anderson

*"You know, there's a saying that goes,*
*'If you want to make God laugh, tell him your plan.'"*

Dave Anderson is an enrolled member of the Chippewa and Choctaw tribes and is the founder of *Famous Dave's of America*, recognized as one of the "Hottest Restaurant Concepts" in America by *Nation's Restaurant News*. Dave's award-winning restaurants are remarkably unique and he is widely recognized for his extraordinary palate, devotion to detail, and dedication to constant improvement.

In Dave's own life, he has experienced frustration and bankruptcy as well as tremendous success. He firmly believes God has had His hand over his life. Dave also believes that if it weren't for other people giving him second chances, he would not be where he is today, having helped found three publicly traded companies on Wall Street and creating over 18,000 new jobs. He has been awarded a Bush Leadership Fellowship, received a Master's degree from Harvard University (without having an undergraduate degree), and been recognized as "Emerging Entrepreneur of the Year" (in Minnesota and the Dakotas) by Ernst & Young, NASDAQ and *USA Today*.

Today, Dave devotes himself to making a difference in his community and in the lives of others less fortunate. As an avid public speaker, he shares his optimism and inspiration with youth groups and community organizations. Oprah Winfrey's Angel Network recently recognized Dave's leadership development work with Native American youth. In 2004, President Bush appointed Dave as the ninth Assistant Secretary for Indian Affairs, The U.S. Department of Interior. This position required a full Senate confirmation and Dave was responsible for a $2 Billion budget and over 10,000 employees.

Dave is also the author of the best selling books *Famous Dave's Life Skills For Success, The Ultimate Manual for Achieving Your Very Best* , Famous Dave's Backroads and Sidestreets, an award winning cookbook that was recognized as "Best Barbeque and Grill Cookbook in America!" by the National Barbeque Association .

Dave's next big idea is a 135 Million Dollar Water Resort called KeyLime Cove, located just north of Chicago. "We believe it's going to revolutionize the way Americans vacation!"

Find out more by visiting www.davidwanderson.com

**Who do you think you are?**

I believe that my higher purpose in life is to make a positive difference in the lives of others.

**What event or series of events led to your discovery?**

In the beginning I didn't really understand that my life had a higher purpose. I think I was like a lot of people. I was struggling to make my way through life, and I lived life for Dave Anderson. I wanted to know how I could get more, how I could satisfy myself. I spent most of my earlier years in that pursuit. I would work hard and I'd get so far, then I'd hit a brick wall and I'd crash and burn. Like most Type A personalities, I'd pick myself up again, get back in the game, work hard, bust my butt, and then hit a brick wall and crash and burn all over again.

I think when someone is seeking self-gratification it's easy to get messed up in substance abuse and drinking. At least it was for me. There are many different ways that people use to feel happy. Maybe they're looking for that magical moment (the high you experience the first time you use). When you experience that first high, you really feel like you've found something. But then like all addictive substances, the next time you go after it, it doesn't quite get you so high. So you drink a little bit more, or you use a little bit more drugs, and you're in that constant search for that gratification, that incredible high, that elusive magical moment, unachievable after the first time experience.

When I reached this point, I started to spiral downward. In that moment of personal failure, I did like a lot of people do; I blamed the economy and I blamed others. I always had an excuse for why I just couldn't get over the hump or why I could never attain my dreams. I was doing it to myself, but I would blame everyone and everything else instead of taking responsibility for my own actions. I didn't understand that it *wasn't* just about Dave Anderson; there were others around me who suffered as a result of my behavior.

Then my wife put me into treatment. For the first couple of weeks I sat around saying, "I can't believe my wife would do something like this to me." Today I've learned that recovery is a gift. It's the gift of healing. When I had been in recovery for about two weeks, contemplating where I had been, I really started to understand that I was my own worst enemy! I found myself on my knees at the side of my bed praying to God, the Holy Spirit, Jesus…I mean I was praying to everybody, and I said, "God I'm tired of being sick and tired, and I'm tired of doing things Dave Anderson's way. It seems like everything that I try just doesn't work. I'm done doing things my way and I want to be forgiven, I want to be cleansed." It was at that moment I discovered the power of the word "surrender." I found that being able to surrender your pride and ego is not a weakness. I think that when you can ask for help and surrender to something greater, it's really a sign of wisdom and strength.

I think a lot of people are still trying to do their plan. You know, there's a saying that goes, *if you want to make God laugh, tell him your plan.* I was so intent on doing it my way and for my reasons that I never understood the spiritual side to all of it. I hadn't realized that there's a reason why we've been given talents or been blessed with certain gifts. Sometimes we get so full of ourselves that we forget to notice the real reason why we've been put on this earth, and that's for a higher purpose. I never understood that until the moment I surrendered my life and gave it over to an almighty power that I know as God. When I got off the floor that day, I felt like the weight of the world had been lifted from my shoulders. I felt free. I felt enlightened. I felt empowered. And from that moment on I started living my life in servitude. I started to read and understand the Bible. The Bible says that *the meek shall inherit the earth* and it talks about humbleness. Jesus was always humble. I started to understand that I was like Mother Teresa or Gandhi. I was a servant of other people, and I could give the best I had to the greatest number of people, and do it without any expectation other than just being able to give to other people.

Once I made this decision, I didn't have to worry about where success came from. All the doors that were so difficult to open before started springing open. It's amazing what I accomplished once I understood that it isn't all about Dave Anderson. Since I've been living a life of giving the best that I have to other people, I've really discovered what my purpose in life is all about.

**If you could give advice to those who are still searching for their purpose in life, what would it be?**

I think almost all successful people recognize that they are spiritual beings. We can go to school to learn disciplines, whether it's art, music or a profession like being an attorney. Those are all technical disciplines which you will become proficient at if you really study. But, the people who really succeed in touching many lives are the ones who understand that they have a spiritual side. Those who are unafraid to recognize this are able to connect to God's great universe, all of its resources, and the unbelievable abundance that is out there. When you live in the realm of only what you can do, well there's only so much you can do as a human being. Once you surrender to a higher power, you're then able to connect with it.

It says in the Bible that we are made in the image and likeness of God; think about that. There is a lot in that incredible statement. God is infinite and we are as well. There may be some limitations to the human side of us, but there is no limit to our creativity. Look at all the scientific breakthroughs with computer technology, bio-technology and nanotechnology. Whenever we reach a philosophical breakthrough, a scientific breakthrough or a technological breakthrough, it opens up new horizons and we keep discovering just how unlimited our creativity is.

I'm a firm believer that if you can get rid of blame, live a life of being forgiven, and live a life of spirituality, when you're not in judgment of others or yourself, that's when you can start connecting with who you really are and make a significant difference in the lives of others.

I would also say that people should just hang on, not give up, and face their problems head on. A lot of people spend their lives running away from problems, cursing God and saying, "What's all this business about living a life full of abundance? All I seem to be getting is adversity and crisis. Why is it that I have to deal with this crushing problem right now that's ruining my life?" And God looks down and says, "Hey, you wanted abundance and abundance only comes through adversity, problems and crises." Once you get through the problem you're going to be wiser and you're going to be stronger. That's when people will start saying we've got to go get Dave, because he's good at handling problems. Every time we run from problems, the good Lord above is saying, "Hey, where are you going? You wanted abundance yet you keep running away from all the problems I send your way. Don't you realize these problems are your opportunities? And this last problem...it's a real doozy; I worked really hard on that one because I wanted to give you your best opportunity to show the world what you're made of!"

When we quit running away from problems, that's when our creativity comes bubbling forth. When you have to work with your mind and your talents to get through the problems, people start to notice your abilities and start to recognize all the good that you've accomplished. That's when people with ideas and resources and their own abundance come to you and say, "Hey, you have a real talent for getting through the tough times, and you always turn problems around. I could sure use someone like you on my team."

# Bill Bartmann

*"The only voice you should listen to is the voice that comes from within."*

America loves a "rags to riches" – an "underdog" – an "against all odds come-back" - a "survivor!" Bill has been a millionaire three times, bankrupt twice, and a billionaire once.

Bill is the ultimate underdog/survivor/achiever overcoming personal circumstances and tragedy to rise to the top of corporate America. Homeless at age fourteen, a member of a street gang and a high-school dropout – he took control of his life by taking the GED exam and putting himself through college and law school.

Bill and his wife Kathy have individually graced the covers of national business magazines, Kathy on the cover of *Forbes*, and Bill on the cover of *Inc.* They were listed individually in the *Forbes* 400 wealthiest people in America. One national magazine ranked them number 25.

In 1998, tragedy struck when Bill's former business partner committed fraud and sent the company into bankruptcy. Although Bill's former business partner told the prosecutors that he had acted without Bill's knowledge, admitted his guilt and was sent to prison – in the post Enron environment, U.S. Attorney General, John Ashcroft, indicted Bill on 57 felony counts relating to Bill's partner's activities. Five years later, after a 2½ month long trial where the Government called 53 witnesses and produced over 1,000 exhibits, Bill rested his case without calling a single witness or producing a single exhibit. The jury unanimously acquitted Bill on all counts.

Ironically, seventeen months after his acquittal and six and a half years after his company was liquidated, the Federal Bankruptcy Trustee issued his report, which publicly acknowledged for the first time, "CFS was not a fraud."

This experience would have embittered most people, but not them. Bill and Kathy now travel the country, sharing their stories of how they created their successes and how they dealt with their challenges. It is their life's goal to do for "failure" what Betty Ford did for alcoholism and Susan Komen did for breast cancer.

Find out more about Bill at: www.BillBartmann.com

## Who do you think you are?

That's a great question, and if you had asked me at any other point in my life I probably would have given you a different answer. It's like when we pick our major in college. We decide in our freshman year what we think we want to be when we grow up, and it almost always changes by the time we become a sophomore. All those things I thought I was during the early part of my life have changed. And last year at age fifty-seven, I finally figured out who I really am, and what I'm really supposed to be doing here on earth.

I have led a very unique life, with some cataclysmic failures and some wonderful successes. It's pretty rare to have both of those in the same individual, and because I posses both, I think that is now my job. I'm supposed to talk to as many people as I can about both my successes and my failures, and I am very open about them both. Quite frankly, I think there is more to be learned from our failures than there is from our successes. So, who I think I am is a spokesman for people who have failed in their lives and who want to learn how to overcome their failures.

## What event or series of events led to your discovery?

It is so much a process of overcoming adversity in life; it's the adversities that introduce us to ourselves. Likewise, it was an adversity that introduced me to the new me, or the "who I think I am now." I had a business partner who committed a crime. The crime tanked my company, put the company into bankruptcy, caused 3,900 people to lose their jobs, caused my wife and I to lose a three-and-a-half billion-dollar fortune, and ultimately got me indicted on fifty-seven felony counts. During all of this adversity I was able to get myself acquitted of all fifty-seven of those counts, but in the process I learned a lot about myself and about the world. It was that adversity that set me on the path I am on now.

## If you could give advice to those who are still searching for their purpose in life, what would it be?

The best advice I can give anybody, and I give it as often as I can whether I'm talking to a high school group (I do over a hundred high school speeches a year) or if I'm talking to adults (I will speak to over 300,000 adults this year), is that the only voice they should listen to is the voice that comes from within. We are so eager and willing to listen to outsiders.

We listen to others when they tell us that we're good enough or we're not good enough, or not smart enough, or we can't do this, we can't do that. The only person who is really qualified to opine on our strengths, our weaknesses, our credibility, and our capabilities is ourselves.

Sure we should be honest with ourselves; we should admit and accept that which we didn't do well and right, or the mistakes that we have made in our life. But at the same time we should be equally honest about all the things we have done well and right. We should be able to embrace and accept and appreciate all the times we didn't screw up, all the times we didn't get it wrong, all the times we didn't make a mess of something, and put them on the same level – on the same scale – as we put our screw ups. And if we were to do that, if people were to do this one simple little drill, just compare their successes against their failures (and a success is any time that you didn't fail) they would see that they have succeeded a hundred times more than they have ever failed. This would give them the strength to overcome whatever adversity they're facing presently.

I think we should keep it simple. There's no need for me to give you the eighty-four steps to success, because honestly there aren't eighty-four steps. There's just learning how to live with yourself, learning how to be yourself, learning how to be happy being who you are, what you are, the way you are right now. It's so important to enjoy the moment. Yes, we can strive for more and be on a path to have more, but we should never be in "deferred gratification" mode where we have the mentality of "well I'm going to be happy later if I work real hard now." No! Let's be happy now.

It doesn't matter which God you believe in. I'm very spiritual and I have a strong sense of personal belief, but I try really hard not to put my beliefs on anybody else because I don't think that's my job. I don't think that's what I'm here to do. No matter which God you believe in, that God believes in YOU, and wants you to be whatever you can be. He also wants you to be happy being what it is he's already made you.

# Gerry Robert

*"Find a mentor and you do what they say."*

Gerry Robert brought himself out of poverty to earning over $1 Million in a single year. Now he's a mentor to some of the highest income earners in numerous industries. He cares about people and is great at what he does. He is the father of three boys and married for over 20 years to Anne, his teenage sweetheart. He is also a former minister.

He is a best-selling author, columnist, speaker and consultant operating throughout North America and Asia. Gerry has spoken to over 1 Million people from around the world. People from IBM, Shell, Air Canada, MacDonald's, Royal Lepage, The Royal Bank of Canada, Nesbitt-Thompson, Scotia Bank, GM, Canada Dry, John Deere, CIBC, Prudential, ReMax, Malaysia Airlines, John Hancock, Bank of Montreal, Trimark, Hewlett Packard, Boeing, Texas Instruments have attended Gerry's power-packed seminars. Last year, he traveled over 250,000 air miles giving lectures and seminars.

He has written several best selling books Including *Conquering Life's Obstacles*, *The Magic of Real Estate* and *The Tale of Two Websites: A Conversation About Boosting Sales On The Internet*, and *The Millionaire Mindset: How Ordinary People Can Create Extraordinary Income*.

His books are endorsed by Dr. Norman Vincent Peale (*Power of Positive Thinking*), Ken Blanchard (*One Minute Manager*), Zig Ziglar (*See You at the Top*), Robert Schuller (*Possibility Thinking*), Mark Victor Hansen (*Chicken Soup for the Soul*) and others. He is a regular columnist for numerous prestigious publications and newspaper the world over. His weekly column provides practical, humorous and innovative ideas on sales and marketing.

His ideas are not conventional. He is provocative and innovative. He gives practical ideas and strategies to build almost any business. He is not part of the "motivational hype" crowd many people associate him with, given his line of work.

He can be reached in Toronto at 1-(800) 473-7134 or by e-mail: gerry@gerryrobert.com

# Who do you think you are? What is the purpose of your life?

I am an expression of who God is. I am part and parcel of what makes up who God is. I'm a reflection of who God is.

When I discovered the purpose for my life, I discovered it in about two minutes at a seminar that literally changed the course of my life forever. Bob Proctor's mentor, Leland Val Vandewall asked us to think for a second, and without giving much more thought than that, simply write the first thing that came to mind when we asked the question, why am I here? What is my purpose? Without thinking, I wrote the following: "My purpose is to demonstrate by my life and my results what a life of faith is, teach that to the world in order to lift their spirits closer to God."

That came out instantly and it was very clear to me that it was what I'm here to do. I want to demonstrate by my life and my results, not my talk, not my wishes, but by my results. I think that results are a demonstration of what's really going on. I want to demonstrate by how I live with life, how I interact with life. I want to demonstrate what a life of faith is. I am not necessarily talking about religious faith, although that is an important part of my life.

The good book says that faith is the evidence of things unseen and the certainty of things hoped for. In my case, it's the certainty of what I hope for. I want to teach people to get their eyes off of their past, and get their eyes off the limitation, and get their eyes on what it is they hope for and have them be certain that it will materialize in physical form in their lives. Faith is seeing things that other people can't see. Faith gives you hope. Faith keeps your eyes on God. Faith keeps you moving.

The next part of that is to teach it to the world. I have been gifted with the ability to teach, and it is important to me to have a global view of teaching the world in order to lift people's spirits closer to God. I think what people need more than money, more than relationships, more than anything, is an intimate connection with the Almighty. If I can participate by lifting people a little bit closer to God, then my purpose in life is being fulfilled.

## What event or series of events led to your discovery?

There have been two major events that took the form of mentorships that transformed my life. My first mentor was a man named Norm

Sharkey, who I met on September 6, 1977. That marked a significant change in my life, because for the first time ever, I opened myself up to the spiritual dimension of life. I was going down the wrong road. I was like a freight train on the tracks of destruction. I met Norm Sharkey, and he got me in touch with God for the first time. He showed me that I could have a personal relationship with God and he introduced me to Jesus and other teachers who have been instrumental in changing the direction of my life. He showed me how to give love and how to receive love. It happened in such a profound way that it completely altered the course of my life.

Then in 1988, I met Bob Proctor. Bob Proctor has become my financial mentor; at least that's what I call him. He's really my internal mentor. He showed me that I could earn in a month what I used to earn in a year. I started making over $1 million a year. In order for that kind of result, something major has to happen inside of you, and that's what Bob's main effect on me was. He showed me how to really think about what was going on in my life and he changed my understanding of who I am and how I tick. We're never taught about how people think. We're never taught about why people do certain things and don't do certain things. And why people don't do the things that they want to. He showed me how to apply that.

I started off by applying this to the earning of money, and I quickly found out that it's just a symptom, a game, or a measuring stick, to understanding more about me and what causes most people in the world to operate on autopilot without thinking. Bob has had a major effect on my life for the past 21 years. And I'm just so grateful that he's been part of my life.

## If you could give advice to those who are still searching for their purpose in life, what would it be?

I was asked that question recently on an Australian radio show. They said in 30 words or less, tell us how a person could achieve what they want to achieve in their life. I told them it wouldn't take me 30 words it would only take me eight words. Those eight words are: *find a mentor, and do what they say.* It's that simple. Find somebody who has the results that you want. Don't ask broke people how to get rich. Don't ask sick people how to get healthy. Don't ask divorced people how to have strong relationships. Find somebody who has the results that you want and do what they say, and the emphasis is on the word *do.*

Now some of us are seminar junkies and go to seminar after seminar after seminar after seminar, and I'm here to tell you that some of you should stop going to seminars. You should start doing the seminar. What I mean by that is people need to start putting into practice what they already know. Most of us know what to do to have more love. Most of us know what to do to have the money. Most of us know what to do to have better physical bodies. The question is why don't people do it?

Again, find a mentor and do what they say. It's not a matter of gathering more information. There are some people who have gone to so many seminars that they can finish the sentence of the speaker on stage because they know the material that well. My mentor told me that you know nothing until you make a permanent change in your behavior. It's behavior, not gathering more information, it's doing what you're mentor says. So you've got to study and learn and get close to them. You've got to invest; be near them and let them influence you. That's what I've found is the easiest and fastest way to grow in any area of your life. Find a person who lives the life you want and do what they say. Follow their advice.

I was in Vancouver yesterday with my first mentor, Norman Sharkey, who really taught me about love and about God. And just watching him interact with people caused me to be more loving. Proximity is good. Read their books, do what they say, go to their events, learn from them - not to simply gather information, but to implement what they say into your life.

# Christine Comaford-Lynch

*"It's important to invest the time to find out who you are. The path doesn't just make itself clear without some searching."*

Christine has led many lives: teenage lingerie model, celibate Buddhist monk, Microsoft engineer, geisha trainee, entrepreneur, and venture capitalist. Her triumphs and disasters have been revealed in her New York Times bestselling business book: *Rules for Renegades: How To Make More Money, Rock Your Career, and Revel in Your Individuality* (see www.RulesForRenegades.com).

Christine is CEO of Mighty Ventures, a business accelerator which helps both startups and established companies to launch and gain traction at rapid speed. She has built and sold 5 of her own businesses with an average 700% return on investment, served as a board director or in-the-trenches advisor to 36 startups, and has invested in over 200 startups (including Google) as a venture capitalist or angel investor. Christine has consulted to the White House (Clinton and Bush), 700 of the Fortune 1000, and hundreds of small businesses. She has repeatedly identified and championed key trends and technologies years before market acceptance. Christine's popular column on www.BusinessWeek.com/SmallBiz launched January 2007.

Christine has appeared on CNN, MSNBC, CNBC, PBS, and CNET and is frequently quoted in the business, technology and general press at large. Stanford Graduate School of Business has done two case studies on her and PBS has featured her in three specials (*Triumph of the Nerds, Nerds 2.0.1,* and *Nerd TV*). CNET has broadcast two specials covering her unconventional rise to success as a woman with neither a high school diploma nor college degree. Christine believes we can do well and do good, using business as a path for personal development, wealth creation, and philanthropy.

Find out more about Christine at: www.mightyventures.com

# Who do you think you are?

Who I am is a person who is very committed to helping people realize their full potential in both their business life and their personal life. I am very service-oriented and helping people to grow, stretch, and learn is very important to me. My personal growth is a high priority.

## What event or series of events led to your discovery?

I've seen a lot of pain and loss in my life. By age seven, I had lost both of my favorite friends. By age thirteen, I was studying different religions, going with friends to their churches, reading Buddhist and other self-discovery texts. It just happened naturally. I was drawn to learning why I was here, what it all meant, and what my place in the universe was.

At age fifteen, I went to EST (Erhard Seminars Training). What struck me as life-altering was the message that we are 100% responsible for our own lives. It was exhilarating! It was all up to me; I could shape my life however I wanted! WOW!

I've had a wild ride since then, trying on different lives. I was a celibate Buddhist monk for 7 years because that's how I thought I could help reduce human suffering. But after a while it became clear that the path for me was to dive into the middle of human existence, roll around in it, and reduce suffering from that vantage point—from helping others to help themselves. So I broke my vows, got a burger and a boyfriend, and continued on my quest.

My volunteer work in hospice has been profound and humbling. It constantly reminds me that we never know how much time we have. We need to live NOW. Serve now. Love now. Be the difference you want to see in the world NOW.

## If you could give advice to those who are still searching for their purpose in life, what would it be?

Well, we're all on the path, and always will be! It's important to invest the time to find out who you are. The path doesn't just make itself clear without some searching. You have to make the time to develop a relationship with your own version of God, to meditate, pray, get still by whatever method works for you. As you practice quieting your mind, you will begin to receive messages that will help you get better direction on your path. Slow down, be still, and listen. Then dive into the world and serve!

# Paul Martinelli

*"One of the lessons I've learned is that the quality of the answers that we get in life is truly determined by the quality of the questions we ask."*

**Paul Martinelli is a self-made entrepreneur born and raised in Pittsburgh, Pennsylvania. His full-service cleaning company, At Your Service, Inc., was established in 1988 with expanded operations in Tampa and Pittsburgh.**

**Mr. Martinelli's business efforts led to a term as President for the Executive Association of the Palm Beaches (1999) and won him the Arthur E. Turner Excellence in Entrepreneurship Award (1998).**

**Mr. Martinelli maintains close ties with Palm Beach communities as a Board Member of ARC (Association of Retarded Children) and has personally worked to make communities safer as the East Coast Regional Director for the Alliance of Guardian Angels in New York City.**

**Mr. Martinelli is currently the President of Bob Proctor's LifeSuccess Consulting. Read more about Paul and LifeSuccess Consulting at: www.lifesuccessconsultants.com**

### Who do you think you are?

I am a child of God who has been gifted with certain intellectual faculties that allow me to co-create my life and to live my purpose. My purpose is very specifically defined: to guide people in discovering their life purpose, and to be the very best in the world at communicating the teachings and ideas of Bob Proctor and Thomas Troward.

### What event or series of events led to your discovery?

I was twenty-two years old and had gotten the entrepreneurial bug to start a business and to express the spiritual side of myself that had built up inside. I had $200 and a dream. I went door-to-door and cleaned offices in the evening time. I used a vacuum cleaner, a bottle of Pledge and a bottle of Windex. I built that business to a certain degree in about three years. I got stuck, as so many of us do, and I could not break out of where I was financially. In hindsight, I realize that I wasn't just stuck financially, I was stuck spiritually, I was stuck in my relationships, I was stuck in every area of my life. I was stuck in my personal development and my health.

I did something that I had never done before in school; I started to read books. I had flunked out of high school. I had limiting beliefs for the first half of my life. I had this terrible speech impediment…I stuttered. Of course, whenever a young person has some kind of weakness the other kids tend to prey on that. I was told that I was stupid and was teased a lot. If you hear these comments over and over again, sooner or later it forms your perception of who you are. It got to a point where I had so much desire that I began to challenge my own core beliefs and values. I began the tough work of self evaluation, of asking, "Why do I believe this?" "Is this true about me?" "Does it have to be?"

I read everything from Anthony Robbins to Zig Ziglar, but I just couldn't get any of it to stick. It seemed like most of the information in those self help books just wanted to motivate me, and I was already motivated. I was a twenty-four-year-old man, who was cleaning toilets and emptying trash cans at night. I did not need a kick in the rear end to move me faster in same direction. I needed a change of course. I needed to change who I was and how I operated. I truly believed that this could happen.

Through divine intervention, somebody gave me a videotape of a seminar called *You Were Born Rich* by Bob Proctor. After watching it for about thirty minutes, I knew that Bob had the answers for me. He made me aware of the universal laws that governed the way I thought and behaved. He showed me that I had intellectual faculties that I was using, but wasn't using properly. I would always imagine the worst-case scenarios instead of using my imagination to look at all the possibilities. I realized that I had the ability to choose my perception and that would ultimately create my reality.

That was the first shift, when I realized I could co-create my life by tapping into the spiritual side of myself, becoming aware of my oneness with my creator, and working with the talents I had been given. I could define who I was and define my purpose and I could live that out loud and boldly. For the first time in my life, what other people thought of me didn't matter anymore. Another person's opinion of me was none of my business. My opinion of me is what mattered most. That was the beginning of my self-discovery. I had gotten to the point where I was sick and tired and frustrated enough to do the necessary work involved in shifting my paradigm, and that's what I did.

**If you could give advice to those who are still searching for their purpose in life, what would it be?**

My advice would be to accept the notion that they already have the answer, and that they always have had the answer. We are taught biblically to seek first the kingdom within us. The answer is there. Now, it gets clouded by all types of beliefs that we may not have chosen as young people. I believe that the average age for somebody to fully develop conscious awareness, where they have the ability to accept or reject ideas about themselves, is around seven to nine years of age. By then we have been filled with so many limiting beliefs from our parents, our grandparents, our teachers or our coaches. They're well-meaning, just ignorant. When I say the word ignorant, most people identify that as being rude. I mean ignorant as a lack of awareness. They just lack the awareness of how human beings operate in the laws that govern our thoughts and behavior.

I recommend that people unplug their TV sets and really dedicate some time to self-study and recognize that wherever they are, whatever the results are in their lives, whatever circumstances have shown up, their best thinking has gotten them there. They didn't just wake up one day and say to themselves, I think I'll make all the wrong decisions in my life today. The results that they have in their lives are an expression of their level of awareness. If they want to change the results of their lives, they must first change the cause, which is what's going on inside. The only way to shift that is to raise their level of awareness through self-contemplation. Spirit contemplates and Spirit expresses itself through contemplation, and we are individualized Spirit.

I would recommend that people study some of the great teachers that we have now and some of the great teachers from the past, and apply the principles they teach. They should never wait for the conditions and circumstances to be "right" in their lives to take the steps necessary to define their purpose and live their purpose. The conditions and circumstances of their lives will never be right. They have to set their own course and move in the direction of their dreams.

One of the lessons I've learned is that the quality of the answers that we get in life is truly determined by the quality of the questions we ask. Often times we ask the wrong questions. When gifted with an idea that is in harmony with our purpose, most people filter that idea through their current belief system and they evaluate whether it is good or bad or right or wrong or ask, "should I or shouldn't I?" Asking those self-limiting questions does them no good. It doesn't serve them at all. I would encourage someone, when gifted with an idea, to ask this question, "If I act on this idea will it move me in the direction of my dream?" If so, regardless of knowing how to achieve it and regardless of the conditions or circumstances, move in that direction. Go as far as you can go, and then the next step will be shown. It always works, it works for everybody, and it works all the time.

# Scott Evans

*"There's nothing we can't do… only things we won't do."*

Scott Evans, AKA, "The Working Inventor" has taken his passion for creating new patents to the big screen in his first feature film *PASS IT ON.*

Evans, an entrepreneur, inventor and international speaker, has co-produced the groundbreaking motivational movie *PASS IT ON. The film* shares a sequence of *ACTION* steps that anyone can apply to become the *inventor* that is hidden within—these are the proven success strategies that Evans applied to develop health and fitness concepts that have made him a multi-millionaire.

Evans was only nine years old when he realized his talent and passions were inventing and marketing. He built his first prototype, a Radio Flyer wagon, which was later immortalized in the movie *Radio Flyer.* Other events in Scott's life lead to the inspiration behind the scripts for the Sandlot movies I and II.

In 2001, Evans thought he had a "million dollar" idea, but he was wrong. What he actually had was a 75 million dollar idea. The BodyBow, a portable gym, grossed millions in its first few months of sales alone, earning him prestigious recognition with the Electronic Retailers Association as a top New Inventor.

Evans' dynamic personality and his track record of success have inspired thousands in the US and Canada. His expertise in taking an idea from concept to the marketplace has made him a highly sought after business consultant for budding inventors.

In addition to owning a successful appliance retail company in Southern California, The Working Inventor is also a Human Movement Science Specialist, and even finds the time to take on an occasional acting gig. His other hobbies include golf, mountain biking and home brewing.

Contact Mr. Evans at: Wish Entertainment, Inc., www.PassItOnToday.com

# Who do you think you are?

I've discovered that my purpose is to create and to have a positive impact on as many lives as possible through innovation, inventions, inspiration and motivation. I'm known worldwide as *The Working Inventor,* because like most people, I've had million dollar ideas. The problem is that most of those millionaire ideas don't go anywhere. What I actually had instead of a million dollar idea was a seventy five million dollar idea. So, it started becoming very easy for me to do what others find it difficult to do. People will concede that most things are simple, just not easy. You know you have a responsibility to dispense this valuable information when the two issues of simplicity and ease of a task collide. When that happened for me, I realized I had to bundle what I know together, how to bring a product, service or business to the marketplace with relative ease and simplicity and bring that to the masses, because the truth is, it only takes one big idea.

## What event or series of events led you to your discovery?

I stopped thinking and I started doing. And believe me, there's a huge difference between thinking and doing. I recognized that most people we remember *for something*, not just their names, but *for something*. They're usually remembered for a discovery or credited for that discovery. I consider a discovery as simply coming up with a plan of attack and implementing it. I do this through simple concepts like: What do you do with an idea? You've got to take the idea and build a core group of people around the idea, then, you've got to develop and execute a plan. So, that's a discovery, and that's what people are remembered for, and at that point they have the responsibility to put that information out there for the people who want it.

## If you could give advice to those who are still searching for their purpose in life, what would it be?

It's all about being challenged. I call it the Snort Factor. It's like a horse or a bull that's going to snort and challenge you or run at the red cape. You've got to find that something that challenges you. At that point you've got the Snort Factor. When you find something that challenges you, go out and tackle it by whatever means possible. I promise anyone who does that is going to bask in the enjoyment of it all, and then they'll be looking for more or larger challenges. Unfortunately, there's no rewind button in life, so it'd be good to either push play or fast-forward. I choose to push fast-forward, and that way I get a lot of things accomplished. I like to say, "If you want to get something done, get busy." That's what I would pass on. Find a challenge, and your talents and passions will come to the forefront, and you'll tackle it. Now validate yourself for the Win, and go on to the next one!

# David Schirmer

*"You already have within you the answers, but sometimes it takes a mentor or a teacher to help you bring them out."*

David Schirmer is an entrepreneur, stock market investor and commodity trader who regularly trades shares, options, warrants, futures and CFD's on the Australian and overseas markets. His market analysis ability is highly sought after by industry experts as he is the leading market cycle analyst in Australia and amongst the best in the world.

David has been involved with the stock market for over 25 years and is committed to the idea that everyone can invest in the stock market. All people need to be successful in the stock market is some simple, practical, technical analysis skills to help them make better decisions.

David's background is the family farm, where he and his brother invented a product that revolutionized the hay industry in Australia. After leaving the farm in central Queensland, David co-founded Schirmer Industries, a company that commercially manufactured computer controlled farm machinery.

David sold his half share in the manufacturing business and went on to build a desktop publishing business. He studied the financial markets and eventually turned his hand to commodity trading. After relocating to Melbourne to establish and build the first interstate office for Hudson Institute, David decided to share his stock market knowledge with others.

David started Trading Edge, Australia's leading stock market education brand, in 1997 with his wife, Lorna. By the end of 2007, over 85,000 people have listened to David share his vast knowledge of the stock market and more than 15,000,000 people around the world have watched, listened to or read David's knowledge on The Secret and Law of Attraction.

Apart from being the CEO of the David Schirmer Group of Companies, David is an accomplished presenter and world class speaker. He presents over 100 workshops, seminars and guest appearances per year on topics ranging from "Mastering the Stock Market", "Entrepreneurship 101 – Legal Structuring to Protect Your Wealth" to "Wealth is a Mindset", a personal development and psychology workshop. David is 'self-taught' and shares from his vast personal experiences in business.

If you think David is not quite busy enough, he and his wife have six boys aged seven to twenty-three. He plays the violin, the occasional game of golf, and likes to keep up with the latest computer technology.

**Read more about David at: www.DavidSchirmer.com**

## Who do you think you are?

I am one of the most successful stock and commodity traders in the world and one of the most brilliant minds on the Law of Attraction. The reason I am a great teacher of the laws of the universe is due to my ability to explain a complex subject in the simplest way possible.

## What event or series of events lead to your discovery?

Thirteen years ago I found myself flat broke. I come from a farming background, and we invented a piece of machinery for handling bales of hay that was cutting edge at the time. I started a manufacturing business with my brother to manufacture this great product. Things were going extremely well until the day that greed set in.

This left me in debt of over fifty thousand dollars and without any share in the business and no assets. With no education, no skills and no money I had no other choice but to go on social security. This fortnightly check barely covered the food and rent, and it surely did not allow for paying back any of the debt I was left with. The bill collectors came knocking and I finally ended up working out plans for payment with them that included a very small monthly pay-off rate. I convinced them that if they got just a little bit of money from me for many years to come, it would still be better than nothing which is what they would get if they said no to my offer.

I started to look at ways to make some money and learned about this new (at the time) form of marketing called network marketing. Through that I was introduced to personal development and over the next few years I attended seminars and read books from authors and speakers like Tom Hopkins, Jim Rohn, Zig Ziglar, and Tony Robbins. I attended Tony Robbins' UPW course 7 times. I learned everything he did, watched his presenting techniques, listened to the way he phrased things and continued to read and educate myself.

A friend loaned me some Bob Proctor cassette tapes of his seminar *You Were Born Rich*. As I listened, Bob explained to me how the mind works and why we get the results we have in our life. The reason I was drawn to his work was because Bob didn't just tell me what to do, he also showed me how the mind works and told me the *why* to do it. Within thirty days of listening to Bob and doing the things he said, things started to change. I went from broke to ten thousand dollars a month within 3 months, then over a million a year within three years.

I became a very successful trader once I realized that the stock market is just a vibration, like everything else. Once you tune into the vibration and really notice the way the energy moves, you can see its patterns and cycles. All you really need to successfully trade is the right knowledge, a ruler, pencil and a half an hour a week.

**If you could give advice to those who are still searching for their purpose in life, what would it be?**

Find a mentor, someone who you feel drawn to. Take their course, buy their products and do what they tell you to do. Make a decision to live an abundant life. Get close to your creator; God is the source of absolute abundance. You already have within you the answers, but sometimes it takes a mentor or a teacher to help you bring them out. My life is totally different because I listened to mentors over and over again. I now have programs that teach how to use the law of attraction to bring you whatever you desire, but there's more to it than just using the law of attraction. Some people think that using affirmations will bring you what you want, and that positive thinking will keep you from getting into trouble. It will help, but you must get clear about exactly what you want in your life. Make success a must! Study the mind every day because wealth is a mindset! The next step is to take action. "Affirmation without emotion *and* action is delusion" and "A dream without emotion and action is but a fleeting thought."

# Armand Morin

*"There may be ten pieces of the puzzle here, but you just need to go to the next step, to the next step, then to the next step."*

Since starting online in 1996, his personal online businesses have generated over $25,000,000 in revenue. This doesn't include the millions of dollars his students have produced from his teachings.

Armand has taught tens of thousands of people his unique and proprietary Internet business building principles and strategies, which work without fail for every single business that has implemented them.

Each year Armand appears at live business trainings and seminars all over world. It's not uncommon to see Armand share the stage with other world famous marketers like Mark Victor Hansen, Robert Allen, Dan Kennedy, Jay Abraham, Alex Mandossian, Joe Polish, Jay Conrad Levinson, Mike Litman, and T. Harv Eker.

Armand Morin's straight to the point teaching style, which has the unique ability to transform any business in 90 minutes or less, has made him a requested speaker in the USA, Australia, the United Kingdom, New Zealand and Singapore.

He has helped thousands of people from all walks of life to increase and enhance their online businesses through automation with his highly acclaimed "Generator" brand of software, used by tens of thousands of people in 101 different countries.

Read more about Armand at: www.armandmorin.com

## Who do you think you are?

I think many people go through life not really knowing where they want to be. As I was going through the various stages of my life, from selling vacuum cleaners to running a long-distance company to running an Internet business, my purpose wasn't clear. I knew I needed to earn an income, but what I needed to understand was what exactly did I need to do, what was my purpose? That was certainly a quest for me.

What I discovered was as I did certain things, all of a sudden everything else came into alignment. When you are doing the right thing, the alignment happens automatically for you. If you're not in sync with everything around you it doesn't happen.

As we go through this process of discovering what we want to do, we need to be aware of what is around us. Meaning, when we take a certain action what is the end result? If we take the right action, all of the rest seems to fall right into place for us. For example, for a long time, even as I built a successful Internet marketing business, I knew that I wanted to talk more about the aspects of a person becoming successful. It's not just our technical abilities that we utilize on a day-to-day basis. What I wanted to talk about was the mindset of success and how success actually happens.

I took a big step. I made the decision to speak on the topic of success. I also made the decision to speak on bigger stages as well. In the course of a few days, several people called me to speak, and they had events with three to five thousand people lined up to attend. This all happened four of five days after I made up my mind. Here's the really interesting part. They didn't ask me to speak about Internet marketing. They wanted me to teach people how to be successful. They wanted me to talk about success. All of a sudden, all of the pieces of the puzzle came into play.

My purpose is to teach people how to become successful by teaching them the techniques to get their minds straight, rather than to depend upon things like technical abilities. At this current time in my life, that is definitely my purpose. Many people have said this but I believe it bears repeating: *When the student is ready the master will appear.* Hopefully, I can be that person teaching those people and appear at the right time in their life, and they can learn from what I've done and from the mistakes I have made.

**What event or series of events led to your discovery?**

I don't think it was a specific event. It was a quest. I believe everybody has what they call a "vision quest." Everyone has one, but they don't always realize that they do.

I was always in search of what everyone else was in search of, meaning, I wanted the life of success. What was that? How did I define it? Actually, I am still in quest of that. That may seem strange coming from me. I have many things that people would certainly want to have: a beautiful home, a thriving business, as much money as I could possibly need, but does that match up with my vision?

Here's what people should understand, it's not a series of events. It's really what you start, what you intend your life to be. People intend their lives to be a certain way when they are young. From the time I was ten or twelve years old I would tell my mother every single day that I was going to become a millionaire by the time I was twenty-five. For some reason that number always stuck in my mind. You can ask my mother and she will tell you the exact same thing. I said this over and over again anytime she asked me, "What do you want to do?" I would tell her, "I'm going to be a millionaire by the time I'm twenty-five." The funny part is I did not become a millionaire by the time I was twenty-five, I was actually twenty-six. Some people might call this a failure, but the fact is that I earned my first million dollars when I was twenty-six years of age. It took me ten months to do it.

So what series of events caused this? Some might say it was the constant reiteration of that goal, even though I didn't even know what I was doing at that time. Some people might say I was in the right place at the right time. But let me tell you this, prior to me starting a business that made me $1 million, I sold vacuum cleaners door-to-door. In selling vacuum cleaners door-to-door, I certainly learned how to deal with people, but I didn't learn anything about how to run a business.

From the time I was very young, I realized that there was a life that was different from the one I was living. Not that my parents didn't provide for us, they did everything they could for me when I was young. But the fact is, I realized that there was a world out there that I didn't know. I saw it on television. I saw it on shows like *Miami Vice*. I saw the houses on *Lifestyles of The Rich and Famous*. The question became how could I access that world? How do I go from where I am today to that place? That's what started me on my quest to find out what that other world was.

Along my way, I met certain other people, and each one of those people taught me something. There were probably nine or ten key people who made a difference in my life.

The first one was a guy named Lenny Epstein. Lenny taught me how to sell vacuum cleaners. He sold me on the idea of selling vacuum cleaners, even though I was 19 years old and had no intention of selling vacuum cleaners. He convinced me to sell vacuum cleaners in about two minutes. The reason this is important is that he showed me how to be a great salesperson. He taught me that you don't push the product on someone; you make them want it so bad that it's their own idea to have it.

And another person was someone I met along the way as I was traveling. (I don't even remember his name actually.) I had a job for a very short time selling timeshares down in Florida. I only did it for two weeks because I felt kind of guilty selling time-shares, quite honestly. This person showed me the next step. I happened to meet one of the people who started the very first time-share in Spain. He was living in Orlando, Florida at a very high-end place called Windermere. Windermere is a beautiful place to live with really big homes. Shaquille O'Neal has a house there and Michael Jackson has a house there. He brought me to his home, which is the biggest house I had never seen and he also showed me his car, which was a Jaguar. I was impressed. Not with the fact that he had a Jaguar, but that he had it shipped all the way from Germany to Orlando in order to drive it. He had given me a taste of what the extra life was. He was an instrumental person because he opened my eyes to see that people actually do live like this.

Another person who probably changed my life the most was a teacher I had during my brief year in college. During one of his classes he talked about one of the greatest books ever written about business and how it had created more millionaires than any other book. It's a book called *Think and Grow Rich.* He explained the story of Napoleon Hill and Drew Carnegie and said that if you ever want to be successful in life you need to buy this book. I took all the change I had and went to the nearest phone booth and started calling all the bookstores in the area in order to find the book.

I grew up in a very small town in upstate New York, and I was really shy at this time. I didn't want to use public transit because I would have to see a bunch of strangers on that bus. I was not willing to use the bus to get to this bookstore. The problem was the bookstore was about 6 miles away. So I ended up walking across town, 6 miles, to this little bookstore, bought the book *Think And Grow Rich,* and walked back another 6 miles.

I read the book on my way back as I walked. I skipped classes the next day to continue reading and I finished the book. Here is where I would like to say that I read it and my life changed and I've never been the same since, but the truth is, I didn't get it. I thought to myself, "Why would someone read this book and become a millionaire- because of what they read in it?" I knew that there must be something in it, but I couldn't place my finger on it. It took me years before I realized the impact, before my mind was ready to accept what I had learned. I hadn't lived the concepts enough to understand them. Eventually, I did get it, and I still read that book to this day. I actually republished it with my own forward.

If I were to name one key event, I would say that it happened on Easter Sunday in 1995. That's the day that my son's mother took my son and left me as I was trying to start my long distance phone company. I sat there alone, in an empty room, saying to myself, "I have to make this work." I had been working four or five months to launch the company, and my wife left me saying "You'll never amount to anything, and you are just playing at this business like it's a game." Her words stuck in my head and will probably continue to stay in my head the rest of my life.

That was the single defining moment. I had my back against the wall. There was no place else to go. I couldn't go any lower. I had no money. The cupboards were absolutely bare, and that's not just a figure of speech. It was absolutely true. There was no food in the whole house. And there I was with this idea of starting a long-distance phone company with nothing more than a background in selling vacuum cleaners.

Within the next two weeks, we launched the company, and in our first seven days we generated over $100,000, and I've never looked back.

**If you could give advice to those who are still searching for their purpose in life, what would it be?**

You can find all the reasons why you shouldn't do something, but what you want to do is find all the reasons that you should. We just need one good reason. For many people it may be their family. For many people it might be in spite of someone else.

My advice to someone who's getting started is to first believe in yourself. That is key. Belief has a success cycle to it. First you have a belief that causes you to take action, or in some cases, causes you not to take action. Based upon that action, we get to a series of results, and based upon the results we either build a bigger or smaller belief. Then the success cycle starts all over again.

In order to grow your success cycle into an ever-growing one, you need to start with something small. By starting with something small, all of a sudden, it grows, and it gets bigger and bigger. Start by achieving small levels of success and building it up from there. What people hear when they go to a seminar, read in a book, or watch in a movie is the end result of what has taken people many years to achieve. They don't see the very beginnings. So, they think that they can just start there, just jump to the end result.

The fact is, that doesn't really happen. There isn't necessarily a quantum leap to get there. There is a faster method, which is to focus on the next logical step, meaning from where you are to the next place. What is your next logical step along the way? There may be ten pieces to the puzzle here, but you need to go to the next step, to the next step, then to the next step. Those are the sequential steps we need in order to make the whole system work for us.

So the question I have for the readers of this book is, based on where you are, what is the next logical step for you to take? What is the one thing that you can do today to move yourself toward your end goal? If we take that premise and we apply it every single day, all of a sudden we achieve those little tiny steps, which eventually add up to a big step when we look at it overall.

Again, what is the next logical step for you, and what is it that you can do for yourself today? Today is the key! Today! If we worry about the future, we are worrying about something that hasn't even happened yet. We need to focus on the present, because the present is what is going to make it work for us. It's all about what we do today. How we can take destiny and put it in our own hands, and allow ourselves to achieve a level of success? Yes, there is a sequence and order of things, and it all starts with your very next step. Just take your next step.

# Alexandria K. Brown

*It's all inside of you. If you haven't found it yet,*
*you probably haven't been paying attention to the signs.*

Alexandria Brown is CEO of Alexandria Brown International Inc., a multi-million dollar company devoted to empowering women around the world with the tools to living the freedom-based lives of their dreams via owning a successful business.

Ali's ezine "Straight Shooter Marketing", has over 22,000 subscribers around the world, and she currently has more than 400 solo-entrepreneurs enrolled in her high-energy coaching programs. Her marketing and success courses and programs have helped thousands of women (and men) use email and the Internet to leverage their expertise, gain a broader reach, and dramatically increase their incomes.

While Ali's best known for her expertise in marketing, her students share that her biggest impact comes from her philosophy of "designing your business to create an extraordinary life™" – ensuring your business revolves around your own personal values and lifestyle. This, Ali says, is the most important key to bringing a business owner their ultimate wealth and happiness.

She most enjoys sharing her message in person, and has spoken on stages around the world, alongside marketing and motivational geniuses including Mark Victor Hansen and Dan Kennedy, sharing her message of empowerment through business. She's also been a guest on hundreds of teleseminars and webinars, sponsored by companies such as Microsoft Live Meeting.

Ali's dynamic businesses have been profiled in *Entrepreneur Magazine, Entrepreneur Magazine's Business Startups*, and *Personal Success* magazine (U.K.). Her marketing and success advice has been featured in the books *Confessions of Shameless Internet Promoters* (2002, Success Showcase Publishing), *Mastering Online Marketing* (2007, Entrepreneur Press), *The Official Get Rich Guide to Information Marketing* (2007, Entrepreneur Press), *Birthing the Elephant: A Woman's Go-for-It Guide to Starting and Growing a Successful Business* (2008, Ten Speed Press), and *Entrepreneur Magazine's Start Your Own Information Marketing Business* guide. (forthcoming in 2008) She has also been interviewed by *The Wall Street Journal*.

Ali herself has been featured on the HGTV network, the "Leading Experts" TV show, and Dan Kennedy's "The Phenomenon" DVD.

Ali's book *Power and Soul* (2007, Love Your Life Publishing), highlights herself and 42 of her coaching members on their personal journeys to finding the power within that brought about the success of their dreams.

Contact Ali at: www.eZineQueen.com

**Who do you think you are?**

Fabulous! Ha ha…well, I am. And you are too. First of all we need to realize that.

Your timing is perfect with this question, because until recently I didn't really know the answer. I think this is true for everyone. Very rarely is a person born already knowing why they're here. The answer is there, but it's a journey to the center of your soul. At some point, the universe takes you through a series of events that show you why you're here, and makes it really clear what your purpose for being is.

I know now that I am here to inspire women around the world — ten million of them or more — to experience wealth, joy, and peace through owning their own business. I am very passionate about this, because I firmly believe that there is no way to have complete freedom in your life unless you are in business for yourself.

**What event or series of events led to your discovery?**

In my experience, when you see things start going wrong, that's usually the very beginning of something really good.

I hopped around from job to job in my 20s, and I was really frustrated. I looked around and it seemed like all of my friends were really happy in their jobs. They looked at me and said, "Why aren't you happy in yours? This is just the way it is. You work from nine to five, you make a certain salary, and that's it." But, I was completely miserable in a job. There was so much I wanted to do and change in each job that I had, and it wasn't very long before I realized that I couldn't work for anyone else. The good thing is that I realized that I was an entrepreneur and that I could own my own business. I was still young, so of course that thought filled me with some fear.

I lived in a tiny 5th floor walk-up apartment that was so small the bed had to fold up into the wall and the bathtub was in the kitchen. It was also over a Mexican restaurant so my clothes always smelled like a big burrito. I was depressed and frustrated.

Then suddenly — this was about nine years ago — I did it. I took the leap and went out on my own not having any idea what I was doing. I just got this message, "Quit! Quit your job and go on your own!" At first I was in for a rude awakening, because what I didn't realize is that marketing is the essential skill that you need in any business. I had to learn about marketing.

I'm always telling people that the marketing is more important than the mastery. No matter what job or thing you do really well, when you own a business, your number one job is now the marketing. It's even more important than how well you do what you do. It's really important. Once I really got this, I started learning everything I could about marketing.

I didn't have a mentor or a role model so I just went to the library, bought books and audio books, and I went to the seminars that I could afford at the time. I learned about e-mail marketing and online marketing, which I really loved. For someone who is on a tight budget, this is a great way to market.

I started with a little e-mail newsletter, and this newsletter started spreading the word about my business. People started asking me, "How are you doing this e-zine?" (An e-zine is short for email magazine.) Then they told me that I should write a book about it. I didn't know the first thing about writing a book, so I decided to publish an e-book instead. I bought an e-book on how to publish an e-book, and learned even more about online marketing. It seemed like whatever I did people would ask me, "How did you do that?" and I'd just teach them.

That's how I got to where I am today, by starting small and working my way up and teaching others as I learned. So, if you're reading this right now, my advice would be to pay attention to all of the small things that you can teach people. You may find that you underestimate what you know, and that people will pay to learn what you already know. Just honor that.

I just kept taking it up a level. I'd teach someone how to publish an e-zine and they would say, "How do you do online marketing?" I came up with an online marketing course – my Online Success Blueprint® system, then I added personal success coaching programs, then I added seminars, and I just kept taking it to another level. And I saw that women entrepreneurs most resonated with me and I with them, so they are my focus now. This year I have a waiting list of 27 women to get into my $19,000 coaching program.

All I need to do is keep honoring myself and honoring why I am here, and when I stay on that path success is effortless. Once I tapped into my true purpose and strengths, I began doubling my business every year – to over a million dollars in 2006 and two million in 2007. Last year I finally purchased my first home right on the beach here in Southern California, I drive a gorgeous luxury convertible, and I'm really living my dreams right now. Best of all, my simply being who I am and staying true to my purpose is helping thousands of other women achieve their own dreams and goals!

I've noticed that if I venture off that path and forget who I am, if I try to be like someone else or act competitive, I don't do as well. I believe that all you need to do is be *who you are*. I tell my students, "I don't compete, I don't compare, I just AM." I believe this has been the key to my success.

There's a great quote I love from Marianne Williamson: "Our deepest fear is not that we are inadequate. Our deepest fear is that we are powerful beyond measure. It is our Light, not our Darkness, that most frightens us. We ask ourselves, who am I to be brilliant, gorgeous, talented, fabulous? Actually, who are you NOT to be? You are a child of God. Your playing small does not serve the world. There is nothing enlightening about shrinking so that other people won't feel unsure around you. We were born to make manifest the glory of God that is within us. It is not just in some of us; it is in everyone. As we let our own Light shine, we unconsciously give other people permission to do the same. As we are liberated from our own fear, our presence automatically liberates others."

That quote always give me chills. You see, holding back your true power, your essence, your greatness actually hurts you, hurts God, and the world.

**If you could give advice to those still searching for their purpose in life, what would it be?**

It's all inside of you. If you haven't found it yet, you probably haven't been paying attention to the signs. Let me share three ideas with you.

First, look at mentors that you want to be like. There are a whole lot of people out there teaching, but are they teaching *HOW you want to be like*? It's really about you, and who you want to be. For example, many people come to me and say, "Ali, I've studied with many internet marketers, but when I saw you, I realized that I wanted to be like you. I want to model you because you have a relaxed lifestyle, you take good care of yourself, you travel and play and give to charities. Also, you don't work yourself into a competitive frenzy and get all crazy about your business, and you teach that business is really just a tool for designing an extraordinary life." Take a really good look and decide which mentors you want to be like, and that will help clue you into what your true purpose or calling is.

The second thing is, you're going to need some time alone. This really freaks some people out. We're used to being distracted all day with the television, with friends, the telephone, our blackberries and all the things going on around us. You cannot connect to Source — the Universe, God, whatever you'd like to call it — unless there is quiet time. I used to have a real problem with this. I'm still not a sit alone and meditate type of girl, but what I do like to do is participate in activities where I'm not over-stimulated, like take walks on the beach or just sit quietly for five minutes. You will find that when you give yourself this quiet time, this is when clarity appears. I would say that finding purpose is more realized from *stripping away your layers* than finding new things. It's not something you need to go search for. It's something that is simply revealed, something that you become aware of. It's something inside of you.

The third thing I would suggest is to work with a coach or a mastermind group. It's really important to do this to stay motivated. Share your purpose with them, and tell them to call you on it when you start to stray away from your purpose. Be very clear with them what it is you want to do, and ask them to call you on it if they see you straying from your purpose or playing small. I remember Jim Rohn saying, "you are the average of the five people you are around the most." That should get you thinking about raising the bar on whom you associate with. It helps pull out who you are more easily when you are around others who have already tapped into their life purpose.

The Universe doesn't like it when you play small, and once you really tap into knowing who you are, that's when it becomes easier and easier to play big. It's really amazing! You'll see. (And I'm here to help you women if you need it.)

# John Assaraf

*"Every day we are exchanging our life energy for what we do, and the trade better be worth it."*

For more than 17 years John Assaraf has helped thousands of entrepreneurs and team leaders achieve outstanding results in life and business. How? By showing them the fastest and most efficient ways to break through their mental limitations.

As a teen, John had to overcome low self-esteem and severe health issues. He was in danger of landing in jail or the morgue. At the age of 19, John left home and began a quest to find mentors and wisdom. At the age of 21, he met two mega-successful entrepreneurs who are the most successful sub-franchisors of real estate offices in the world. Their 1,500 offices in 19 countries produce over $15 billion a year in real estate sales.

His vivid and sometimes embarrassing life stories have touched the lives of millions of people worldwide through his appearances on national TV and radio.

John's passion and warmth have made him a highly regarded entrepreneur and one of the most sought after consultants and keynote speakers in North America and Europe today. His first book, *Having it All, Achieving Your Life's Goals and Dreams*, made it to the New York Times and Wall Street Journal's bestseller lists as well as #1 at Barnes and Noble.

In addition, John volunteers his time to help at-risk kids develop their skills to believe "the power of their minds and hearts."

Find out more about John by visiting: www.JohnAssaraf.com or www.onecoach.com

## Who do you think you are?

I am at a unique stage in my life, where my purpose is to contribute and to really help other people achieve financial freedom so that they can live an extraordinary life. That's the business purpose of my life. In conjunction with that, my life purpose is to be a great dad to my children and to be a great husband to my wife.

**What event or series of events led to your discovery?**

Well, when I was younger I focused only on money, and I ended up with something called Ulcerated Colitis. I became very sick and that wasn't any fun. I was taking 25 pills a day and taking cortisone shots. I realized that money really wasn't the be-all and end-all, and that I had to have some semblance of balance in my health and wealth, and in my career, spiritual activity, and in relationships. For me this was a discovery that; number one – you can have more than money, and number two – that I was able to, and I just needed to learn the skills and strategies. So that is the series of events that led to some of my discoveries.

**If you could give advice to people who are still searching for their answers to this question, what would it be?**

The first thing I would advise people to do is not to ask themselves whether they are worthy of the goals that they have, but to ask if the goals the they have are worthy of their lives. Every day we are exchanging our life energy for what we do, and the trade better be worth it. Life is too short. So let's switch the question around and ask, "Am I prepared to exchange my life for these relationships?" "Am I prepared to exchange my life for this business?" "Am I prepared to exchange my life for the relationship that I have with God right now?" because that is exactly what we are doing every day. If the answer is "no," well then, let's make those changes. Let's learn the skills and the strategies to get the support around us to be able to make the necessary shifts.

# Are You Here To Be In Show Business?

# Daniel Nahmod

*"If you can't decide whether to be a hardware manager or a trumpet player, rent a trumpet for a month and see if you gravitate towards playing it."*

**Los Angeles-based singer/songwriter and humanitarian Daniel Nahmod, has performed his profound, heart-opening original music for over 500,000 people in 40 U.S. states and in Canada. Since beginning his music career in 1999, Daniel has sold over 50,000 CDs while receiving thousands of standing ovations along the way.**

**Daniel's poetic and evocative message of peace, love and compassion across all nations, cultures and faiths has found overwhelming acceptance wherever he has performed. Daniel has presented his spectacular music and message for nearly all of the world's major faiths, including Christian, Catholic, Muslim, Hindu, Buddhist, Jewish, Bahai, Mormon and Unity audiences, and has worked with some of the most influential and brilliant speakers and leaders in the world.**

**In response to Hurricane Katrina, Daniel visited the Houston Astrodome for two days, walking amongst the survivors talking, shaking hands and singing songs. Following late 2004's humanitarian crisis in Asia, Daniel organized, produced and hosted two soul-stirring benefit concerts, raising over $15,000 for Operation USA, a Los Angeles-based relief agency working in Indonesia and Sri Lanka. In 2000, he was nominated as National Hospital Volunteer Of The Year for his musical work at Cedars Sinai Hospital in Los Angeles.**

**Learn more about Daniel Nahmod at: www.danielnahmod.com**

## Who do you think you are?

I am here to channel my musical talents towards inspiring and supporting humanity.

## What event or series of events led to your discovery?

The musical side of that self-awareness has been with me since I was very young. I was aware of my innate musical ability when I was seven or eight, playing songs by ear. In high school I was learning an instrument in a week or two and then when I was in college I started writing songs. I've always recognized it. I remember reading a little snippet of an interview a slightly bitter at the time John Lennon, in which he said that he always knew he was a musical genius and he couldn't believe that no one else saw it in him. It was just something he knew about himself his whole childhood. I always knew I had a musical gift, and it came out in small ways over the years, playing piano and writing songs, playing trombone in high school and college and that sort of thing.

Even though I knew I had this musical ability, I wasn't raised to be an artist. I was raised to be a lawyer, or a doctor, or something with intellectual credentials. Therefore I was induced to do my homework, study hard, get good grades and go to college. I majored in economics in college, and having the life of an artist never occurred to me until after college. I was twenty-one. I was listening to Sarah McLachlan on a Walkman, and all of a sudden it occurred to me that this is a woman who sits at a piano, plays a song, records it, sings it, sells it, and that is her job. But, even then, it didn't really permeate my awareness of what I was to be until years later.

In 1997, when I was twenty-seven years old, I had the realization that computer programming (which is what I was doing at the time) was really not my life. I've always had the natural inclination to give joy, to make someone smile. I used to visit my grandmother in the hospital and sing to her. When I'd sing for her in the hospital I would always find anyone else on the floor who was open to hearing music and visit them as well…I've always done that. I realized that this was mine to do! The exact form of it wasn't clear, but in 1998 I moved to Los Angeles and started saying "yes" to every musical invitation I could find. Rather than doing the computer programming I'd been doing, I just dove all the way into my music and allowed it to take shape however it was going to take shape. What ended up happening was that this music with a message, this inspirational music for humanity, filled with songs of healing, compassion and connection, music that I innately write, found an audience in a magnetic, beautiful, graceful, organic way.

Now, eight years later, after bringing these songs to whoever will have me, singing them for hundreds of thousands of people, being very persistent using the other side of my brain, and doing all of the business work necessary, I find that my exact purpose in life is being fulfilled. I am now in a position to sing songs for all of humanity in every language they can be translated into, and at every event around the world that will have me. All these things conspire to create the exact career of musical service to humanity that I had imagined, but never would have known how to build if I hadn't done it one day at a time. I took that huge leap in 1997, moved to Los Angeles and just started! Starting is very important. Right where I was I just started, and I certainly could not have planned most of what's come.

**If you could give advice to those who are still searching for their purpose in life, what would it be?**

Well, there's the simple answer I always shared with kids, which is do for a job what makes you giggle. Do the thing that is so fun that you can't even imagine people would pay you for it. Because somewhere, somebody is making a good living doing that thing.

I used to think that was the whole answer, but it's really not. For a lot of people, that thing that they "came to do" really isn't all that clear and could in fact be completely hidden. People who aren't clear gravitate towards me, because I am so clear about who I am and what I do now. They come up and share with me that they are touched by that clarity and inspired by it. I think the advice I would give to a person who just doesn't know how to answer the questions, "What am I here to do?"and "Who am I?" is that we all fear making a mistake that we can't take back. I think that fear keeps people from quitting the job, leaving the relationship, moving to the city, recording an album, writing the book. We view these things as one-way tickets, as no-going-back choices. The fact is that there is no one way (and this is a song from my new album), there is no foolproof plan, there is no fateful final chance. And I really do believe that.

Face the fear of not knowing, face all of those uncertainties, and particularly face the fear that you're going to make a fatal mistake, that this is your one big shot. If you don't know what it is you dream of doing, try something! If you can't decide whether to be a hardware manager or a trumpet player, rent a trumpet for a month and see if you gravitate towards playing it. See if you have a knack for it, or go work in a hardware store, and if you don't like it after six days, quit. It sounds a little freewheeling and perhaps a little idealistic if you have significant financial responsibilities or "ties that bind you." But, it is possible to experiment and find out, and I'm a big believer in the path of least resistance.

If you step forward and try it – whether it's a mystery or something you would love, love, love to do – if you just step forward and try it, you will find the path of least resistance, it will pull you onto your perfect path. That's exactly what's happened to me. If you encounter tons of resistance, pay attention to that resistance – which I would call a "no" – it's as good as a "yes" because it tells you as much as a fluid, graceful entrance into something would. Resistance is just as informative and valuable. So my advice would be to just try something. Even on a hunch. In fact, the crazier the better!

For somebody who has an inkling of what they came here to do and just hasn't stepped into it, I would say just start where you are. Face the feeling of inadequacy, face the mystery, face the feeling of being unqualified, just feel all those things. Face all those fears: I don't have any business doing it, I don't know how to make it happen, I don't have the relationships, I don't have the money, I don't have the capital, I don't have the friends, I don't have the experience, I don't have the office, I don't have the music equipment, I don't have the word processor, I don't know any publishers in New York, I don't know any venture capitalists, I've never manufactured a product before, I don't know how to trademark my invention.

Take the first tiny step forward. Make a single phone call, take out a single book from the library, just take a step forward. Anyone from Donald Trump on down to the ten year old who opened up the lemonade stand will tell you that they had no idea how it was going to turn out. They just did the first thing they could think of towards that goal.

Of course, experience serves you. In other words, you do gain experience over the years, but the only way to get that experience is by trying it. The first time you open up a lemonade stand you may buy too many lemons or not get enough ice. But the second time, your estimate will be closer. The third time you won't run out of quarters to change people's dollars. By the eleventh time you'll be teaching classes on how to run the lemonade stand. Donald Trump did the same thing, I am sure. Even if you began with a billion dollars, you'd still need to learn how to manage that kind of money, how to build a beautiful building. You'd still need to learn how to grow a company, how to hire and fire, and how to manage assets. No matter who you are, you'd still need to learn all of those things, and all those things come with time and experience. We all begin with a blank slate or a blank sheet of paper.

# Craig Shoemaker

*"I used to have a lot of fear until I learned what fear really is —
False Evidence Appearing Real."*

**Craig Shoemaker was named Comedian of the Year by the American Comedy Awards, won two NATAS Emmy Awards, was named Best Supporting Actor at the 2007 Elevate Film Festival, performed at every major comedy venue in the country and was seen by over two million people last year. His "Lovemaster" routine was voted Most Popular Comedy on XM Radio's Big Schtick Award and was voted one of the top 20 stand-up specials on Comedy Central. Additionally, he had his own nationally syndicated radio show, which after only ten months on the air, won the prestigious Communicator Award "Crystal" prize. Craig has appeared on over 100 television shows – including ABC's *The View* (where he was Joy Behar's first guest in her Comedy Corner), HBO's *Comic Relief* (in '06 he co-hosted in New Orleans), Showtime's *Comedy All-Stars*, and *The New Hollywood Squares*.**

**As an actor, Craig has co-starred with Patrick Stewart in the film *Safe House,* was featured in the box office hit *Scream 2*, and starred in *Dark Honeymoon* opposite Daryl Hannah. His own movie *The Lovemaster* (with Farrah Fawcett) won "Best Film" honors at the Independent Film Festival in Los Angeles and garnered rave reviews.**

**His latest hit DVD entitled *Craig Shoemaker Live: That's a True Story* was filmed live at the San Jose Improv Theatre and features 90 minutes of non-stop stand-up comedy. Craig's new live concert DVD is now in post-production and will be distributed through Universal.**

**Learn more about Craig by visiting his website at: www.craigshoemaker.com**

## Who do you think you are?

I am a guy that really, truly, fundamentally, profoundly loves to make people laugh! I like to be around laughter, whatever that looks like. If I can be the inspiration for the laugh, that's all the better. I really cherish being in the company of others, whether I am having them over for dinner or just hanging out. I have always enjoyed this. Now, the performing aspect of my life has moved to a different level. I have gone from my little fort, hanging out with my friends, to being in front of 70,000 people at the University of Florida. To sum it all up, I am a person who enjoys life and likes to spread that joy. I am like Johnny Laughterseed.

**What event or series of events led you to your discovery?**

Internally throughout my whole life I knew what my purpose was. But I ignored it, shunned it, and turned my head to it. I wasn't encouraged to bring that part of me out, the spark that was inside of me. I was actually discouraged from original thought and feeling, and that really bothered me for a long time. But I know the moment it all changed; it was the moment my first child was born. That's when a new connection took place. That's when I started to look deeper inside of myself and found those truths that were always lying within, affirmed and confirmed them, and went from there. It was a monumental moment in my life, and it happened the second I locked eyes with him. I knew right then that it had all changed.

The journey became more intentional, because I realized that everything I do has an affect on him, Justin, and my other child, Jared. Every move or decision I make, everything I am about, I have to answer to someone directly, and I have to be an example. This has helped me bring focus to my life, because my road is narrower now. I can't have so many distractions or so many people in my life because I need to go coach little league, I've got to go to mommy and me classes for the little one! My time is scheduled now, and it's purposeful and meaningful. Whether it's coaching little league or setting up a production meeting for a movie that's coming out, everything has its place in time. It's moment to moment.

**If you could give advice to those who are still searching for their purpose in life, what would it be?**

I'd say the most important thing I ever did was to decide not to be a victim anymore. I participate in my own life, and I understand that only I can dictate what happens. I will constantly find my part in an equation. What is my role in this relationship? I always have a part in my relationships, whether it's a business relationship, a love relationship or whatever it is. If I can define my part in the relationship, then it makes the fear go away. I used to have a lot of fear until I learned what fear really is - False Evidence Appearing Real. Now I'll find evidence that

I've gathered that keeps me from going any further, because that's what fear does, then I'll wipe that fear away and move forward.

There are so many detractors, doubters, and cynical people out there who want you to join their pity party, and my suggestion would be to stop and move away from them. I have had to do that in my life. And, I'm not being harsh by doing that. I will always be there for them; I am a loyal friend…I still have the same friends from kindergarten. There are ten of us, and we go away every year together even though I live three thousand miles away. It's still important for me to have those friendships. If someone is toxic and they're trying to bring me down, I will extend my hand, help them, and share of my experiences of how I have overcome a fear. But if they're not willing to face their fears or their part in something, I can't just pull them along with me, because they'll drag me down.

I think it's really important to live like that, and that's what I try to teach my children. I hope that I am a good example to them; when I see an obstacle, I don't run from it. I make it dissipate. The bigger the obstacle, the higher the hurdle, and the better I feel having overcome it. For instance, when I went skydiving, I dealt with the greatest amount of fear I have ever had. Yet I experienced a huge amount of joy in going through the process. When I landed safely (barely, by the way, because my radio didn't work and I landed in electrical barbwire…talk about landing shock), the feeling of elation and accomplishment that took place was incredible. It was a metaphor for my life. There are so many fears and people and obstacles that get in your way. You know, things we are powerless over like the prime rate or an ex-wife who is a debtor. What am I going to do about it? When I get over those fears and those types of things in my life, it's incredible.

Ultimately, I would say that it's important to face your fear head on, and welcome it, because it's your friend. The avoidance of fear is far worse then the actual fear itself. It's much more painful.

# Michael Colyar

*"Who are you? Ask you who you are. Ask yourself.*
*And if you know who you are, then everything just gets to be easier."*

Dubbed "The King of Venice Beach," Colyar made his mark in the hearts and minds of his audiences on the Boardwalk of Venice Beach California with his thought-provoking humor. Every Saturday and Sunday for over nine years he would perform five one-hour shows a day to audiences of all ages, races, and backgrounds.

Colyar's informative and highly entertaining brand of comedy not only demands but guarantees positive response. As "Host" of "*Live From LA*," his point blank delivery and razor-sharp insight connected with the guests who joined him on the sofa, as-well-as audiences of all ages, coast to coast.

Colyar gained notable attention in 1990 when he was the $100,000 Grand Prize Comedy champion of "Star Search", the nationally televised talent competition, donating $50,000 to homeless charities in the Los Angeles area.

In addition to Hosting "*Live From LA*," one of cable televisions most popular talk shows four nights a week, Colyar had had feature roles in numerous films and TV shows, "Hosted" HBO *Def Comedy Jam*, and performs at comedy clubs and concert halls, continues to be active in fundraisers and benefits for community and national organizations, and whenever possible, if Colyar is in concert performance, you will find him stopping by a neighborhood school, youth center, or homeless shelter sharing the laughter practicing what he preaches; "What I give my brother, I give myself."

Michael can be contacted at:  www.MichaelColyar.com

## Who do you think you are?

I think that I am a healer, a healer and a humorist, and in fact it's through humor that I do my healing. I also think I am a discoverer and an adventurer of this life, you know, I really dig being here. Every day is a great adventure for me, and although what I do now is comedy and act, it wouldn't matter. Whatever I was doing, I would go at it with the same energy. I get up in the morning and I can't wait to get the day started. I don't need an alarm clock. What I try to do everyday is just live my dream.

You know what's really funny, I had learned how to do comedy in the streets of Chicago, telling jokes and passing my hat, and I became like the king of street performance in one summer in Chicago. But then winter came, and nobody wanted to hear jokes in December on State Street. I packed everything that would fit in my 1967 Buick LeSabre, sold everything else, and drove to California so I could stand in the street and do comedy for living. I really came to become a millionaire, but when I got to Venice Beach I discovered my brother, and I discovered that the world ain't about me, and that I can't find me until I find you. Because I ain't at my place; I'm where you are. Once I embrace you I embrace myself, and only then am I free to be who I am.

Instead of trying to be a millionaire, I now attempt to be a billionaire of being. Instead of trying to make my living, I live my making, and my making shall make my living. That's how I try to walk through this thing called life. That's why I get up in the morning. I'm living life to the fullest each day. It ain't necessarily whether I'm doing comedy, or acting, or being a grandparent, or flying to Chicago to feed my mama collard greens every three weeks. She's seventy-seven years young and just got past breast cancer, and now she's fighting liver cancer, but when I feed her, she's up and about and her energy is good again. I'm just living the life.

I think my purpose is to discover who I am. I think that is the only job, the only curriculum, in this entire course of life. To discover who I am and my connection to life and to that pulse and the energy. I discover that by being honest and true to myself every day. And I try to keep revealing a little bit more of myself every day, to myself.

**What event or series of events led to your discovery?**

I think it's more like a series of events, because it didn't just come to me; it's been coming to me, continually, over the years. When I got to Venice Beach, I saw a life force that I had never seen before, where everybody was interacting with everybody and so many people were about life and Spirit. They weren't necessarily putting a name on Spirit, but they were about the goodness of the land and healing each other and raising folks up. I saw that all mixed in, in the area where people were absolutely crazy, and drug addicts, and wild gangsters, and all of that was blended together in this area known as Venice Beach.

When I got there it was like I discovered a new world. It allowed my mind to be open for new things. I think the first thing I did was run into a guy who later became one of my spiritual gurus, Ostarius. This brother started talking to me and automatically I started getting connection to Spirit and to those people who lived out on that beach and to the homeless people, to people who were dealing with drugs, who still came to my show just to cool out and be regular folk. Life meant something to me. I will always tell everybody I didn't even start knowing what life was until I was twenty-nine years old. That's what I think was the beginning of the series of things which culminated with *The Secret.*

I hit about eight things, and each one sent me flying. Like if you were driving then all of a sudden you hit the turbo button. Eight things in my life have done that to me, and *The Secret* is the eighth in that series. I just keep on growing, and more and more things happen. I think it's about the discovery of self and that's what made me come to it. I wanted to know more about who I am.

Another thing in the series of events was talking with Anthony Robbins. He had this infomercial back then, and I was the first black person on his infomercial. When I did his infomercial, I did it because I really believed in that guy! Casey Kasem invited me to see an animal rights seminar. I hadn't even heard of anything like that. Anthony Robbins was running it. He talked about how bad it is to kill animals just so you can have their skin or you can eat them. He showed what happens to the animals and at the same time he showed the educational value of it, how to be in love with the animal and in love with the world and the planet. It blew my mind that he cared that much. I said to myself, I want to meet this white dude. So, I went to meet him. I had just won Star Search and given half of the money to the homeless and I told him that. He looked at me and said, "Well I want you to be my friend." So he sent me those tapes. In thirty days those tapes had me so focused and so clear on where I wanted to go and how to go about it. It was truly one of those moments that put me in turbo. It just sent me out there! I connected that with the connection to the Spirit I was already getting from talking to Ostarius out on Venice Beach and every few years something great like that has happened.

**If you could give advice to those who are still searching for their purpose in life, what would it be?**

Try as hard as you can not to lie to yourself. If we can just get to the point where we can be 100% honest with ourselves, then everything in our lives becomes more workable, more manageable, more real and more loving. A lot of us are so terrified that somebody's going to get what's ours, or we won't get the radial tires, or that's not going to be our DVD that we deal with that fear thing instead of that love thing, and we miss the whole point. It's not about the destination. We don't know whether we're ever going to get where were trying to get to. It's about the journey. Have a blast; you might not make it till tomorrow. You might say, I ain't getting in no plane because they crash too much, but you could be driving down the street and a plane could crash into your car and kill you. You don't want to rationalize anything more than God is Love and you're part of that. You get to be this continuing explosion of energy and positivity if you want to be. You can get there by not lying to yourself.

Who are you? Ask you who you are. Ask yourself. And if you know who you are, then everything just gets to be easier. The way you treat other people gets easier. Every thing gets easier when you are truthful with yourself. I don't maintain that any of this is right. I'm just saying that this is what I've been doing. This is what's been working for me.

Another thing I would recommend is *Agape*. Way before I saw *The Secret*, I saw Michael Beckwith. He was one of those eight things that happened to me. People were talking to me about *Agape* on Venice Beach fifteen years ago. I'm talking about teenagers, 12-year-olds, 10-year-olds would come up to me after my show in Venice Beach and say, "You would love my church. It's called *Agape*. Do you know what that means?" I'd say "no." And they'd say, "It means all encompassing love."

I blew that off, I never paid any attention to it, but I was on a search for churches. Every time I would see some place on Sunday, where there were black people standing outside in suits talking to each other, I'd pull over and go inside and see what they were talking about. I was in *Agape* for eight minutes, and I knew that I was at home. There was no two ways about it. This was before Michael even started speaking. He created such an atmosphere of love and energy in that place. You can just walk in, and it's like the Bodhi Tree (The Bodhi Tree was another one of those eight things for me). When you walk in the Bodhi Tree you feel the love of the spirit that's in that room. There ain't nobody there to hurt nobody; everybody's there to embrace everybody. When you walk into *Agape*, you feel that warm energy and that love right way, before anybody even opens their mouth. Then when Michael goes up and starts talking, forget about it.

# Debra Wilson Skelton

*"It depends on one's belief system, but I personally think the universe has a plan for each and every one of us."*

**Debra Wilson Skelton is best known for her eight seasons on Fox's late night sketch comedy series *MADtv*. Her other television credits include *CSI: Crime Scene Investigation, Without a Trace, E*! and *VH1* specials, as well as various other guest star appearances. Her film work includes *B.A.P.S, Skin Deep, Nine Lives, Scary Movie 4, Super Sweet 16, Gridlock'd, American History X* and *Avatar*.**

**Skelton is most proud of her community service work with elementary schools, at-risk-youth programs, and a number of animal organizations including Linda Blair's World Heart Foundation, New Leash On Life Animal Rescue and Farm Sanctuary. Debra is married to writer/ director Cliff Skelton and lives in Los Angeles.**

## Who do you think you are?

My purpose is the same as everyone else's; it's just that I have asked to discover what that is. I have taken the journey to discover it and have come to the understanding that everything around me is a byproduct of what I am supposed to do in the universe. I think other people allow *it* to define them. I think we are here for our healing and for other people's healings. We're here to uplift, support, validate, appreciate, recognize and continue to move forward to make this planet register on a higher vibration. Everything we're given is a circumstance to do that.

Some people get defined by their careers. They're defined by how much money they make, the status of their relationships, the car they drive, the clothes they wear or their jewelry. They're defined by a lot of status symbols. But it is the investment in self that doesn't go away. All the other things that we are defined by go away. You're clothes, your money, your shoes, and your house; when you pass from this planet, what will people say about you, other than the fact that they liked what you did as an actor? What will they say of you as a human being? When you strip the acting away, what you have left is the human.

My purpose is to ensure that when I pass from this planet people have wonderful things to say, and that, like Obi-Wan Kenobi said, "If you strike me down I shall become more powerful than you could possibly imagine." So, it's not in my acting, it's in my living and doing that creates the person I am on this planet. I think that I am an amazing human being that the universe created to do wondrous work for other human beings. That's what really defines me. If someone says, "Oh my god she's great because she took the time, she prayed with me, she spent time with me, I got to know her," I have created a personal relationship with that person. That's the thing that lasts when the celluloid disappears.

**What event or series of events led to your discovery?**

There have been so many it's not funny. I think that everybody has a downfall at one point in their life in order to find the make and measure of who they are as a human being, and I have had many downfalls. Significant ones. Dramatic ones that were basically do or die, at least in my mind. They forced me to ask the question, "Who am I?" They forced me to ask the question, "Is there a God?" They forced me to cry out in need of something beyond myself. They made me say, "If there is a God, prove to me that I am worthy to be here. Help me understand the journey of my purpose on this planet."

When Spirit speaks it feels so good. Having a giving nature, and knowing how to do that is a part of every being's journey on this planet. When you give, it feels good. So, part of it is, I am grateful that I am recognized as someone who is worthy to give, and at the same time my ego enjoys the "feel good" of it.

**If you could give advice to those who are still searching for their purpose in life, what would it be?**

It depends on one's belief system, but I personally think the universe has a plan for each and every one of us. Each and every one of us is significant. I volunteer at a lot of "at risk" teen organizations in conjunction with the Department of Juvenile Justice and the California Youth Authority, and this is something I always tell them. Say you were a Rolex watch, and that Rolex watch was made of platinum, diamonds, the most fantastic metals, the most fantastic artistry and workings in the world. What if the smallest mechanism broke down, and you were that small mechanism. What happens to the entire watch? It breaks down. It doesn't serve its purpose, which is to tell time. It may still be a nice looking piece of jewelry, but it was created to be a watch. It has now lost its purpose. Now did that small mechanism need to be any larger to be part of that entire breakdown? No. So, it doesn't matter how large you are or how small you are, you are essential to that watch, which means you are essential to the universe.

The universe is essentially that watch, that timepiece. We are mandated by time on this planet, and so I liken human beings to that watch. Even the smallest mechanism is important to the watch. Without you here fulfilling your purpose on this planet, there is a part of the universe that breaks down. There is someone in the future that needs you and you won't be there for them. It's vital for you to find your success, your balance, find your truth and offer these back to the world.

# Keb' Mo'

*"Start going toward what you love to do, even if you feel like for some reason you're not able to do that right now."*

Keb' Mo' draws heavily on the old-fashioned country blues style of Robert Johnson, but keeps his sound contemporary with touches of soul and folksy storytelling. He writes much of his own material and has applied his acoustic, electric, and slide guitar skills to jazz- and rock-oriented bands in the past as well.

Born Kevin Moore in Los Angeles to parents of Southern descent, he was exposed to gospel music at a young age. At 21, Moore joined an R&B band later hired for a tour by Papa John Creach and played on three of Creach's albums. Opening for jazz and rock artists such as the Mahavishnu Orchestra, Jefferson Starship, and Loggins & Messina helped broaden Moore's horizons and musical abilities. Moore cut an R&B-based solo album, *Rainmaker*, in 1980 for Casablanca, which promptly folded.

In 1983, he joined Monk Higgins' band as a guitarist and met a number of blues musicians who collectively increased his understanding of the music. He subsequently joined a vocal group called the Rose Brothers and gigged around L.A. 1990 found Moore portraying a Delta Bluesman in a local play called +Rabbit Foot and later playing Robert Johnson in a docudrama called *Can't You Hear the Wind Howl*?

He released his self-titled debut album as Keb' Mo' in 1994, featuring two Robert Johnson covers, eleven songs he wrote or co-wrote, and his guitar and banjo work. His second album, Just Like You, was equally well received. Slow Down followed in 1998 and Door was issued two years later. Big Wide Grin followed in 2001, while 2004 saw the release of two albums, Keep It Simple and Peace, Back by Popular Demand. Suitcase was issued in 2006 on Red Ink Records.

Read more about Keb Mo at: www.KebMo.com

## Who do you think you are?

I am who I am, and who I think I am is probably not who I am. I think who I am is already hardwired into my DNA. I think of myself as a servant and a participant. The word "leader" never comes to mind, because I think "leader" is a strange word. It connotes someone else is maybe sheep-like. What it boils down to is to hourly know who I am.

When I interact with the world and nature, I feel a part of the whole thing. I'm a cog in the wheel. I'm a lot of things, dependent on what's going on. I'm kind of like, what is plastic? It's the dashboard on your car, it's the bag you put your groceries in, it's the covering of your TV set, and it's the outside of your computer. What is anything really? At any given time, that role could morph into several different versions of myself.

**What events or series of events led to your discovery?**

For me it was more surrender than discovery. I surrendered myself and then let go. Often times, depending on who you are, it's difficult to find out how you fit into society. For instance, if you grow up with a knack for science, or a knack for writing, or you have a knack for playing a musical instrument everyone knows what you're going to be at young age. But if your knack is to be, let's say, the Rodney King of this lifetime, who knew you were going to grow up to say one of the famous quotes of all time, "Can't we all just get along?"

There's a guy who may have appeared to be a loser, when in fact, he's not a loser. He's just a cog in the big wheel. He's a part that affects all of us in some way. Even in what appeared to be his darkest hour, he affected the world in a really powerful way. He affected his city. He made a difference.

It's easy to recognize the Einsteins, the Nobel Peace Prize winners, the Oscar winners and the presidents of the world. Those people are easy to spot. It's the "not-so- significant" people who aren't as easy to spot, but they have so much to offer the world and so much to contribute to society if we'd only listen to them.

**If you could give advice to those who are still searching for their purpose in life, what would it be?**

I'd say the search is over; start going toward what you enjoy. Start going toward what you love to do, even if you feel like for some reason you're not able to do that right now. If you're looking for yourself, you need to walk toward it. Don't let fear stop you in your tracks. Don't let fear keep you from doing what you were put here to do. Sometimes, you'll have to walk into the mouth of the beast, and if you do…the beast will just turn into a bunny rabbit.

# Charles Holt

*"If you don't know what you want to do or what the path is for you, do something. Do what's calling you now, because what's calling you now will lead you down the path to what the call is for you later."*

Charles Holt is an Actor, Singer, Writer, Transformational Speaker, and Entrepreneur. Even though he grew up in Nashville, Tennesee, Charles does not recall ever aspiring to be a performing artist. Instead, he dreamed of one day playing professional football and becoming one of the game's most memorable players. In high school, he garnered many awards and accolades for his outstanding athleticism, earning him local and national recognition along with the opportunity to attend college on an athletic scholarship. After graduating, Charles worked out for several professional football teams as defensive back and return specialist, but despite his valiant efforts and persistence he was not selected in the NFL Draft and pursued a career in corporate America.

Charles has starred in some of the most celebrated productions in American theatre history including *Jesus Christ Superstar, Smokey Joe's Café*, and the *Lion King*. Charles was the first person of color to star as 'Rocky' in the European tour of *The Rocky Horror Picture Show*. He adds guest starring and lead roles to his television and film credits: *Law & Order: Criminal Intent, All My Children*, the award winning independent film, *Anne B. Real* (Universal Home Video), and the penetrating comedy, *Ed's Trip*, presently being featured in national film festivals. In Fall 2001, following the tragedies of 9/11, Charles created and produced his critically acclaimed national collegiate touring series of the one-man play based on Richard Wright's autobiographical landmark, *Black Boy*, as a vehicle of inspiration, healing and freedom.

Over the past five seasons Charles has performed for sold-out audiences for top, national venues, including The John F. Kennedy Center, receiving rave reviews for his 20-character portrayal. In the show's first national review, *The Washington Post* praised, "Holt turned in a lucid and self-possessed performance. Shifting among personalities, Holt flared into moments of idiosyncratic animation, always settling back into the grave tones and dignified posture of Wright the narrator."

As a transformational speaker, Charles hosts numerous workshops and forums around the country. He is founder and creator of *'Miracle Monday,'* a program that encourages members of The Lion King family on Broadway and the youth at Covenant House/New York to empower and inspire one another in a group forum. Read more about Charles Holt at: www.charlesholtproductions.com

# Who do you think you are?

I am inspiration, freedom and healing manifested in form. That's exactly who I am. All of the things I do in terms of my career - singing, acting, stage, film, television, transformational speaking - are a platform for those things to show up and for people to see them. I realized three or four years ago that I no longer had to try to be anybody or be anything. I realized that as soon as I walked into the room people knew exactly who I was. The only person who was kind of clueless at that time was me. I thought that I had to do certain things or dress a certain way. I finally got it, that whenever I step into the room I am inspiration and freedom, I am healing. That's what I've been put on the planet to be. I'm just using the platforms of stage, film, television, music and speaking to get that message across, to inspire somebody to heal the planet. That's what I'm about. I'm about the greater good of the planet, and seeing in people the brilliance and magnificence that we all have.

## What events or series of events led to your discovery?

I've always been guided by divine beings, by spirit, by my ancestors. I had moved to Atlanta to spearhead a new company and a year from the date I started they terminated me. I was talking to one of my friends, who is now one of my mentors, and I was telling him that I got fired. I was actually on the phone with him while I was in my office reading the letter of termination. For some reason, I was not at all shaken by it. I could not understand it. I was sitting there thinking, "I just got fired, I don't know what I'm going to do, but everything is perfect. I am at peace."

The first thing he said was, "You got fired; good, now you can start doing what you're supposed to be doing."

"What is that?" I asked.

"You're an entertainer, Charles," he said.

I said "Okay, how do you know?" This guy was Stevie Wonder's choreographer for his world tour in 1988 and 1989 so I believed him.

I've always had the gift of song. I've always been able to sing and act. I'd do skits and stuff like that, nothing really big. But music and storytelling have always been a big part of my life. So I took his advice and I took an acting class at the Alliance Theatre in Atlanta. That's where my career as a performing artist began. While I was doing a show at The Alliance in 1996, I got a big break during the intermission. I sat down in my dressing room and I heard a voice. I know now that it was the voice of God and the voice told me, "It's time to move, it's time to go." I knew exactly what it meant and I knew where to look. I immediately went to Oxford Books (no longer in existence) on Peach Tree Street. I thumbed through these books called *How To Be A Working Actor In New York* and *How To Be An Actor In Los Angeles*. I chose New York and moved on July 6, 1996.

I was as green as grass gets, but before I went to New York I said to God, "You know I'm supposed to move here. I'm going. I have $400 in my pocket, but it's what I'm going to do." I got to New York and a month later I auditioned for *Jesus Christ Superstar*, the national tour, and I was cast. That's where I met Carl Anderson.

Carl Anderson was my first introduction to Agape. Carl was Judas in Jesus Christ Superstar and I was playing Simon. Carl would always tell me if I ever came to L.A. he wanted me to come to church with him. Carl really took me under his wing and helped me out. He said, "Anything you need, you just let me know, and I'll take care of you while you're on the road."

He made his transition before we ever made it to Agape together, our schedules just didn't match, but Carl was very instrumental in my knowing that someone really cared about me out there. It's a big world, or at least it seems like a big world when all of your family lives in the South and you move to New York. My mom had asked me if I was crazy when I decided to move to New York. I said, "No, I'm going because I know that something is calling me," and I followed that voice.

Since then I've had several experiences of voices speaking to me. Not just in an everyday tone, but in a very declarative one. I get input every now and then, and I know exactly what it's about. I've listened to the voice inside, the voice of God, my higher self speaking to me. It's the spirit within saying it's time to do this, time to do that. It's the guidance of inner self and spirit, universal substance, universal consciousness, and my ancestors.

I started a dialogue with my grandfather while I was living in New York in 2003. It came as a result of someone bumping into me and not saying excuse me for the ninetieth time. I was tired of it. I was marching back to give that person a piece of my mind and I heard his voice say, *"Don't do it, just let it go, don't get yourself all worked up, is not worth it."* The voice kept coming to me, anytime I would get upset or if I thought I was being taken advantage of. I wasn't one to let people just say anything to me. I'd be like, "You're not going to talk to me like

I'm crazy." Then I would see my grandfather's face and hear his gentle voice, "*What is that all about?*"

One day I described him to my mom. "Who is it in our family who has gray hair, no teeth, broad shoulders, and is easy-going?"

"That's your father's father," she said, "your granddaddy."

I said, "Oh wow, well, he talks to me."

"He made his transition when you were three, and you were the light of his life. He loved your dearly."

"He comes and talks to me," I said.

Then I started speaking to my grandmother, and after my grandmother were my aunt and my uncle, and then more people came. Every time they came it would always be extremely uplifting. They still say the greatest things. I know by spirit inside. It's very sacred to me and I'm so thankful that I have that guidance.

What has occurred in my life since moving to Los Angeles has been miraculous. I drove from Nashville to LA and I got here at 10:30 at night on September the 12th. I stayed in a Beverly Hills hotel, because the Polyurethane on the floor in my apartment was not dry. I woke up the next morning and my car and everything I had in it was gone. All I had was a change of clothes and some toiletries. While the sheriff was on the way over to take a stolen car report, I declared that this is exactly where I was supposed to be. And I knew that without a shadow of a doubt. I just declared that, and when I did, the universe opened up to me. I know that the universe is conspiring for my good. I know that for myself.

So that's how I've come to where I am now. It's about trusting, believing, knowing, and just continuing to go. I have a motto that I got from one of Reverend Michael's sermons, and it's that no matter what… whatever it is that I am down here to fulfill, there's nothing that can stop it from unfolding. Nothing. I don't care what appearances may look like, it will be done.

**If you could give advice to those who are still searching for their purpose in life, what would it be?**

I think my advice would be this. If you don't know what you want to do or what the path is for you, do something. Do what's calling you now, because what's calling you now will lead you down the path to what the call is for you later. All paths lead to where you're supposed to be, but you have to travel the path. You have to go towards what looks like the end, which is not really an end. It's just something that leads to another path. When I do my one-man shows I always tell my students maybe you majored in history, or law, or English, or sociology or business and you're thinking now, "I don't know if I want to go to law school, I don't know if I want to go to business school." If you don't know what you want to do, that's okay, but do something. Do something constructive.

I know that once you get on that path doing something constructive, and something that you like, it will help you. It will catapult you into that thing that you would do without getting paid. All of us want to get paid; all of us want to be rewarded financially for us for what we do. When I started singing, I used to sing for free. Then I got to a place where I was like, I'm a little too talented for people not to pay me. I needed to tell myself, "You're worth whatever money you ask for." So do something that moves you so much that you could do it for free, something that brings you that type of passion. If you don't know what your passion is, do something constructive, because it will help you to getting into that place where what you're doing is your passion. It works for everybody, there's something in it for everybody. Just trust your intuition, go down the road, and keep following the path.

# Paul Ryan

*"I'd say that we are given the gift of life from God
and our gift to God is what we do with it".*

**Paul's acclaimed new book, *The Art of Comedy…Getting Serious about Being Funny* was just published by Backstage Books, a division of Watson-Guptill Publishing in New York. His new TV Talk show is *Feel Good TV with Paul Ryan & Friends*, which focuses on optimum health and the entire world of wellness and self-help for the entire family. His speaking engagements on *Hollywood, Health, & Humor* have literally taken him around the globe. Paul is known as Hollywood's premier comedy acting coach and teaches corporations and companies how to bring humor into their presentations in the workplace. He is in his tenth year conducting his very successful monthly *TV Hosting Intensives*, where he hones the skills of TV hosts and those who want to be guest experts in every area of the media.**

**He has hosted and interviewed over 2,000 celebrities internationally as celebrity correspondent for *Entertainment Tonight*, series co-host for *Mid-Morning L.A.*, host/producer/owner of 675 in-depth TV celebrity talk shows with guests including Robin Williams, Jerry Seinfeld, and Sophia Loren, as well as legendary directors, writers and producers. As an actor he's co-starred in films with Michelle Pfeiffer, Goldie Hawn, and Sir Peter Ustinov, movies directed by Sidney Pointier and Gil Cates, guest starred on many TV shows. He is currently in pre-production for a staged reading for his new comedy screenplay.**

**Find out more about Paul Ryan at: www.paulryanproductions.com**

## Who do you think you are?

I am a child of God, made in the image and likeness of God, God loving itself so much that it duplicated itself as me. And I feel that my purpose is to accept fully who I am on the deepest possible level. If there were one word that I hope described Paul Ryan, a.k.a. Bernard Paul Feldman, it would be joy. My life is really about me being in my joy and sharing it unconditionally with others. That's the playing field I like to live in and on. I'm very turned on to performing in the arts. I love the creativity of the entertainment industry, the arena of laughter, making people laugh, and spreading joy. I feel a sense of accomplishment from writing my book, *The Art of Comedy, Getting Serious about Being Funny*. It's definitely a validation of my message.

More than that is living life to the fullest every day and opening up new horizons inside myself. As we all know, life is completely an inside job, and I've always been drawn to those who can inspire my inner growth. That has always been first and foremost in my life. It's about being in synchronicity with those I feel a connection with, where others can help me feel my own deeper connection with truth, love and expansion.

## What events or series of events led to your discovery?

I was an only child growing up in the city of Philadelphia, and I felt there were certainly areas that were very gray to me. Upon reflection, it probably wasn't the perfect environment, but I think I grew up learning what didn't work for me. In my teen years I tried everything that was trendy like smoking, drugs, and alcohol. Fortunately I was terrible at being trendy. I did it, I didn't feel good about it, and couldn't figure out why I didn't feel good about it. I was desperately trying to fit in and trying to be someone I was not.

Then I came to California, and got into transcendental meditation, which I've been doing twice a day for over 20 years. That led me to eating extremely healthy, and watching what I put in my body. My main focus was to have my body feeling as great as possible and that led me to embracing the world of exercise. I speak on the topic of optimum health and well-being, and it's truly all about the balance of mental, physical, emotional and spiritual. One thing led me to another. It was like connecting the dots in my life. Transcendental meditation led me to Arnold Ehret's Mucousless Diet, which allowed me to purify my nervous system and purify my body. This led me to a plethora of seminars. You name a seminar, and I've done it. I've done a lot of personal growth work and am very proud of it. Attending the Agape International Spiritual Center on a regular basis has been the major excavation of my heart and soul. I took the classes to be a practitioner because I was so drawn to the expansion of consciousness available to me. My body got into the car every single Sunday to go to Agape because my spirit undeniably wanted to be there.

I'm very clear that my heart wants to be somewhere where it soars. I like to put myself in places where my soul and spirit are able to play in a high vibration. Everything works together. I guess I'm really attracted to "upliftment." I'd say that the "event" was acutely tuning in to my inner voice and following my own bliss. I followed where my heart wanted to go and people showed up to trigger the next step. I feel incredibly blessed for the people who have come forward in my life. I know that I am well protected and guided, because spirit is taking me where I need to go.

**If you could give advice to those who are still searching for their purpose in life, what would it be?**

I think we learn best by example. I started something recently called Conscious Conversations, and just love it. I bring a group of 20 to 30 people together to have empowering conversation. My advice is to put yourself in environments where you can learn and grow. A lot of people put themselves into circumstances to do what everybody else is doing. I am certainly still a work-in-progress, but what has really helped me was putting myself in environments where I could continually unfold and expand my consciousness. The days of going to places to numb myself are definitely over. Places filled with smoking, drinking, drugging, and processed foods don't lend themselves to optimum living.

We live in a world today where there's so much information about how to have more qualitative living. If you're ignoring it, you're ignoring the possibility of a life filled with inner fulfillment. There are so many trappings around us, whether it's shopping or drinking or over indulgence. Once you find your center and find out who you are there's more possibility for discovering you inner rainbows.

I'd also recommend spending a lot of time in nature to see examples of perfection. Watch and observe the flowers blooming, the trees swaying, feeling the air all around you, and looking up at the sky. That's true perfection. When we know that we are one with that, it's the most exciting journey possible. I'd say that we are given the gift of life from God and our gift to God is what we do with it. I think the key to life is to keep loving more and more. How much more loving can you be? How much more loving are you willing to become? That's the greatest question that one can ask, and the greatest answer is to go for the gold. Give and receive love all the time, freely and with unabashed joy. Enjoy the process of your life at the deepest possible level. Enjoy the whole enchilada!

# J. Karen Thomas

*"Go within, go within, go within, go within, go within,*
*go within, go within."*

**J. Karen Thomas is an Actress, Singer/ Songwriter, Dancer and Voice Over Artist, who is grateful to have worked alongside Ellen Degeneres, Ossie Davis, and Oscar Winners; Jennifer Hudson and Jamie Foxx. Recurring TV roles include:** *Alley McBeal, City of Angels and Melrose Place.* **Recent Guest Stars:** *Criminal Minds, Crossing Jordan* **and HBO's** *Big Love.*

**She and her environmental activism are central to the Sony Classics' Documentary;** *Who Killed the Electric Car?* **On stage she's played Lorrell in** *DREAMGIRLS,* **the Nurse in** *ROMEO and JULIET,* **Velma Kelly in** *CHICAGO,* **Yvette in** *MOTHER COURAGE,* **and most recently Titania Hippolyta in Shakespeare Festival/LA's jazzy** *A MIDSUMMER NIGHT'S DREAM.*

**J. Karen's volunteer roster includes Agape Spiritual Center's** *Music and Dance Ministries, Outfest, POWER UP,* **and SAG's** *Bookpals.* **She loves dogs, nature, her family, and sharing her gifts with the world.**

**You can contact J. Karen Thomas through  Met Talent Management 323-924-1194 or by visiting: www.jkarenthomas.com**

## Who do you think you are?

I am a queen, a goddess, and a blessed loyal holy child of God. I know I am here to do great things. I'm here to heal, to bless, and to inspire through my talents, my gifts, and through my service. That's what I think I am on a spiritual level. That's the journey isn't it? To always be able to keep that foremost in my view of who I am.

On the physical level, I would say I am an actress, a singer, and a dancer. On the mental level, where the worry, doubts, and fears live, there is the part that says, "Aw, you aint doing nothing'. You're going too slow." So, as I go along on my journey I'm knowing that I'm in the perfect place at the right time and living my purpose, and that I'm not here to question what time it is. It's about God's timing, and there are so many breakthroughs happening in my life right now. There's this gigantic energy flow coming through me to create more and have it out there on a global level.

**What events or series of events led to your discovery?**

I always knew that I was here to do great things; I just didn't know what. I've always seen myself as an actress, and "singer" is a label that I'm starting to wear more fully. I am a singer. There are a lot of people who sing, and I thought I was an actress who sang and moved well or danced. Now I'm learning that I am all of these things fully, there are no parts in God, things are fully what they are.

I used to be a radio DJ in Nashville, Memphis, and Atlanta. I am originally from Nashville, Tennessee. In fact, I call myself an international Southern Belle. For a while, I had loved radio, but it got to the point where I was only a liking it, and I wasn't completely focused on what I was doing. I really wanted to be a full performer; I really wanted to be an actress and a singer.

At that time I was working mid-days at a radio station and my boss called me in and told me I was getting a demotion. I said, "I'm not doing that - I can't do that." He told me he was putting me on overnights for a while. I told him, "I am not doing overnights." I didn't know what I was going to do, but it was a turning point for me. There was something else I was supposed to do, so I went on a leave of absence for a while to figure it out.

After a week on leave, I got a call to perform, in a theatrical production in Boston. It was a lead role in a musical that I loved, *Ain't Misbehavin*, so I got to use all of my performance gifts: acting, singing, and dancing. I was being paid well as an actor in a full equity show. And I absolutely took that opportunity to make a change in my career path, because I had gotten disillusioned with radio. I was ready for a change, but I didn't know how to make the change. It took that low point for me to recognize that it's tough for me surrender and let something more come in.

I didn't know what it is or where it was coming from, but I knew there was something greater for me to do. I realized that I am only here to do great things. If you're asking me to do something that's not great, it's not for me. And it wasn't just for my ego. What I was really working on was being in that stillness and being in that presence all of the time. Where it's not just about "How did I look?" or "How did I sound? Did you see me? What did you think?" But knowing that I am here to share a service.

Another turning point was moving to LA. I've lived here for about eleven years now. And another was meeting my divine life partner, Colette

Divine. She and I are featured as Documentary subjects in the film *Who Killed the Electric Car?* She always challenges me and holds me accountable to stand in my truth and my greatness. Making a choice to be with her (we've been together ten years now) has confirmed to me that everything I was feeling and knowing deep within me was true.

My dear dad, who was always such a strong, honorable, and forthright man passed away in 2004. That really reminded me that tomorrow is not promised, so the things that we want to do here on this planet we need to do them now!

**If you could give advice to those who are still searching for their life's purpose, what would it be?**

Go within, go within, go within, go within, go within, go within, go within. When I was first getting ready to move to LA, I had a lot of questions. I've written a song about it, too. I was asking everybody what they thought. "Should I move here, do you think it's time, should I move here, I've got a good life there, should I stay with this person, should I break up with that person, should be with this new person, should I live here this house, should I do this, should I do that?"

I talked to psychics, highly recommended psychics, looking at it on a spiritual level. I asked what they saw for me, what I should be doing for my career, what I should be for my relationship… and I already knew all of these things. All of these things were right within me. I'm not saying don't go to a psychic, if that's the perfect right thing to do for you at that moment. Maybe I would do it again, but the biggest lesson for me was that it's all within.

Go into the stillness, into the closet and sanctuary of your soul, go into meditation and prayer, journal even. Journaling has been a great tool for me to reveal what spirit wants me to do, how spirit moves through me. Find a spiritual practice. Find a spiritual center that works for you. Where there are people who reflect the truth to you when you get into questions. We all have points where we get into questions and confusion, when we look to people to stand in the truth and know the truth for us, even when we don't know it ourselves. It's great to have that sense of community. That's what Agape is for me, does for me.

Again, to sum it up in two words, go within.

# Chantelle Paige

*"God puts people and circumstances in your life for a reason!"*

Chantelle Paige is a young California girl who grew up in the Bay Area and currently lives near Los Angeles. She has had a great deal of success in the realms of modeling, acting, dancing, academics and music.

She began modeling at the age of three and has been on the cover of over 35 catalogs, magazines, brochures and billboards. When she was 8, a "Chantelle" doll & book series were made in her name and image for a catalog (Storybook Heirlooms) that she worked with for over ten years. If you were born after 1985, you most likely opened a toy box with her image on it when you were younger.

Chantelle attended a private Christian high school where she graduated in 2006 with a 4.1 GPA. In addition to performing, she enjoys helping people and in 05/06 she volunteered for Big Brothers/Big Sisters & Hurricane Katrina Relief.

Despite her success in a variety of arenas, Chantelle's first love is music. She enjoys expressing herself through singing and songwriting. Her six-song Demo EP (April 2006) was produced by Tone, whose credits include artists such as Santana, Green Day, Outkast, Gwen Stefani, and The Black-Eyed Peas. The day after posting her first song on MySpace Music, Chantelle became one of the top 20 unsigned artists on the site. Since then, she has gained over 243,000+ fans and close to 6 million song spins (plays) on the popular website. She has recently opened for The Pussycat Dolls, Pretty Ricky, Bobbie Valentino and Robin Thicke.

## Who do you think you are?

Everyone has a purpose in life that benefits others. Whether we allow God to use us to fulfill that purpose or not is up to us as individuals. Wrong choices, laziness and even fear can veer us away from what we were created to be. No one is perfect, but we must strive to be our best and we have to work hard and not sit around waiting for something to fall in our laps! I try to use all of my mishaps along the way to learn and grow, and eventually, hopefully fulfill even part of the purpose that was intended for my life!

The purpose of my life is to be what I was created to be and from a very early age I knew that everything about me belonged in the entertainment industry. It's not work, it's joy! But, I don't sit around waiting for something to come to me and hit me in the face. I take voice lessons, acting lessons, I go on auditions, I perform, and I record. I'm appreciative of my fans and to everyone in my life who's helping me with my foundation.

Even though I went to a Christian High School and constantly had teachers telling me to sing Christian music, I knew that wasn't for me. Circumstances made me certain of that. I feel that I can have more of an impact on a secular crowd, and that's where my heart is, at least for now.

### What event or series of events led you to your discovery?

I've been falling into discoveries since the age of three when my mom put me in dance! When I was five, my dance teacher auditioned my team to sing a solo for a charity event. I was picked and my teacher told my mom she had to put me in voice lessons. My mom always tells me, "If it wasn't for Alison, voice lessons NEVER would have crossed my mind." Crazy how God places people in our lives!

When I was three I was approached about modeling and that led to acting. I've honestly never really pursued anything, it just all fell into place. I have strong work ethics, I try hard to stay humble, people refer me because of my attitude and I often get things that much more talented people probably deserve simply because I'm a hard worker and not a diva.

After my dance teacher made up a little song and dance number for me at age five, I started singing at fairs, at competitions and at festivals. At an art and wine festival, I was approached by someone who suggested that I audition for a musical theatre production. CMTSJ is one of the best theater groups in the nation. I auditioned at age nine, got a great part, and fell in love with theatre.

Acting, modeling, singing, and dancing have all been training grounds for my purpose in life. So many other things have made me who I am as well though! My parents raised me to have morals and took me to church. They've been married for 25 years and have shown me so much love and support. I would NEVER be able to be a performer if it wasn't for all of their sacrifices, time, and cheering me on through the years. God puts people and circumstances in your life for a reason!

I was home schooled in grade school because I was modeling and acting so much. Okay, I know what you're thinking... she's one of those weird home-schooled kids. Nope. My mom was an amazing teacher and because of all the dancing and theater I did I was always around kids my age and being social. I think that being home-schooled not only made me a hard worker, because I had the best teacher pushing me, but it also made me an independent person.

As for the future, I want to keep a high standard in an industry full of immorality, and hopefully not only make an impact on my fans but other artists as well. I want to always have a few songs on my album that challenge or lift people up.

**If you could give advice to those who are still searching for their purpose in life, what would it be?**

I'd ask them, "What are you good at? What brings you joy?" Be honest about your circumstances, how they have shaped you as a person. Are they there to show you your purpose? What are you afraid of?

I really believe that we know what our purpose in life is. At least I do. Not everyone was created to be a rock star or a pro athlete and it's not about money. I remember an example about a hammer. A hammer was created to pound nails. That hammer can be used to hit and destroy things, even to harm others. It can be used to hold a window or door open. It can sit useless in a toolbox. But, it was still created to pound nails and that's what its "creator" had in mind when he made that hammer. It's pretty simple. Look for the obvious, AND BELIEVE!

# ARE YOU HERE TO BE A SPEAKER?

# John Demartini

*"I believe very strongly that everything in your life*
*is actually directing you."*

**Dr. John Demartini is a world leading inspirational speaker and author at the forefront of the burgeoning personal and professional development industry. His scope of knowledge and experience is a culmination of 35 years of research and studies of more than 28,600 texts into over 250 different disciplines ranging from psychology, philosophy, metaphysics, theology, anthropology, neurology and physiology.**

**Today, Dr. Demartini speaks 300 days a year in over fifty countries across the globe and is the author of over forty books. Some of his best-selling titles include *The Breakthrough Experience – a Revolutionary New Approach to Personal Transformation*, *Count Your Blessings – The Healing Power of Gratitude and Love*, *How to Make One Hell of a Profit and Still Get to Heaven* and *The Heart of Love*.**

**As a presenter, Dr. Demartini has shared the stage with such noted speakers as Stephen Covey, Dr. Donald Beck, Les Brown, Mark Victor Hansen, Dr. Deepak Chopra, Dr. Wayne Dyer, Dr. Patch Adams and many others. He has been a welcomed guest on over 2,000 radio and television talk shows including: CNN Larry King Live, CBS's The Early Show, PBS's This is America with Dennis Wholey, CNBC's Alive and Wellness, Mornings with Kerri-Anne, Good Morning Australia, Carte Blanche, 3 Talk, and Voice of America.**

**Learn more about Dr. Demartini at: www.DrDemartini.com**

## Who do you think you are?

This is a question that philosophers have been asking for millenniums. How and why did this whole universe begin? Why are human beings here? What is their purpose? We could get very broad and deep about the answers, or we could just probe our own selves and say that we are here to integrate our lives and to take everything that we haven't appreciated and loved, and appreciate and love it. We are here to live our lives to the fullest. We are here to be inspired by and thankful for our existence and reach out to expand and explore our greatest human awareness and potential and live to the farthest reaches of our capacities during our physical earthly existence.

## What event or series of events led to your discovery?

When I was seventeen, I had the opportunity to meet a great teacher named Paul C. Bragg. My life changed as a result of meeting him on the North Shore of Oahu in the Sunset Recreation Hall at Weimea Bay. I listened to him speak that night. He was an elderly man who taught great wisdom. That night I listened to him speak about the body, mind, and soul and the impact they have on our life potential. Listening to him at that meeting that special night was certainly a life-changing event for me. I became inspired and decided that I wanted to dedicate the rest of my life to studying what he termed Universal Laws as they relate to the body, mind and soul, particularly as they relate to healing, probably because I had a health problem at the time. I wanted to become a teacher, healer and philosopher, step foot in every country on the face of the earth and share my research findings with people to help them live inspired and magnificent lives. That is what came to me that night and that's all I've been focusing on and living for the last thirty-five years.

## If you could give advice to people who are still searching for their purpose in life, what would it be?

It is wise to scan your life and look at all the actions that you've taken that have inspired you and find the common thread in each of them. Look at where your skills are most profound. Look at what you have done that has been most inspiring, most meaningful and most purposeful to you and synthesize these. This will point you in a meaningful direction. Everything in your life is actually directing you. When you experience tears of gratitude in your eyes, you're on track. So pay close attention to those moments.

Doing what you love and loving what you do is the key to living a fulfilling life. If you look at who your heroes have been, what you've studied most, what you thought about most, what you've mastered most, what you're inspired by most, and integrate them, you'll discover what your mission in life really is.

I wrote my initial mission statement when I was with Paul Bragg in 1972 and refined it fifty-seven times since then. I read it every day. I have it in front of me right now. My mission is what I'm up to; it's the highest priority I have in my life. I've also focused on documenting all the objectives that I intend to accomplish in my life and keep record of them all as they emerge and become fulfilled. I have the largest collection of goals, and the largest collection of experiences to feel gratitude for, of anyone I know. If you can imagine thirty-five years worth – every single day, that's a lot of gratitudes.

I've been writing, reading and refining my mission statement, goal book, gratitude book and accomplishment book since I was seventeen, and I'm fifty-three now. So I'm a big believer in defining and refining and re-defining and re-refining your dreams, constantly polishing exactly how you would love your life to be, and being realistic and inspired by the vision of your destiny. Making sure it's truly what you would love to have as your destiny. If you can't wait to get up in the morning and go and live it then you're clear and on track. If for some reason you're still not inspired by your life and your mission, then you obviously have not yet clearly defined and refined enough.

# Paul Scheele

*"I realized that my job was to be a de-hypnotist, to awaken people from negative, self-limiting trances that they have accepted in life and to help them reclaim the magnificence of who they are."*

You are brilliant beyond your imagination! Paul R. Scheele has facilitated this realization in millions of lives. He guides people to achieve extraordinary results in relationships, work, money and health. Paul is an expert on learning how to tap the other 90% of your mind. He believes everyone has an inner genius just waiting to be awakened.

Paul, co-founder of Learning Strategies Corporation, is the developer of programs such as *PhotoReading,* a powerful system for processing the written page at 25,000 words per minute, *Natural Brilliance, Genius Code, Abundance for Life, the Paraliminals* self-development series, and many other courses to stimulate personal and professional success. These programs allow people to go beyond what the logical mind believes possible and break through stuck states. When you want high impact, Paul will entertain, educate, inspire, and move audiences to use their genius minds and achieve amazing abundance.

Paul Scheele has activated the natural brilliance within millions of people around the globe during the past thirty years. He educates audiences how to access their full potential using powerful learning strategies. His unique combination of expertise includes degrees in Biology and Learning and Human Development plus a rich background in neuro-linguistic programming (NLP), accelerated learning, preconscious processing, and universal energy. Paul uses his specialized knowledge to deliver leading-edge, thought-provoking programs and helps people acquire information many times faster than through traditional methods. His programs provide the rare experience of tapping the vast innate potential of the mind to attain more success in life. Sharing how to activate these rich resources within the mind and connecting this natural power with spiritual wisdom is Paul's passion.

His work has been translated into more than fifteen languages and purchased by enthusiastic clients in 155 countries. Paul is also a founding member of the *Transformational Leadership Council.*

Read more about Paul at: www.LearningStrategies.com

**Who do you think you are?**

Who I am is defined by goals as well as passions, and the roles that I play are varied. I'm chairman of an organization. I'm a participant of communities of various sizes. I'm a father and a husband. When you really get back to the concept of purpose, I stand to testify to the genius in you, assisting you in reclaiming that genius capacity and healing the wounded learner in you. So the work that I do flows out of that. It's helping people reclaim the natural brilliance that they are and the genius capacity within them.

**What event or series of events led to your discovery?**

While I was at the University of Minnesota as a student in biological sciences, I had an opportunity to be trained as a professional hypnotist. At the age of nineteen I began to do individual consultations using hypnosis out of a clinic in the Twin Cities. Two years later I took over that practice, and it was the oldest established hypnosis practice in the Twin Cities of Minneapolis and St. Paul.

　　During that time I had the opportunity to present a demonstration of hypnosis for a church youth group. I had about ten of the kids in the deep trance state, and I was demonstrating the power of hypnotic suggestion. I told one of the kids, "Your foot is glued to the floor, you can try to move it but you cannot, it's glued to the floor!" and he couldn't move his foot. Since it was early in my career, and I had just learned these techniques, I was kind of surprised and was thinking, "Wow, this works; I'll try something even more powerful!" Then I said, "You've forgotten your name, you can try to tell me your name, but you can't do it. You've forgotten it. Try to tell me your name."　As I watched this kid struggle - completely unable to say his own name - I realized that's what we're doing to ourselves all the time. We're taking perfectly reasonable resources of mind and body and we're essentially throwing them out because we accept the suggestion of "I cannot." So, at about 20 years old, I realized my job wasn't about putting people into trances, they're already there. They're in self-limiting, self-defeating trances, accepting a belief in what they're incapable of doing. I realized that my job was to be a de-hypnotist to awaken people from negative, self-limiting trances that they have accepted in life, and to help them reclaim the magnificence of who they are.

**If you could give advice to people who are still searching for their purpose in life, what would it be?**

There's a great quotation by Ralph Waldo Emerson. He said, "Find your soul, and if it's still alive, poke it with a stick, find out which way it moves and then follow it."

The idea is to tune in to yourself and find out what your passion is. Make a commitment to follow your own passion. You'll always be making the best choices. The second part to that is to stay with it. To stay with whatever it is you make a commitment to and find out which way it goes, where it takes you.

Understanding your purpose and living a life of purpose is a process of discovery. It's not something that you sit down and write out as an interesting pithy phrase. It's really something that emerges. When you start seeing your life as a co-creative emergent activity with a loving, supportive universe that's trying to express itself through you as you, then you know that you have an immense power on your side to get you where you want to go.

# Les Brown

*"You have greatness within you. Know that and be with that thought on a daily basis. Know that greatness is a choice; it's not your destiny."*

As a renowned professional speaker, author and television personality, Les Brown has risen to national prominence by delivering a high-energy message, which tells people how to shake off mediocrity and live up to their greatness. It is a message Les Brown has learned from his own life and one he is helping others apply to their lives.

Born a twin in low-income Liberty City in Miami, Florida, Les and his twin brother, Wes, were adopted when they were six weeks old by Mrs. Mamie Brown. Mrs. Brown was a single woman who had very little education or financial means, but a very big heart. As a child, Les' inattention to school work, his restless energy, and the failure of his teachers to recognize his true potential resulted in him being mislabeled as a slow learner. The label and the stigma stayed with him, damaging self-esteem to such an extent that it took several years to overcome.

Les has had no formal education beyond high school, but with persistence and determination he has initiated and continued a process of unending self-education, which has distinguished him as an authority on harnessing human potential. Les Brown's passion to learn and his hunger to realize greatness in himself and others helped him to achieve greatness. He rose from a hip-talking morning DJ to broadcast manager; from community activist to community leader; from political commentator to three-term legislator; and from a banquet and nightclub emcee to premier keynote speaker.

Les Brown is an internationally recognized speaker and CEO of Les Brown Enterprises, Inc., he is also the author of the highly acclaimed and successful books, *Live Your Dreams,* and newly released book, *It's Not Over Until You Win.* Les is the former host of *The Les Brown Show,* a nationally syndicated daily television talk show that focused on solutions rather than problems. He is one of the nation's leading authorities in understanding and stimulating human potential. Utilizing powerful delivery and newly emerging insights, Les' customized presentation teaches, inspires, and channels audiences to new levels of achievement.

Read more about Les Brown at: www.LesBrown.com

# Who do you think you are?

I think that the calling on my life is to help people get a larger vision of themselves beyond their circumstances and mental conditioning. I came to that level of awareness in terms of my purpose because of what has happened in my own life: born in an abandoned building on the floor, adopted, labeled educable mentally retarded, put back from fifth to fourth grade, having no formal college training. I then experienced a life-transforming event when I met someone who interrupted the story I believed about myself, the things that had been said about me, and based upon the results that I had produced at that particular time. I had this limited vision of myself, and as a result of this relationship, it dramatically changed the way I saw myself. As a result of that, in my own mind and spirit I wanted to be that type of person to other people. I wanted to impact and inspire others to get an expanded vision of themselves and realize what was said in The Lion King, "Samba, you're more than that which you have become." That to me has become my theme and the mantra of my life and that's where I have been living from.

## What event or series of events led to your discovery?

There have been three events. One, when I was adopted. I believe something that Abraham Lincoln said, "All that I am, and all that I ever hope to be, I owe to my mother." I realized something that really impacted me. God took me out of my mother's biological womb and placed me in the heart of my adoptive mother. So, my mother, Mrs. Mamie Brown, always made me feel special, and I was one of seven kids that she adopted.

The other person who impacted me was Mr. Leroy Washington, a high school teacher who I met my junior year in high school. He was a substitute instructor, and he asked me to go to the board to work something out. I was in his class waiting for another student, so I said, "Sir, I can't do what you asked me to do."

He asked me, "Why not?"

I replied, "I'm not one of your students."

He said, "It doesn't matter, follow my directions anyhow."

The other students began to laugh, because they knew that I was in special education. They knew my twin brother, Wesley, and one of the kids said, "That's Leslie not Wesley, that's DT."

That's what they called me, DT, which stood for the "dumb twin."

I said, "I'm not the smart one."

He came out from behind his desk and said, "Don't ever say that again. Someone's opinion of you does not have to become your reality."

That was a defining moment in my life. On one hand, I was humiliated, but on the other hand, I was liberated. The students were laughing at me when I turned around and tried to follow the directions that he was giving me. But at that moment I felt like he was looking at me with the eyes of Goethe who said, "Look at a man the way that he is, he only becomes worse. But look at him as if he were what he could be, and then he becomes what he should be."

That moment was a life-transforming moment because he had given me a vision of myself beyond that which I had believed about myself. Because of what had been spoken to me, the results of my life academically had convinced me that I was far less than what I was.

The other person is a gentleman named Mike Williams, who's been my mentor for the last thirty-eight years. I hired him as my first newsman and through talking in between the records I was spinning, he convinced me that I was more than a disc jockey. I believed that I was a disc jockey. I was "Les Brown, man about town. There were none before me; there will be none after me. Therefore that makes me the one and only. Young and single and love to mingle." So this guy talked to me about having a larger vision of myself beyond radio. He talked to me about being a communicator, not just seeing myself as a disc jockey. He talked to me about seeing myself as a catalyst of action and a messenger of hope.

That vision he had of me I did not see at the time. But, I came to understand that sometimes you have to believe in somebody's belief in you until your belief in you catches up. This gave birth to a Les Brown that I did not know existed. That relationship so empowered me that it inspired me to give up who I was for who I could become and who I am still becoming. I am much like George Bernard Shaw, who was asked if he had it in his power to come back as anyone throughout all of history who would it be? He said, "I'd like to become the man I never was."

That's where I am. I'm still reaching, I'm still searching, I'm still groping and I'm still learning. I'm like the woman who said, "Lord, I ain't what I want to be, I ain't what I'm gonna be, but thank God I sure ain't what I was.

It's because of my relationships with Mike Williams, Mr. Washington and my mother that this Les Brown, who's communicating with you right now, has become the person he is today.

**If you could give advice to those who are still searching for their purpose in life, what would it be?**

I would say that number one it is very important that you don't settle for what life is giving you. Judge not according to appearances. There is a mind-sight and then there's eyesight. There are a lot of people who define their lives, and the possibilities for less, based upon what they see in terms of their education, their bank accounts, their circumstances, and what they've accomplished.

Mind-sight you live out of your imagination as opposed to your memory. Einstein said, "The imagination is the preview of what's to come." Go through life with a vision of yourself beyond where you are. If you are aware of what your purpose is, work on it with everything that's in you and through persistence and perseverance you'll discover some things about yourself that you didn't even know. You'll create some magic moments in your life and you'll make an impact with your life that you can't even imagine.

If you don't know, continue to search until you find out what it is that resonates with you, what turns you on, what is it that you could do twenty-four hours a day for free. A career is something you love so much that you would do it for nothing, but you do it so well that people are willing to pay you for it.

Something else I heard that I believe very strongly in, and is the place from which I live my life: Man was not born to make a living, but to live his making; and living his making will make his living. What is the making? Why were you chosen out of 400 million sperm? Once you discover why that is, and what it is you're supposed to do, your life takes on a whole new meaning. But it's up to you.

You have greatness within you. Know that and be with that thought on a daily basis. Know that greatness is a choice; it's not your destiny. Live your life from a place of knowing that you are something special, that you have greatness within you, that you were chosen to be here. Know that there's something you have that if you don't deliver it, if you don't leave it here, then all of the world will be deprived. In historical context, the world will be a better place because you came here and did what it is that you were supposed to do. Move in life with the spirit of expectation, curiosity, discovery, and know that there's always more.

# Rudy Ruettiger

*"Once you know what you want, ask yourself, 'Why Not Me?'*
*Why shouldn't you be the one who achieves your goals*
*and lives your dreams?"*

**Against all odds on a gridiron in South Bend, Indiana, Daniel "Rudy" Ruettiger in twenty-seven seconds carved his name into history books as perhaps the most famous graduate of the University of Notre Dame. The son of an oil refinery worker and third of 14 children, Rudy rose from valleys of discouragement and despair to the pinnacles of success.**

**Today, he is one of the most popular motivational speakers in the United States. It took years of fierce determination to overcome obstacles and criticisms, yet Rudy achieved his first dream - to attend Notre Dame and play football for the Fighting Irish. As fans cheered RU-DY, RU-DY, he sacked the quarterback in the last 27 seconds of the only play in the only game of his college football career. He is the only player in the school's history to be carried off the field on his teammates' shoulders.**

**In 1993, TRISTAR Productions immortalized his life story with the blockbuster film, RUDY. Written and produced by Angelo Pizzo and David Anspaugh, the award-winning team who brought us HOOSIERS, the critically acclaimed RUDY received "Two Thumbs Up" from Siskel and Ebert and continues to inspire millions worldwide.**

**Today, a highly sought after motivational speaker, Rudy entertains international corporate audiences with a unique, passionate, and heartfelt style of communicating. He reaches school children, university students, and professional athletes with the same enthusiasm, portraying the human spirit that comes from his personal experiences of adversity and triumph. In addition to his motivational speaking, Rudy has co-authored several books, including: *Rudy's Insights for Winning in Life*, *Rudy's Lessons for Young Champions*, and *Rudy & Friends*, and has produced the Dream Power tape series.**

**Read more about Rudy Ruettiger at: www.Rudyinternational.com**

### Who do you think you are?

My mission is to be an example and a source of hope. It's to be an inspiration and to encourage people to dream. And I mean dream big!  I am a person who believes in making goals and committing to achieving those goals. I believe in being accountable for my own outcome, whether it's in my personal achievements or in my business. I'm always looking for ways to stretch myself and for new ways to grow.

**What event or series of events led you to your discovery?**

Well, I knew who everyone else wanted me to be, but that's not what I had in mind. I had a completely different idea. I wanted to play football for Notre Dame and no one was going to convince me otherwise. I had my doubts at one point, and I went inside myself, redefined who I was, and I became very clear that I could do it. I knew that if I put my mind to it and kept moving forward I could reach my goals. Not only could I play football for Notre Dame, but I could achieve my academic goals, and moving forward I could achieve my business goals as well. The bottom line is this, "If I can do it, anyone can do it."

**If you could give advice to people who are still searching for their purpose in life, what would it be?**

First you should define who you are, then discover what it is that you want. What do you want? So many people can't answer this question, and yet they wonder why they keep getting more of what they don't want. What do you like, what are your passions, what would you do all day long if money were no object?

Once you know what you want, ask yourself, "Why Not Me?" Why shouldn't you be the one who achieves your goals and lives your dreams? You deserve great things just as much as anyone else does. Make positive thinking a habit, and you will start to see your thoughts manifest right in front of your eyes. Read positive books for motivation, and surround yourself with positive people. Surrounding yourself with nothing but positive energy can't help but attract more positive to you! It's just how it is. You CAN do anything you want to do, and be anyone you want to be, if you have faith in yourself and the courage to finish what you started.

# Marcia Martin

*"Realize how much you do know, and really come from yourself. Bring your inner power into the world rather than searching for yourself in the outside world."*

Marcia Martin has been a Teacher of Success for over 30 years in the Transformational Training Business. She is renowned internationally for being one of the leading Life & Executive Coaches, and Transformational Trainers in the World today.

Marcia is considered to be one of the original pioneers of the Human Potential Movement, and was instrumental in training many of the executives and managers of the leading transformational training companies, including *Esalen Institute, Landmark Forum, Technico, Life Spring, Insight, Actualizations, International Federation of Coaches (IFC), Sports Mind, Self Esteem Seminars, Tony Robbins Seminars, Human Potential Project, Money & You, Accelerated Learning,* and *Delfin International.*

She is the Executive Vice President and a Board Member of *The Transformational Leadership Council* (TLC), a not-for-profit association she helped co-found in 2004 with Jack Canfield, the famed author of the *Chicken Soup for the Soul* book series. As the Executive Vice President of TLC she is responsible for Program Development, Event Production, Media, and Communication.

In 1971, Marcia was one of the original founding members of est, *Erhard Seminars Training,* the largest human potential training and educational company in the world. As the Senior Vice President of est, Marcia was responsible for training the trainers, graduate, and guest seminar leaders in the arena of enrollment, sales, and presentation skills. She managed the Communication Registration Division and created the Guest Seminar Leaders Training Program (GSLP).

In 1985, Marcia founded her own consulting and transformational training company, MM Productions (also known as Power Speaking Seminars). As the CEO and President, Marcia currently delivers corporate and public trainings, seminars, and courses that teach people to be successful and how to create the results they want in their lives and in their organizations. Marcia's clients include: Inter-Continental Hotels International, Loews Hotels International, Capital One Financial Services Inc, Chase Manhattan Bank, and Warner Brothers. She has personally trained and coached over 150,000 people worldwide to be more effective in their lives and communication.

In July of 2005, she was selected by Rhonda Byrne, the Executive Producer of the world phenomena DVD and Book *The Secret,* to be one of the TLC Teachers interviewed for the film, and is a recognized expert in teaching the Law of Attraction. She is also the Associate Producer and a regular guest host of the international television series *Positive Living TV,* to be shown in over 100 countries by the end of 2008.

Marcia Martin holds a BS degree from the University of San Francisco in Communication Arts & Business Development. She currently lives in Aspen, Colorado with her family.

# Who do you think you are?

I am definitely about one purpose, and I think I'm part of the human family and a part of the universe that's all connected. I think my purpose is to do the best I can to express myself and to be in life in a way that I learn as much as I can, and am able to give back as much as I can by the end of my life. When I get there I'd like to say, at this time I have done my best to leave it a better place. I will have made sure that the people I interacted with are in a better place as a result of knowing me and they were touched by me in some way. It's an expression of life that's growing and evolving.

## What event or series of events led to your discovery?

I think the first major thing was my teachers when I was young growing up. They always told me that I could have anything and do anything, and that anything was possible. So that's how I viewed the world. When I was twenty-one I met my aunt, who is a clairvoyant healer. She suggested I study world religions, meditate, understand how my body and mind worked, and understand how energy worked. She taught me the perspective that we're all connected. That humanity and the earth and nature are all connected, and that I could come from a higher power by going deep inside myself and connecting to that.

Next, I met Werner Erhard. I was about twenty-three years old when I met him, and he had just been made an instructor for a company called Mind Dynamics. I took his first seminar for Mind Dynamics and I soon became one of his staff members. Later that year, we created a seminar company called est. About ten people were the original founders.

I spent ten years with Werner as the Vice President of est, which later became The Landmark Forum. During those years I was the spokesperson for est and in charge of all the marketing, promotion, production, and enrollment. I trained the guest seminar leaders and the trainers, taught the seminar leaders how to speak effectively in front of groups, and was in charge of filling all of the events.

During those ten years of my life I learned so much about how one manifests, how one creates results in this universe, about the law of attraction, the power of the word and how we use language, and how to connect with other people. Life since then has been an ever-evolving process. It's being about growing, learning more, connecting more, and been able to make a bigger contribution as I move through life.

**If you could give advice to those who are still searching for their life's purpose, what would it be?**

The search is not outside of your self, the search is within. For those of you who are looking for something outside of yourself to find the answer to who you are, if you redirect your energy and look within, all of your answers are there. Come from that place of knowing, rather than trying to search out something that you don't know. Realize how much you do know, and really come from yourself. Find yourself in your inner world.

I would also say to read as much as you can, attend as many courses, workshops, seminars and classes as you can, and see as many speakers as possible. Really keep your mind open, alert, and always learning. Don't think that learning is over just because you graduate from high school or college or get some kind of title at work. As a human being you are always evolving, always emerging, and always expanding. To the degree that you are doing that, you are still alive. And to the degree that you think the learning process is over, you're really in the process of dying.

# Greg Scott Reid

*"When you do what you love, and love what you do,*
*you'll have success, your whole life through."*

Filmmaker Gregory Scott Reid is a #1 best-selling author, entrepreneur, and the CEO of several successful corporations who has dedicated his life to helping others achieve the ultimate fulfillment of finding and living a life of purpose.

In his first feature film *Pass It On*, Reid guides the viewer through a virtual tour of what it takes to create an abundant life. The motion picture features modern-day masters who share the proven success strategies that Reid has applied to inspire thousands with his books and to motivate audiences around the country for the last two decades.

Reid's work has been published in 21 books, eight bestsellers and three #1 bestsellers, and can be found worldwide. His most popular titles *The Millionaire Mentor, Positive Impact,* and *Wake Up, Live the Life You Love* teach the principles he learned from his mentors: to achieve extraordinary success one must first help others to succeed.

His unique style has made him a highly sought-after keynote speaker for corporations, universities, and charitable organizations. He's even earned praise from the White House: "Making your own outstanding contributions...you have devoted your time, talents and energy to fulfill America's bright promise for all our people," said former President Bill Clinton.

A native Californian, Reid is the founder and former CEO of Work$mart, Inc. an innovative advertising firm. He's also the CEO of three rapidly growing corporations in San Diego including WISH Entertainment, The Millionaire Mentor, Inc., Reliable Furniture, LLC, and the co-owner of BASIC, the hottest new restaurant in downtown San Diego.

Ask Reid how he's doing, and he'll respond with "always good." And when you part ways he'll likely offer a suggestion to "keep smiling" – a friendly reflection of his powerful message to maintain a positive, solution-seeking attitude, and a reminder to others that true success comes in the giving, not the keeping.

For media or speaking inquires contact:  WISH Entertainment, Inc. To learn more about his movie, go to: www.PassItonToday.com or email media@passitontoday.com

**Who do you think you are?**

I am a mentor to many. In fact the majority of my purpose on this planet is to be a beacon and guide to help others define their goals and their mission. A lot of people think I got the name *The Millionaire Mentor* because I only work with millionaires and corporations, and although that's the majority of what I do, I actually mentor many inner city gang kids in San Diego, California. That's where my passion is.

It seems like society keeps telling kids, and even adults, where we shouldn't go, what we shouldn't say, and what we shouldn't do. I thought to myself, wouldn't it be cool to be that one voice of reason that asks, "What can you do? What are you capable of? What could you do with your life if you didn't have any obstacles and limitations?" Then help guide them towards what their answer is to those questions. Everyone has a different mission and purpose on this planet, and it's just an awesome life to live helping people to discover what that is.

**What event or series of events led you to your discovery?**

I believe that we're hardwired. I don't know that there's been an epiphany for myself, or that one day a light went on. My entire life has been built around being of service to people. Even as a kid, I would do things like help another kid play a sport better, because I realized for myself that I kept getting better and learning and growing by simply helping others around me to do the same. You learn the most when you are teaching others. So, again, I don't think I had some epiphany as much as I realized I was born to be of service and this is truly who I am.

**If you could give advice to people who are still searching for their purpose in life, what would it be?**

I've come up with a solution for that. In fact, it's something in our film *Pass It On.* It's called the success equation. I came up with this to help people, because a lot of people come up to me and say, "It's easy for you, but how did you actually do it? Is there a system?" I think that a lot of people do this already, consciously and subconsciously. For me, it was subconsciously.

It works like this.

The success equation is:  $P + T \times A^2 = \textbf{Success}$

**P = Passion**
**T = Talent**
**A² = Action and Association**

It works like this; **P** is your passion (What would you do, if you could do it for free?). Then you combine that with **T,** which stands for talent, and a lot of people miss this. You hear these late night infomercial guys say, "Go and find your passion" but they're missing something. Just like you see these people on these television singing contests, they have a lot of passion but they're not very talented, therefore they don't keep going. You combine what you're passionate about with your talent, and then include the multiplication of **A²**, which is taking **A**ction with the right **A**ssociation.

Imagine if your **P**assion was that you loved stuffed animals, they're all over the house, you drove everyone else nuts, but you just loved stuffed animals. And say your **T**alent happens to be working on the computer. You're pretty good on the Internet. Now, how could you take **A**ction with the right **A**ssociation? And the answer is, your passion or your purpose might just be selling beanie-babies on eBay, because you combined what your passion was with your talent and you took action with the right people. And, that's the true manner, in my opinion, in which all great leaders have found their purpose on the planet.

# Dan Poynter

*"Each step that you take reveals a new horizon."*

Dan Poynter is author of more than 120 books, has been a publisher since 1969, and is a Certified Speaking Professional (CSP).

He is an evangelist for books, an ombudsman for authors, an advocate for publishers, and the godfather to thousands of successfully published books.

His seminars have been featured on *CNN*, his books have been pictured in *The Wall Street Journal* and his story has been told in *US News & World Report*. The media come to Dan because he is the leading authority on book publishing.

He has starred in an online interactive book writing-publishing-promoting program. His 20-year-old newsletter, *Publishing Poynters*, has a circulation of more than 33,000.

Dan travels more than 5,000 miles each week to share, inspire, and empower writers, publishers, and professional speakers through keynotes and seminars. Some of his books are *Writing Nonfiction, The Self-Publishing Manual, The Skydiver's Handbook, The Expert Witness Handbook* and *The Older Cat*.

Dan shows people how to make a difference while making a living by coaching them on the writing, publishing and promoting of their books.

He has turned thousands of people into successful authors. His mission is to see that people do not die with a book still inside them.

See his Para Publishing website at: *http://ParaPublishing.com*

## Who do you think you are?

I often ask myself that question. I guess that I'm a researcher and information disseminator. I love to study, I love to research, and I disseminate that information in my books, my speeches, my articles, and of course my website. I don't like to think of myself as being an author, or publisher, or even a publicist. We are all information providers, and we have to think about our audience and provide that information to them in any form they want.

For example, I write books, but some people out there can't read my books. Perhaps they're a long-haul trucker or behind the wheel for many hours at a time. So they can listen to my books, I try to put most of them into an audio format, to serve those people. And we also have eBooks and large PRINT books so that we can serve all of those different audiences.

## What event or series of events led to your discovery?

There are a series of things, but I think the most moving event for me was back in 1962. I was taking finals in law school in San Francisco and a friend of mine said, "I know where we can go skydiving." Well, I had always wanted to do that and there was a place about an hour and a half away in Calistoga. So, I finished my exams, went up there on a Saturday and made the jump. I was so excited I stayed overnight and on Sunday I made three more. I was right back there the next weekend. I think my eighth jump I landed in the tree. My ninth jump was a water jump into Clear Lake, and I did pretty well in the water jump competition.

From there I decided that I would rather be a parachute designer than a lawyer. Maybe because they have more friends. (: That completely changed my life, because I was able to turn my passion center into my profit center. I spent many years collecting information and published a huge manual on parachutes, a very technical book that's purchased by the manufacturers, technicians, and designers.

I rose in the politics of the parachute industry and the sport of skydiving, and I've just had a wonderful life ever since. If I hadn't gone out there, if I didn't have that experience of skydiving, I just don't know where I would be today. I just can't imagine that I'd be as happy as I am.

This is why I tell young people today to get out of the house, try something different every weekend. Don't do the same things, don't go out with the same people. Hopefully something like skydiving will grab you and you can turn your passion center into your profit center, turn your avocation into your vocation. Do something that you really enjoy, rather than punching a time clock, doing your job and trying to pay the bills. It seems most people are unhappy with what they're doing. They are unhappy with their job, their lot in life, and they just need more experiences when they're young to help them discover the direction they want to go.

**If you could give advice to those who are still searching for their purpose in life, what would it be?**

Get out of the house! Now this may really be hard if you are a person who is introverted, you don't like crowds of people, or perhaps you are so low on the scales of introvert that you're agoraphobic. But you have to force yourself. I'm an introvert; I'm very low on the scale. I work all by myself, I work in a solitary manner, but I forced myself to get out, and that's one of the things that lead me to professional speaking.

I believe it was Loa Tzu the Chinese philosopher who said, "The journey of a thousand leagues begins with the first step." I like to take that further and say that each step that you take reveals a new horizon. Each step you take, each thing that you do, is a learning experience, and that opens up new ideas, new doors, and then you can take another step. Every time you do something new, every time you do something different, you're taking one of the steps.

Benjamin Disraeli said, "The best way to become acquainted with the subject is to write a book about it." Remember Disraeli was that famous British statesmen who was born in 1804 and died in 1881. What he was saying is that in order to write a book you not only use your accumulated knowledge but you research everything that's been done on it before. You read all the other books, you read all the magazine articles, you interview other people, and so on. You come up with all of this information, and then you write your book directly toward a particular type of reader or consumer.

So, if you write a book you're going to learn a great deal about your subject. You may not be the expert on it when you start, but by the time you finish that book, you become the expert on that subject. And of course, everyone holds you in high regard as a published author, and they just accept the fact that you're an expert. As a matter of fact, Joe Vitale points out that the word authority contains the word author. So by definition, you're an authority on the subject. On my website we have some lengthy information kits on how to write, publish and promote your books, and they're free. Each is about 20 pages long and that's at www.parapub.com. Just think parachutes and publishing dot com.

# Hale Dwoskin

*"There's nothing you need to do, and nothing you need to fix
or change in order to be what you already are."*

**Hale Dwoskin, New York Times Best-Selling author of *The Sedona Method*, and co-author of the best-selling *Happiness Is Free* (five-book series) is the CEO and Director of Training of Sedona Training Associates, an organization that teaches courses based on the emotional releasing techniques originated by his mentor, Lester Levenson. Dwoskin is an international speaker and featured faculty member at Esalen and the Omega Institute. He is also one of the 24-featured teachers of the book and movie phenomenon, *"The Secret."* For thirty years, he has regularly been teaching The Sedona Method techniques to individuals and corporations throughout the United States, Canada and the United Kingdom.**
**Learn more about Hale and his work at: www.sedona.com**

## Who do you think you are?  What is your life's purpose?

To me they're two distinctly different things.  Who I am is more of a "what," and my purpose in life is not necessarily related.  So, I may be different than most of the people that you are interviewing.  Let me see if I can explain.  I'll start with what my purpose is.  My purpose in life is to share happiness, peace and joy with the planet by sharing the technique that I co-created called, The Sedona Method.  So, that's my purpose. But what I am is the presence of awareness, that's aware of this conversation, yet completely uninvolved; that is the same energy or awareness that is listening both through these ears and those ears; that's seeing both through these eyes and those eyes; that has no boundaries, no location, that's beyond space and time.  And it's not just who I am. In my experience, that's who everyone is. The sense of a separate individual is made up.  In fact, it doesn't bear direct examination.  If you, right now, try to find the separate "you" that you believe you are, I challenge you to find it.  I've yet to speak to anyone who can actually find it.  They can remember it, because it just exists as a function of mind.  It has nothing to do with what's here and now, and it has nothing to do with what we are.  Again, in my experience, what we are is effortless, choiceless, pure presence or awareness, being-ness or what ever you want to call it. And it's always here, and it's always now. Now, in the appearance we call life there are imagined individuals, and these individuals definitely have purposes.

That is part of the dance. I feel very fortunate and grateful that this particular body/mind has been chosen or is being used to share freedom and aliveness, joy and peace with the world. It's a great pleasure to have that be what I'm engaged in every day.

**What event or series of events lead you to your discovery?**

Again, they're paralleled tracks. The purpose I discovered, very fortunately, when I met Lester Levinson back in 1976 (the man who inspired The Sedona Method). I was organizing a seminar for another seminar leader, and Lester came as a guest. I didn't even notice him in the seminar, but when I met Lester I was blown away by who he was. He was calm, happy, centered, peaceful and equal minded, and at the same time he was not at all full of himself for what he had discovered. In other words, he didn't think anything of what he had discovered, he just thought it was natural. I was really blown away by who he was a living example of, so I asked him what he did and he said, "Well, we teach this technique called releasing (The Sedona Method), and it's taught over two weekends, and you basically sit around a table and release." Of course, I had no idea what he was talking about, but I knew that if he gave me just *some* of what he was a living example of...I wanted it. I took the course the very next weekend, and before the course was even over, I knew that my life was going to be dedicated to sharing his discoveries, and as it turned out, improving them and expanding upon them and reaching a much broader audience then he ever could. So, my life purpose has been sharing this good news with the world. That was 1976, and I'm still very happily engaged in doing that.

Since I've been doing this work, I have continued to explore inwardly and as I've been letting go...at first I was letting go of my sense of inner limitation and manifesting in my life more joy, more happiness, more abundance, more health, more loving and satisfying relationships, and helping literally hundreds of thousands of people to do the same thing. Somewhere along the way, I also started investigating the nature of this person that we believe we are. Through self-exploration and continuing to explore, I discovered that what we are is not the person. What we are is that which is beyond the person, and is even beyond purpose. Because what we are doesn't need a purpose to be. There's nothing you need to do, and nothing you need to fix or change in order to be what you already are. So, after discovering that, this is now an integral part of the advanced work that we do, helping people discover this for themselves.

**If you could give advice to those who are still searching for their purpose in life, what would it be?**

The first thing I would say is: continue the search until you get the answers that you're looking for – whether it be having more money or better relationships or better health or the ultimate understanding of your true nature. Even when you hit obstacles and things don't seem to going the way you would like, just be persistent. As you can tell, I've been pretty persistent. I've been doing the same thing now for over thirty years, and it wasn't always easy. There were times when I guess many people would have given up. But I was persistent and consistent in my efforts to discover my true nature and to help others do the same, and it's bearing fruit. So persistence is very useful.

   The other thing is earnestness. If you're earnest in your endeavors to improve yourself or discover you true nature, that earnestness will lead to toward the right source of information. Most of us have so many choices every day in the spiritual path, self-evolution or evolvement, or self help, and it can be very confusing. But if you're really earnest and you follow your heart, your heart will never lead you wrong. Your mind may, and your beliefs and programs from the past may, but your heart always knows. There is a knowingness that I'm calling heart that is just part of our basic nature. This presence of awareness that we are is all knowingness. It's not all knowing, as that implies there's is a person, it's all knowingness. And that knowingness will guide you to the right things if you're just simply open to it. It's always there, always here, always now, and always guiding you in the right direction, it's just that often it has to do things repeatedly to get our attention. So if you trust your knowingness and trust your heart and you're earnest, you'll be lead in the right direction. Just add persistence to that and you're in really good shape.

   The other thing that I have found personally very helpful, and has the hundreds and thousands of people that do the work that I do, is that simply holding in mind what you want without letting go, without letting go of the old beliefs and patterns, programs and experiences that are holding you back for most people is an IOU for failure. The thing that distracts us from our life purpose and the things that we're trying to pursue is all the excess emotional and mental baggage that we carry around. What the Sedona Method does is show you how to shed this emotional baggage so that you don't have to carry it around anymore. To me that's been critically important, and it has been for the hundreds and thousands of people doing this work. It's a critically an important step to do the work required to uncover this knowingness. It's to uncover your intuitive knowing and your clear reason, and also to help you get off your butt. A lot of us know what we should do, but we've chose not to do it or to stop doing it because of all this emotional conflict that we carry inside. If you commit to dissolving it and to letting it go with some technique like the Sedona Method, which is, in my experience, the best one, but it's not the only one. I recommend you do something to dissolve the sense of inner limitation that prevents you from achieving your goals, and staying on course. So, that would be what I would recommend.

# Debbie Allen

*"When you improve yourself personally along with the professional growth,*
*that's when you become who you're truly supposed to be."*

Debbie Allen has built and sold numerous highly successful companies in diverse industries. She now teaches the lessons of massive success with her insightful business-building strategies. Her contagious enthusiasm inspires others to move past limited personal beliefs that may be holding them back from reaching their peak potential in business and in life.

As an international business speaker for over 12 years, Debbie Allen has presented before thousands of people in 10 countries around the world. She is one of less than 10% of professional speakers worldwide to have achieved the honor of CSP, Certified Speaking Professional, by the National Speakers Association and International Speakers Federation. Debbie was also honored by the National Chamber of Commerce with the prestigious Blue Chip Enterprise Award for overcoming obstacles and achieving fast business growth.

Debbie is the author of five books on business and personal development including her bestsellers *Confessions of Shameless Self Promoters* and *Skyrocketing Sales*. Both books have been published by major publishing houses and also published in numerous languages around the world.

Her expertise has been featured in dozens of publications including *Entrepreneur, Selling Power* and *Sales & Marketing Excellence*. She is also a featured in three motivational movies including, *Pass It On*, *Windows on the Secrets for Success* and *The Opus*.

Find out more by visiting: www.DebbieAllen.com

## Who do you think you are?

I discovered that I am a leader and an inspirational teacher. At first I didn't really accept myself as a teacher. I knew I was a speaker and a writer, but I hadn't really realized that being a teacher was my purpose and that's what I was put on this earth to do. Now I know that my passion has really been discovered, and that's what I will continue to do for the rest of my life.

## What event or series of events led you to your discovery?

I know that I am passionate about speaking and teaching people how to have successful businesses. I've been doing this for twelve years, seven of those years full-time. But it only became clear that this was my life's purpose in December of 2006. I attended a breakthrough workshop with best-selling author, Barbara De Angeles for two days, and it just hit me like a lightening bolt, "This is what I was put on the earth for!" The reason I had been doing all these other things in my life, such as being successful in business and building and selling businesses, was to get the expertise and the knowledge to do what I was really put on this earth to do, which is to teach others. That teaching is not only about business, there's a message of personal growth mixed in. My presentations aren't just business seminars anymore, they deal with mental belief systems and inner work. I discovered that teaching in this way is really my true gift.

I was innately transitioning into that type of work, but I didn't realize it until I discovered my own personal breakthrough. Like I said, before I was a business teacher, and now I've realized that there's much more to my motivational message. I'm like an evangelist of business and personal growth. I'm real, passionate and enthusiastic about what I have to share. I truly care about helping others achieve more in life.

Before I discovered both professional and personal balance in my own life, I could not teach it to others. We need to first become students of what we need most in our own lives and experience it full on before we can share our message from the heart with others. Today, I tie personal development with business strategies into one lesson and it's much more effective. I enjoy sharing this type of information with people because they get the message from multiple angles, not just "here's a business strategy, now go to work." Rarely do speakers talk about "dream stealers", "negative self-talk" or "growing from your failures" … yet these are all part of life we all go through. Once you address the issues we all have we can then take the right steps to move ahead.

## If you could give advice to those still searching for their life's purpose, what would it be?

Never stop learning. Be a life-long student, not just a student of what you think you have to learn in your field (whether you're learning real estate or the insurance business). Become a life-long student learning about yourself. When you improve yourself personally along with professional growth, that's when you become the person you were supposed to be to make a difference in other peoples lives. You cannot fully be of service to other people until you are of service to yourself, and the only way to be of service to yourself is to be true to yourself and never settle for less than you deserve. When you work on yourself inwardly, emotionally and psychologically, along with continually learning new business skills, that's when you really become a master. That's when you become the best that you can be.

# Lissa Coffey

*"We grow as people through our relationships with others.*
*We're not in this alone. We're all connected."*

**Whether you're looking for dating or relationship advice, or the latest in home and fashion trends, Coffey-Talk is an inspiring blend of ancient wisdom and modern style!**

**Author Lissa Coffey is a lifestyle expert who offers dating and relationship advice. She is the CoffeyTalk barista, serving up an inspiring blend of ancient wisdom and modern style. A frequent guest on radio and TV, Lissa's keen insight into interpersonal and cultural dynamics offers guidance for anyone looking to fill the void in their harried lives.**

**Lissa Coffey is the author of several books, including *What's Your Dosha, Baby? Discover the Vedic Way for Compatibility in Life and Love*. She has been featured as a relationship expert on television shows such as *The Today Show* and on the Fox News Network.**

**Sign up for Lissa's free e-mail newsletters at: www.coffeytalk.com.**

## Who do you think you are?

Who I "think" I am varies depending on the time or space that my human form happens to be in. In one realm I might think that I'm a wife, a mother, a writer, a friend, or a teacher. If I've just bumped into some furniture I may think I'm a klutz. If I've just made a delicious meal I may think I'm a gourmet chef! But who I "know" I am never changes. I know in my heart, and without question, that I am, as we all are, an important part of this vast and beautiful Universe. I know that I am here to learn and to grow and to experience Life and all that comes with it. I am a creative being, just as we all are, here to express myself, and my unique gifts with the world. We all have this in common. We all need to look within to discover just what our unique gifts are, and how we can bring them into being to help others. This is our dharma, or purpose in life. When we are living our dharma, we are our happiest and healthiest.

I can go about my day playing all the roles I play, and learning along the way, taking in the essence of Spirit as it is expressed in a variety of scenarios. When I face a challenge, or get stressed, I remind myself to see the Truth, to look beyond any temporary disturbances. Everything has a purpose.

As we learn about ourselves we learn about Life. It's all part of the process. We gain compassion, wisdom, and understanding as we go. We grow as people through our relationships with others. We're not in this alone. We're all connected.

**What event or series of events led you to your discovery?**

Even when I was very young, I loved reading biographies. I have always found true stories so much more interesting than made-up ones. Life is fascinating, and we can learn from the experiences of other people. It makes me more aware of the choices I am making, and I see the things that we all have in common. I have also always loved writing. I remember writing songs in grade school, and entering speech contests, and producing plays in high school. I think I got "off track" a little bit when I entered the corporate world and didn't have the chance to be creative.

All that changed when I was pregnant with my first son. I had morning sickness so bad that I couldn't work, so I took classes, and began to find myself again. I got back into the practice of meditation, and remembered my connection with Spirit. And the blessings continued when I became a mother, and learned from my children. I expressed what was in my heart, and wrote songs and books and expanded my awareness in so many ways.

Parenthood comes with its own challenges and I managed to work through them, learning and growing, seeing Spirit expressed in my children. Life changed for me dramatically when I went to India with my son. We spent his 14th birthday at the Taj Mahal. Something shifted within me that day. Any questions I had were answered. I felt calm and clear and connected on every level possible. Time stood still, and I wanted to stay in that space forever. It was as if everything I had ever lived through had led me to this moment, and I felt totally in love with life, with Spirit, with everything and everyone. That feeling stays with me, it is who I know in my heart I really am. In the hectic pace of daily life I may need reminding every once in awhile, but it's there.

**If you could give advice to people who are still searching for their life's purpose, what would it be?**

Take time to get to know you. Spend time in silence. Meditate. Be with nature. Find what you love to do and do it. Help people. Open your heart to opportunities to learn and grow. Allow yourself to love and be loved. Trust your instincts; you know more than you think you know.

# *Lee Brower*

*"I think all great things come from the rich soil of gratitude,*
*and celebration is a wonderful form of expressing gratitude."*

Lee Brower is a multigenerational wealth expert and founder of The Quadrant Living Experience, LLC, an internationally recognized educational and philanthropic organization teaching a radically successful system called The Brower Quadrant. A noted authority on helping prestigious families create enduring legacies that flourish generation after generation, he is also an accomplished teacher and mentor for entrepreneurs and CEOs. His breakthrough ideas and concepts on preserving wealth are changing the landscape of leadership in a variety of places, from private homes and small businesses, to public corporations and large educational institutions. Most recently, he was featured in the blockbuster book and film The Secret, where he shares invaluable insights about gratitude and other tools to success.

With more than 30 years experience, Lee utilizes his transformational Brower Quadrant System to guide people to successfully protect, empower, and honor their "true wealth" - which isn't just about money and property. Put simply, he helps people recognize and tap into all of their assets, including those one doesn't typically think about, such as wisdom, experience, reputation, networks, health, skills, talents, values, and habits. Through this system, he offers realistic roadmaps for achieving a lasting legacy that can stand the test of time.

Passionate, dedicated, and highly engaging, Lee mixes keynote speeches and seminars with his ongoing role as an active founder or board member of numerous charitable, community, and corporate organizations. His entrepreneurial pursuits include several Quadrant-based companies around the world that spawn out-of-the-box intellectual capital with a focus on real estate, corporate compliance, communication, health, and education.

Co-author of Wealth Enhancement & Preservation, he is recognized in Who's Who in the West and Who's Who Worldwide. His new book, The Brower Quadrant, is slated to arrive in bookstores early 2008. In it, he shares the specifics of applying Quadrant Living principles.

Visionary in thought and action, Lee is a change agent of our time. He's on a mission to revolutionize how people create and nourish their wealth—at home, at work and beyond.

Lee resides in the Salt Lake City area with his wife, Lori, where they enjoy the outdoors and the pleasures that come with having a classic blended family of eight children and six grandchildren.

**Who do you think you are?**

That question can go really deep, so I'll walk through it sequentially. First of all, I see myself as a child of God and an heir to all that God has. Secondly, I see myself as a husband and a partner with my eternal companion, and that together synergistically one plus one is much greater than two. We are building an eternal life together. The first measure of our building is through our children and our grandchildren, which leads me to number three. It is incumbent upon me that I transfer my true wealth, not just my financial wealth, to my children, grandchildren and so forth so that they can continue growing and being contributors to this world rather than just takers and receivers. I see those as my three primary purposes for being here in life.

I also believe that I have a unique ability to innovate, generate, communicate and motivate. I am an intellectual capitalist who takes new concepts and ideas, systemizes them in a way that people are willing to pay money to learn so they can easily and effortlessly accomplish their true potential. If we can help others develop their unique abilities and talents by implementing systems that allow them to optimize their potential and achieve peace of mind, true happiness, and success that's very rewarding and gratifying to me. I get excited about developing and then communicating easily understood systems that achieve individual, family and corporate objectives faster and more efficiently. That's my passion. That's what I love doing. So I utilize my unique talents to serve who I am.

**What event or series of events led to your discovery?**

If you always make your learning greater than your experience, then all of your cumulative experiences are the assets that make up who you are. Using number three from above as the example, when I identify my unique talents as being able to serve the other three, that came about as a result of being in the financial services industry since 1973. My passion had been estate planning, working with financially affluent families to transfer their financial wealth into future generations. Along that road I had a unique experience that totally changed my life.

I had the opportunity to collect a very sizable check from a young entrepreneur who was approaching billionaire status. I walked into his office, and he had his head down working, and all he said was, "Lee, I've been wondering, what's a guy like you worth?" When I heard that statement, because of my own ego, the hair on the back of my neck stood up. I went into an uncalled-for "reaction."

The answer that came out really shocked me, because I said to him (after a long pause and much consideration about whether or not I was going to throw his check into the wind), "To my family, I am worth a heck of a lot. Some people are born with their own particular trials, maybe they're born ugly, or they're born with certain handicaps, mentally or physically, and others have to deal with handicaps physically or mentally that occur after they are born. Your handicap may be that you're rich. I don't think God cares as much about what handicaps we have or how much we have or don't have. What I do think he cares about is how we deal with them." And I just kind of left it there. Fortunately for me, a few long seconds (and lots of sweat) later he replied, "You know I was just thinking the same thing."

This was one of three impactful events that happened right on the heels of each other that caused me to ask the question, "What is my stewardship responsibility to my financial wealth, and when does it end?" In that quest, I discovered that among affluent families worldwide statistically 97% of all family wealth, or less than 4%, ever survives beyond the third generation. I felt like all the work I was doing was in some way for not. I've come to learn that the intellectual ability to structure trusts and other legal instruments to transfer the family financial wealth has very little to do with the long term result of sustaining that family wealth from one generation to the other. Once we value and develop systems that transfer not just the tangible assets, but the intangible assets of values, character, self esteem, confidence, wisdom, and charity - those intangible assets that we value more than money - from generation to generation, then the financial assets have the greatest odds to survive as well.

The Brower Quadrant and The Quadrant Living Systems are truly designed to transfer all of a family's true wealth, not just the financial. It is very exciting.

There was another event, an intervention of sorts, where I was attending a workshop on public speaking in Canada. The participants, were completely unrelated to my industry and had been listening to me speak. Near the end of the seminar they came to me and said, "Lee, what you are doing is not just for the very affluent, it's for everybody. We see your mission as being one who will share these principles with everybody, regardless of their current financial situation."

Those are but two of several significant events that have caused me to focus on how to discover and establish systems that transfer all of our assets, not just our financial assets, to future generations. Right now, each day of our living life, we can we enrich all of the quadrants in our lives, including the financial quadrants so that we can reach that level of happiness and peace we all search for.

**If you could give advice to those who are still searching for their life's purpose, what would it be?**

First, I would suggest that you celebrate who you are and where you are now. In other words, celebrate your accomplishments. I think all great things come from the rich soil of gratitude, and celebration is a wonderful form of expressing gratitude. If you can celebrate your activities of the day, celebrate who you are, the talents and the unique abilities that you have, then happiness comes to you. Unhappiness stems from comparing. When we compare ourselves to others, many times it creates unhappiness in our lives. So, when we celebrate where we are and what we are doing and eliminate the comparisons in our lives, then we can increase the happiness. So, I would recommend first and foremost gratitude and celebration.

Secondly, you must be willing to let go. You have to let go. When most people get a good idea, they want to cling to it, or they've achieved some success in their lives and they've become comfortable. Letting go is huge. Once you've set your vision of what you're capable of, and maybe it's only as far as you can see right now, and you set that horizon for yourself, then to move forward you must let go.

Sometimes you'll have to let go of past habits, past relationships, and past conditions in order to move forward. Surrender to that vision or horizon, and when you let go, then you start moving toward that new horizon, and guess what, you can navigate to that new horizon. The new horizon continues to move with you, and so you get new horizons as you let go.

# ARE YOU HERE TO BE A SUCCESSFUL AUTHOR?

# Jack Canfield

*"The way you see the world, your definition of its perfection is a mirror back to you about what your purpose is."*

Jack Canfield is best known as the co-creator and coauthor of the #1 New York Times best-selling *Chicken Soup for the Soul®* book series. As the CEO of Chicken Soup for the Soul Enterprises he has also helped grow the Chicken Soup for the Soul® brand into a virtual empire of books, children's books, audios, videos, CDs, classroom materials, a syndicated column and a television show, as well as a vigorous program of licensed products.

He is also a highly sought after world-class corporate trainer and public speaker who has spoken to over 600 organizations in over 20 countries around the world. With a background that includes being a high school teacher, a psychotherapist, a corporate trainer, and a success coach, Jack has been an internationally recognized leader in the fields of self-esteem and peak performance. He is the Chairman of the Board of The Foundation for Self-Esteem in Culver City, CA, was appointed in 1987 by the California Legislature to the historic California Task Force to Promote Self-Esteem and Personal and Social Responsibility, and was a co-founder of the National Association for Self-Esteem.

Jack has conducted intensive personal and professional development seminars for over 750,000 people worldwide. He has spoken to hundreds of thousands of others at numerous conferences and conventions and has been seen by millions more on television shows such as *Oprah Winfrey, The Today Show, Fox and Friends, America's Talking AM, The Caryl & Marilyn Show, 20/20, Eye to Eye,* CNN's *Talk Back Live!, The John Bradshaw Show, Home Team with Terry Bradshaw,* PBS, the BBC, QVC, Home Shopping Network and the NBC and CBS Nightly News shows.

He has conducted over 2500 workshops and seminars and has consulted with over 600 school systems, universities, corporations and associations in all 50 states and in over 20 countries including Canada, Mexico, Dominican Republic, British West Indies, Great Britain, Ireland, Greece, Norway, Iceland, Denmark, Morocco, Oman, Turkey, Australia, Tahiti, Singapore, Malaysia, India, and Hong Kong.

His publications include over 120 books (including the best-selling *Chicken Soup for the Soul®* series with eleven #1 *New York Times* bestsellers) as well as *The Aladdin Factor, Dare to Win, Heart at Work, Self-Esteem in the Classroom, 100 Ways to Enhance Self-Concept in the Classroom, The Power of Focus: How to Hit Your Personal, Financial and Business Goals with Absolute Certainty* and his most recent book—

*The Success Principles: How to Get from Where You Are to Where You Want to Be.* **He is also the creator of a three-and-a-half-hour video training program originally developed for California welfare recipients entitled** *The GOALS Program,* **now with over 2,000,000 welfare recipients and people-at-risk in 25 states having participated in this motivational success program over the last eight years.**

**Jack has been a member of the faculties of several entrepreneurial and business training programs including The Million Dollar Forum, Income Builders International, The Street Smart Business Camp, the Life Success Academy, Peak Potentials, and organizations serving the presidents of corporations such as the Young Presidents Organization, the Chief Executives Organization, The Executive Committee and The World Business Council.**

**Jack is a graduate of Harvard, earned his M.Ed. from the University of Massachusetts and has received 3 honorary doctorates in psychology and public service. He is married, has 3 wonderful children and 2 stepchildren, and lives in Santa Barbara, California.**

**Read more about Jack by visiting: www.jackcanfield.com**

## Who do you think you are?

The core of who I am is a pure center of conscious awareness and will, and by that I mean I'm pure consciousness that has incarnated into a body, and I have the function of awareness and choice. Who I am in terms of life purpose is someone who is here to inspire and empower people to live their highest vision in a context of love and joy. By that I mean I inspire people through my speeches, through the *Chicken Soup for the Soul®* books, and through media projects like *The Secret* that I participate in. I empower people through my books like *The Success Principles™, The Power of Focus, The Aladdin Factor,* and the forthcoming *Effortless Success™ Living the Law of Attraction,* my *Breakthrough to Success* workshops, and my monthly "Ask Jack" calls (see www.AskJackCanfield.com) where I give people concrete, practical ways to manifest their vision. That's my purpose and how I work to manifest it.

## What event or series of events led to your discovery?

I have to say that discovering my life purpose has been a result of a series of events over time. It just kept forming and eventually it congealed into the words "inspiring and empowering people to live their highest vision in a context of love and joy." I think it's true that love and joy have always been my two hallmarks, the principle qualities of my life. People that know me say, "Oh yeah, Jack's a fun guy. He's very inspiring, and he's really very loving." That part of me has seemingly been there forever.

I started my career as a high school teacher in an inner-city school in Chicago, and then I became a teacher trainer for a number of years. Back when I was an educator, in one of the weekend human potential trainings that I attended, we were asked to visualize going up to the top of a mountain, entering a temple, and receiving a gift in a golden box from a wise old person, who had descended down into the temple through a beam of white light. We were told that the gift in the box would be a symbol that would represent our life purpose. The gift I received was a golden heart. It is clear to me that the essence of what I was here to experience, express, and teach is love.

Over time, whenever I would think about my purpose, I would get this image of myself climbing to the top of a tall mountain, where I would then gather up a huge ball of light in my arms (the light representing the healing power of love). Then I would take this big giant ball of light, and I would come back down the mountain and hand out snowball sized handful's of light to everyone I encountered. That seemed to be a representation of my teaching, running seminars, coaching, counseling, and doing therapy. When I would run out of light, I would walk back up to the top of the mountain and gather more light. This would play itself out in real life as me going to another spiritual retreat or meditating more—any way to go to a higher level and take in that inspiration of love and light, and then bring it back down and share it with others.

Then there were a number of years that I was a trainer for a company called Insight Training Seminars. The names of our courses I taught were *Awakening The Heart, Centering In The Heart,* and *Opening The Heart*; so for a couple of years there I was very focused on teaching people to experience and express more of the love that they truly are.

Paul McCartney said, "All you need is love," and I truly believe that, but what I also find is that in this lifetime here on earth I am equally interested in helping people manifest their vision, but always in the context of love.

Another major event that occurred for me was that I took a 10-day Vipassana meditation retreat. It's an ancient Buddhist technique, over 2500 years old, and you just basically follow your breath for the first three days, and then after that, you just observe your mind as it goes where it goes. You simply observe your physical sensations, thoughts, memories, and fantasies. I found that after about eight days, I got into a very compassionate state. I remember driving home with my wife, and we were driving about 30 miles an hour on the freeway. Everything was so slowed down. The most amazing experience was when we passed a dead cat on the side of the road, and I noticed that there were a bunch of maggots eating the dead cat. I thought to myself, *Five years ago I would have really been upset for the cat, and now I'm really happy that the maggots have something to eat.* So I had attained a state of pure joy, where I was deeply appreciating whatever reality presented itself, an experience that everything is perfect just the way it is.

Then in 1984, I read a book called *You Can Have It All* by Arnold Patent. In that book he had a written exercise for identifying and articulating your life purpose. The first step was to come up with two qualities and that you most enjoy expressing, and I wrote down *love* and *joy*. Then he asked, what are two ways that you most enjoy expressing those qualities? I wrote down *inspiring and empowering people.* Then he said, imagine the world was perfect from your point of view. What would be happening? And I wrote down, *everyone would be living their highest vision.* I've always believed that when people are living their highest vision—not their parents', society's or their teachers' vision— then the world would work.

It's like everyone is a cell in the body we call humanity, and when every cell is performing its unique function perfectly, then the whole body functions perfectly. It would be as if you were a liver cell, and I were a kidney cell, and Michael Beckwith were a heart cell, and Raymond Aaron were a brain cell, and if everyone were fully being themselves with no holdbacks, then the body would work perfectly. And to carry that metaphor out to the world, if everyone fully lived *their* highest vision, the world would work perfectly as well.

The last thing that Arnold Patent said to do was combine all of those previous parts into one sentence. So I ended up with "to inspire and empower people to live their highest vision in the context of love and joy." For 22 years now, that has been my stated life purpose, my deepest sense of myself, and what guides all of my behavior. I literally ask myself, is this project going to inspire and empower people to live their highest vision? If the answer is yes and I feel drawn to it, I'll participate. If it doesn't, I won't.

**If you could give advice to those who are still searching for their life's purpose, what would it be?**

Number one would be to look over your life both past and present and notice when you experienced the most joy. You see, I believe and teach that we all have an inner guidance system and it's our experience of joy. So when you're experiencing joy in the work you do, joy in your relationships, you're on track. You're on purpose. When you're walking down the beach, and the experience of joy stops, then obviously you're being called to do something else in that moment like maybe go back home and read or write, talk to your friends or pet your cat.

The idea is that normally we can trust that if we're on track we'll be feeling excitement, enthusiasm and joy. There's an opening or an expansion that occurs. If we're feeling a contraction or feeling less than joy, then basically we're off course.

For me when I look back on the times when I was teaching, when I was coaching, when I was speaking, when I was creating products that had to do with expanding human potential and growth, I was really happy. When I'm doing other things, I'm not. So I can then say my purpose is to engage in teaching and coaching and training.

Let me give you an example. In my book, *The Success Principles™*, I write about a young woman named Julie Laipply, who was selected as Miss Virginia in the Miss America competition. When she was at Ohio State University, she was studying biology because as a kid she loved animals. Everyone would say, "Oh, you love animals so much you should be vet." However, while she was studying microbiology in England on a Rotary Fellowship, she realized she was miserable. So she asked herself, *When was I happy?* She was looking for some clues, and then she remembered. *Whenever I was in a leadership role, when I was a student leader, when I went to the state leadership conventions for high school, and when I was at OSU and was chaperoning kids who had come to the campus as part of their leadership retreats—that's when I was really happy.*     She realized that she experienced the most joy out of leadership. So, she went back to OSU and said she wanted to create a new major that didn't yet exist. It would be a major in leadership by combining classes in psychology, journalism, media, and speech. Well, they let her do it, and it took an extra year for her to graduate. But by the time she was 26, she was working at the Pentagon and coaching high-ranking military officers in leadership. She had found her life purpose— what the Buddhists call your "right livelihood" and the Hawaiians call your "kuliana"—, which was teaching leadership.

In my own life, when I look back to where I experienced the most joy, it was when I was learning about developing human potential and when I was conducting seminars and trainings, speaking about, and writing about what I had learned.

The other thing that people can do to discover their life purpose is to do the exercise I mentioned above, in which you write down the two words or qualities that you most enjoy expressing, the two ways that you most enjoy expressing them and then add what would be happening in the world if it were working perfectly *according to you*. Then combine all of that into one sentence. Someone whose life purpose has to do with peace might say the world would be working perfectly if everybody were peacefully and harmoniously interacting with each other.

A recent attendee in one of my seminars who was a professional organizer wrote, "Everything would be well organized and working efficiently." So the way you see your ideal world, your definition of its perfection, is a mirror back to you about what your purpose is. The things that you get excited about, the things you get upset about are the things you care deeply about.

The third thing you can do is to look at your talents. Ask yourself, "What talents do I have?" You are given the talents you need to fulfill your life purpose. If your natural talents have to do with singing and dancing, then maybe your purpose is to be an entertainer. If your talents have to do with being someone who is intuitive and psychic, it may have to do with being a medical intuitive or doing psychic healing. If your talents have to do with easily and effortlessly persuading people, your life purpose may have to do with communication, sales, or leadership. So look at what talents you've been given and figure out clues they are giving you about what your purpose is. I find that to be really powerful pathway to clarity about your life purpose. We each have a set of what I call "core geniuses" that when we are expressing them, we find that success comes easily and effortlessly.

# Joe Vitale

*"I not only have to set the fire underneath them, but I have to show them the way. So, my mission is to inspire people to go for and achieve their dreams, whatever those happen to be."*

**Dr. Joe Vitale has become known as one of the world's most powerful copywriters and marketing minds. He is the author of the international #1 best-seller *The Attractor Factor*, the #1 best-seller *Life's Missing Instruction Manual,* the #1 best-selling e-book *Hypnotic Writing*, and the #1 best-selling Nightingale-Conant audio program *The Power of Outrageous Marketing* among numerous other works. Dr. Vitale is also one of the stars of the hit movie *The Secret.***

**Dr. Vitale wrote the only business book on P.T. Barnum, *There's A Customer Born Every Minute.* He also wrote *The AMA Complete Guide to Small Business Advertising* for the American Marketing Association. His most recent book, co-authored with Jo Han Mok, is *The E-Code: 47 Secrets for Making Money Online Almost Instantly*. Be on the lookout for his new books: *Inspired Marketing, Your Internet Cash Machine, Zero Limits, The Seven Lost Secrets of Success,* and *The Key*.**

**Besides being one of the five top marketing specialists in the world today, and the world's first hypnotic writer, Joe is also a certified hypnotherapist, a certified metaphysical practitioner, a certified Chi Kung healer, and an ordained minister. He also holds a doctorate degree in Metaphysical Science and another doctorate degree in Marketing. He is a proud member of the National Speakers Association.**

**Dr. Vitale has numerous websites, books, tapes, free articles, guest columns, and more on his site at: www.mrfire.com**

## Who do you think you are?

I've decided my purpose is to inspire people to achieve their dreams, whatever those happen to be. It's important to realize there are two parts to that. I don't just want to inspire people, because a lot of people will feel good momentarily, but not take action or not know what action to take. So to complete my mission I not only have to set the fire underneath them, I have to show them the way.

**What event or series of events led you to your discovery?**

When I was a teenager, I decided that most of the world I saw around me was unhappy, and what I wanted to do at that time was to cheer them up. I took on this noble cause by deciding I wanted to write comedy, I wanted to write fiction, I wanted to write plays, I wanted to write humorous materials, I wanted to write jokes. I wanted to write things that would uplift people. And I did do that. I created magic tricks, jokes, some entertainment, and I had a play produced in 1979 that was a one-act comedy.

I saw that people did want to be happy, they wanted to laugh, they wanted to smile, but they also wanted to be inspired. I then realized that I didn't just want them to be inspired for the hour or two that they watched the comedy routine, I needed to give then the tools for success. That evolved into me become a self-help inspirational marketer.

I often refer to myself as a spiritual marketer because I've learned from many other milestones in my career, like my book *The Attractor Factor* doing so well, that people really want this. I've come to the conclusion that people like to be entertained, but what they want more than anything else is to feel good. They want to be inspired, they want to go for their dreams and achieve them, and they want to feel like a success.

**If you could give advice to those who are still searching for life's purpose, what would it be?**

Look to what you truly love, and look to what you truly fear. Joseph Campbell said, "follow your bliss," and I often encourage people to follow what they love, to follow their passion, to follow their enthusiasm. I've also learned that if you look into the area of what you're afraid to do, you may uncover the thing that you are supposed to do.

I discovered that years ago when I came out with a book called, *Spiritual Marketing,* which I later re-wrote and re-titled *The Attractor Factor.* I was terrified. I really thought people would think I had lost my lid or something because I was talking about new age things, and creating your own reality, and the law of attraction; things that weren't really talked about before the movie *The Secret* had come out and swept the nation. I was really afraid of it. What I found is if I face my fears and come out with it, more often than not, the world will accept me. More often than not I will have greater applause and greater wealth from doing the very thing I fear.

I had been a conservative marketer for all those years, and I was hiding the spiritual side of myself. When I faced my fear and came out with *Spiritual Marketing,* which led to *The Attractor Factor,* which led me into being in the movie *The Secret,* which led to me being on *Larry King,* a whole long line of things occurred all because I faced my fears.

I would encourage people to look at what you really love to do, and look at what you really fear to do. Either one of those doors will lead to the same place, and that is your ticket to success.

# Marci Shimoff

*"Move in the direction of what expands you,
what brings you more joy, what brings you happiness."*

Marci Shimoff is the woman's face of the biggest self-help book phenomenon in history, *Chicken Soup for the Soul.* Her six bestselling titles in the series, including *Chicken Soup for the Woman's Soul and Chicken Soup for the Mother's Soul,* have met with stunning success, selling more than 13 million copies worldwide in 33 languages. They have been on the *New York Times* bestseller list for a total of 108 weeks, making Marci one of the bestselling female nonfiction authors of all time. In addition, she's a featured teacher in the international film and book phenomenon, *The Secret.* Her new book, *HAPPY FOR NO REASON: 7 Steps to Being Happy from the Inside Out,* offers a revolutionary approach to experiencing deep and lasting happiness. Upon its release in January of 2008, it soared to the top of all the bestseller lists including #1 on Amazon, and #2 on the *New York Times* and the *Wall Street Journal* bestseller lists.

A celebrated transformational leader and one of the nation's leading experts on happiness, success, and the law of attraction, Marci has inspired millions of people around the world, sharing her breakthrough methods for personal fulfillment and professional success. President and co-founder of The Esteem Group, she delivers keynote addresses and seminars on self-esteem, self-empowerment, and peak performance to corporations, professional and non-profit organizations, and women's associations. She has been a top-rated trainer for numerous Fortune 500 companies, including AT&T, General Motors, Sears, Kaiser Permanente, and Bristol-Myers Squibb.

As an acclaimed authority on success and happiness, Marci is often approached by media for her insights and advice. She has been on more than 500 national and regional television and radio shows and has been interviewed for over 100 newspaper articles nationwide. Her writing has appeared in national women's magazines, including *Ladies Home Journal* and *Woman's World.*

Marci earned her MBA from UCLA and holds an advanced certificate as a stress management consultant. She is a founding member and on the board of directors of the Transformational Leadership Council, a group of 100 top leaders serving over ten million people in the self-development market.

Through her books and her presentations, Marci's message has touched the hearts and rekindled the spirits of millions of people throughout the world. She is dedicated to fulfilling her life's purpose of helping people live more empowered and joy-filled lives.

You can reach Marci at: www.MarciShimoff.com

## Who Do You Think You Are?

I'm a person committed to living my highest potential and inspiring and guiding others to live their highest potential. Ultimately, I think every single one of us is a being of light and love, whatever disguise we might be wearing, and our purpose in being here on this earth is to discover the truth of the essence of who we are.

## What the event or series of events led to your discovery?

I did not win the happiness jackpot at birth. It seemed like I came out of the womb with existential angst. And so, since my earliest years I have been searching for the meaning and purpose of my life.

My first "Aha!" came when I was in the sixth grade. One day I snitched a book out of my sister's bedroom to read while tanning in the backyard. It was a very thin book called *Siddhartha*. As I was lying there, slathered with suntan oil and engrossed in this book about a young man's search for truth, I suddenly burst into tears. I realized for the first time that I wasn't alone on this search. Ever since then, I have spent my life seeking out the best books, teachers and any knowledge I could find that answers the questions, "Who am I?" "Why am I on this planet?" and "How can I live my highest potential?"

When I was sixteen, I started meditating and a huge piece of the puzzle fell into place for me. I realized that I was able to tune in and connect on a regular basis with a profoundly peaceful place at the core of my being. I could plug into Spirit and get a much deeper sense of who I am. This was a huge gift that I was so happy to have discovered.

And even earlier, when I was thirteen years old, I made a major discovery when I saw my first inspirational speaker. His name was Zig Ziglar. As I sat and listened to him speak, I said to myself, "That's it! That's what I'm going to be when I grow up." I knew immediately that it was my calling in life, even though it was certainly a very unusual calling for a thirteen-year-old girl in the early 1970's! I remember going home and telling my parents. They had wanted me to be a dental hygienist, so they weren't very thrilled with the idea that I was going to be a professional speaker. Nobody had even heard of that as a profession in the 70's. But they supported me, as always, though my mother teased me, saying, "Honey, you sure talk enough, so you might as well get paid for it!"

That's when I set my sights on the path that would lead to the work I do now. You couldn't get a degree in professional speaking so I did the next best thing. I earned an MBA in training and development, and I began my career teaching corporate training programs at Fortune 500 companies. I was standing in front of people and talking all day, so I felt I was on the right track. The only problem was that I was training people in business writing, and I hated writing! I didn't think I knew how to write well myself, and I really struggled with that job in the beginning. But I followed the curriculum they gave me and had a lot of success helping others learn to write. And after a number of years, lo and behold, I had become a very good writer too.

Little did I know that this job was preparing me for the day when I would actually edit and author books myself. When I realized this years later, I had to smile—it was as though everything I had done in the past had been perfectly designed to lead me to where I wanted to be and where I am thrilled to be today.

Over time I began to teach corporate training programs on stress management and self-esteem as well. My mentor was Jack Canfield, an expert in the field of self-esteem and not yet the author of *Chicken Soup for the Soul*. Before long, I had founded The Esteem Group and shifted from corporate training to teaching self-esteem programs to women's audiences. This is what I was doing when Jack published the original *Chicken Soup for the Soul* book in 1993.

Then, one day about a year-and-a-half later, I had an epiphany. I was deep in the middle of a meditation when a light bulb went off in my head and I clearly saw the words *Chicken Soup for the Woman's Soul*. I knew immediately that creating a *Chicken Soup for the Soul* book for a specific market was a great idea. I shared it with Jack and he immediately agreed. He then shared the idea with the publisher (Health Communications International) who also loved it, and a year later I had completed my first *Chicken Soup for the Soul* book.

I never could have figured out the *how* of what happened; I just knew what I wanted: to inspire millions of people around the world to live their best life possible. That was my mission. The way it unfolded was like magic, looking back on it. I ended up having the right skills and being in the right place at the right time. People say that I'm lucky, and I agree to a certain extent, but I like to say that luck is when preparedness meets opportunity.

After co-authoring seven of the *Chicken Soup for the Soul* books, I knew it was time to write something else. I also knew that the only thing that I had enough passion to write a book about—because I knew you have to throw your whole life into it when you write a book—was happiness. I've seen so many people who have all the good reasons in the world to be happy, but they're not. I wanted to discover what it is that brings people lasting happiness. So I started studying happiness and interviewing hundreds of people. What I found was that the people who have lasting happiness have an inner state of peace and well being that goes beyond their circumstances. That's why I called my new book *Happy For No Reason*. People who are truly happy are simply happy; they don't need a reason.

My life has been led by doing what was next for me. I know that when I do what's right for me, what draws my interest, what I care about, this is the greatest gift I can give to the world. I think this is true for everybody. We all have an inner spark of knowing what we are here for. When we are actually fulfilling that particular purpose, it serves not only our life—it can't help but serve the whole world.

**If you could give advice to those who are still searching for their purpose in life, what would it be?**

First and foremost, listen to what your heart is telling you. We are all so used to listening to the "should's", whether it's people telling us what we should do or our conditioning telling us what we should do. But deep inside your heart is planted your purpose, and when you listen to that—and when you have the courage and the guts to *follow* that inner knowing in your heart—that's when the magic in life happens. Everyone I've met or interviewed who is living a life that is full of joy, love, juiciness, vitality and aliveness is always listening to their heart and following it. The best advice I could give anybody is, "to thine own self be true," and listen, listen, listen to your heart. Move in the direction of what expands you, what brings you more joy, what brings you happiness.

As I mentioned earlier, I didn't win the happiness jackpot at birth, but my father was one of the happiest people I've ever known. He passed away when he was 91, and every morning he woke up with a smile on his face. His motto was, "If I'm breathing, it's a good day." Once when I was 19, we were driving down the road and I asked him, "Dad, what's your best advice for life?"

He looked at me and said four words. "Honey, just be happy."

At this point I threw my arms up in the air and said, "Dad, that's so easy for you to say! You just *are* happy. What do I do? I'm not happy like you are."

Again, he looked at me and said four more words. He said, "Honey, I don't know."

At that point, I realized it was my job to find out what it was that made him so happy and by extension, what makes some people happy no matter what, and others unhappy no matter what. And that's just what I did.

What I've found is that we live in a culture where we are deeply habituated to searching outside of ourselves for fulfillment, and it's not there. I'm all for having wonderful things in life; there is nothing wrong with that. But ultimately the deepest and truest fulfillment in life is not to be found *out there*. Research is actually showing this. Recent studies show that we all have a "happiness set point," a level of happiness that we tend to stay at, no matter what happens to us (yes, including winning the lottery!), *unless* we consciously do something to change it.

So, can we change it? It turns out that fifty percent of our set point is determined by our genes; we're born with it. The great news is that only ten percent is based on our circumstances, and the other forty percent is based on our habitual thoughts and behaviors. That's what we *can* change, and forty percent can make a huge difference.

We're all so busy trying to change our circumstances in life and gather all the things and achievements we think will make us happy. But that's not where happiness is to be found; all that stuff accounts for just 10 percent of our happiness. According to science, the way we can significantly raise our happiness set point and enjoy a stable state of happiness is by changing our habitual thoughts, attitudes and behaviors. So that's what I show people how to do in *Happy for No Reason*.

The ultimate thing we all want in life is to be happy. It's why we do anything. Ask yourself: Why do I want this better job? Why do I want a raise? Why do I want a spouse? Why do I want a great home? It's because ultimately you think it will make you happy. My advice is, cut to the chase. Go for the happiness first and all the rest will follow.

# John Kehoe

*"At different phases of our lives, different things are appropriate to us. What was appropriate to us at twenty-five isn't necessarily appropriate to us at forty-five."*

For over three decades, Canadian John Kehoe has earned worldwide recognition for his pioneering work in the field of Mind Power. He is a warm and energetic teacher, author, socially conscious individual, and proponent of the amazing human potential to transform the world and our lives with our thoughts.

John has lectured on every continent, and his seminal book, *Mind Power Into the 21st Century*, has topped bestseller lists in over a dozen countries. His teachings relate directly to the powers held within every person to conclusively shape his or her destiny.

In 1975, John Kehoe withdrew to the wooded seclusion of the British Columbia wilderness to spend three years in intensive study and contemplation of the inner workings of the human mind. During this time, Kehoe forged the first straightforward and successful program for developing Mind Power. In 1978, he began traveling and teaching people the principles he had formulated, and the phenomenal success of his speaking tours soon grew to encompass the world.

John Kehoe has taught the Mind Power system to over 100,000 people around the globe and, though he no longer physically teaches the course, has made it available to people everywhere with the Mind Power Home Study Program.

His book *Mind Power Into the 21st Century* has sold millions of copies, and has become an international bestseller, translated and published in a multitude of languages including French, German, Japanese, Korean, and Russian. John has also written four other books, *Money Success & You*, *A Vision of Power and Glory*, *The Practice of Happiness* and *Mind Power for Children*.

Learn more about John at: www.learnmindpower.com

## Who do you think you are?

I am a multiplicity. I am made up of a conscious mind, a subconscious mind, a body, and a soul. Each part of me has its needs, functions, and dysfunctions. Each part of me needs to be listened to and accounted for. This is who I am.

## What event or series of events led to your discovery?

I have been searching and seeking and am an ardent follower of personal growth for thirty-five years now. So I've put in a lot of work on myself. I have researched many different areas such as quantum physics, positive thinking, mind power, religion, psychology, medicine - anything that has something to do with the human mind. The mind is my specialty. I've written the number one best-selling book, *Mind Power Into The 21st Century*, which has sold over 2 million copies, so I've obviously hit a real note with people out there. I just devoted myself to understanding who I am and the nature of reality so I can effectively work with it.

## If you could give advice to those who are still searching for their life's purpose, what would it be?

Follow your passion. That's the single most important thing that I can advise people to do, because following your passion is real and honest. I made a discovery years ago when I was doing research on my book *Money, Success & You*. What I discovered is that when someone's sole objective is just about making money, they almost always don't. The reason for that is because their whole aim is only money-oriented. Now there is nothing wrong with making money, I mean I am very wealthy myself, but to just go after the money without going after what you are most passionate about can lead you astray.

My advice is do what turns you on, follow what makes you passionate and what makes you excited. Do you wake up every day really excited about what you're doing? If you don't, then you're not passionate about what you're doing. Many people do make a living without being passionate about what they do, but they will never be tremendously successful. You must find something that you are passionate about.

The same is also true in your spiritual growth. It's important to find a system that awakens you, that feels right. It doesn't matter whether it's a traditional religion or a very esoteric practice that nobody knows, just find something that nurtures you deeply and follow it for as long as it nurtures you deeply. When it no longer nurtures you move on to something else.

At different phases of our lives, different things are appropriate to us. What was appropriate to us at twenty-five isn't necessarily appropriate to us at forty-five. Just follow your passion and follow what makes you feel alive. The model that I live by is simple: be kind, be aware, be positive, be joyful, do good work, and live life one day at a time. Do this and you will have a very successful life.

# Janet Attwood

*"What you love and God's will for you are one in the same."*

**Janet Attwood combines a unique blend of spirituality and practical, useful knowledge that can be put to use immediately. Her passion and focus is supporting people, in every part of the world, in knowing their personal greatness. She shows her students how it's possible to have a life of abundance while living their dreams. Janet is sought after because of her authenticity, clarity and the power of the tools she shares.**

**Janet is presently co-founder of Enlightened Alliances with Chris Attwood. Enlightened Alliances creates relationships between individuals and organizations that are doing work to create a world of abundance, harmony, and mutual support. Janet is also co-founder of one of the largest online transformational magazines in the world, Healthy Wealthy n Wise (www.healthywealthynwise.com) and co-host of the magazine's Passions of Real Life Legends twice-monthly interviews.**

**Janet is the co-author of the New York Times bestseller The Passion Test: the Effortless Path to Discovering Your Destiny, and co-author of the popular e-book From Sad to Glad: 7 Steps to Facing Change with Love and Power. To find out more about Janet and her work, go to www.thepassiontest.com or www.janetattwood.com.**

## Who do you think you are?

I think that I'm not the "I." I think that I'm silence and bliss, absolute and unbounded eternal, never dying, unchanging, and one with all that is in unity. It's only my mind that gets in the way of me knowing who I am. I love what Nisargadatta Maharaj said, "That I am that."

How we come to that is different for everyone. It's interesting to hear how Nisargadatta Maharaj came to this. Let me share a quick story from his book *The Sense of "I am."*

When I met my Guru, he told me, "You are not what you take yourself to be. Find out what you are. Watch the sense I am, find your real Self." I obeyed him, because I trusted him. I did as he told me. All my spare time I would spend looking at myself in silence. And what a difference it made, and how soon!

My teacher told me to hold on to the sense "I am" tenaciously and not to swerve from it even for a moment. I did my best to follow his advice and in a comparatively short time I realized within myself the truth of his teaching. All I did was to remember his teaching, his face, and his words constantly. This brought an end to the mind; in the stillness of the mind I saw myself as I am — unbounded.

I simply followed (my teacher's) instruction, which was to focus the mind on pure being "I am," and stay in it. I used to sit for hours together, with nothing but the "I am" in my mind and soon peace and joy and a deep all-embracing love became my normal state. In it all disappeared — myself, my Guru, the life I lived, the world around me. Only peace remained and unfathomable silence.

**What event or series of events lead to your discovery?**

When I was young I had a really tough life, but I always knew that there was something more. I started out happy, and then it started to get tough. When I was about 19 years old I was really deep into drugs, and I was thoroughly stuck. I called my brother up and cried over the phone (he was living in Los Angeles and I was living in Northern California). He said to me, "Janet, I just found something so wonderful, and don't worry, everything's going to be okay."

Four days later, I heard a knock on my door and it was my brother. He'd driven all the way up to Northern California with all of his belongings in his car. He packed me up and we moved to Santa Barbara. It was there that I learned how to meditate using the Transcendental Meditation® technique. That was really the beginning for me, when I experienced what they call an awakening (Being awake – Being more conscious).

I love what Maharishi Mehesh Yogi (founder of the Transcendental Meditation® program) said, "Meditation is the direct means of enjoying the greatest happiness, and it's the only means to quench the thirst for happiness on earth. Meditation is the only means to the harmonious development of the body, mind, and soul." I love this quote as well: "Meditation makes the man divine and brings the divine to the world of man."

# If you could give advice to those who are still searching for their life's purpose, what would it be?

I would say to find a meditation that allows you to transcend. And when I say transcend I mean go beyond the thinking process, go beyond the mind, and experience the source of thought, that state of unbounded awareness. It's that unified field where all knowledge comes from. If God said to me, "you can only take one thing in your life with you, and everything else has to go," there would be no doubt, it would be my meditation program. I have been practicing the TM® technique for 35 years now, and it really works for me. I would say to anyone, find a meditation practice that transcends the mind.

Another thing I would recommend is The Work of Byron Katie. The Work is a simple process of inquiry that teaches people how to identify and question the stressful thoughts that cause suffering. Suffering arises from the mind, and The Work is a way to understand what's hurting us. It's also way to end the suffering and the stress we have. I love this quote by Byron Katie: "I don't let go of my concepts. I meet them through inquiry and they let go of me."

The last thing is to take The Passion Test®. I am co-author of the book, *The Passion Test*, along with Chris Attwood, who is my ex-husband, one of my very best friends, and my business partner. It's a really easy process that aligns people with what they are passionate about, those things that are most important to them. Using the processes we teach in The Passion Test book, it effortlessly draws all of these things to you.

In our book we say, "Whenever you are faced with a decision, a choice, or an opportunity choose in favor of your passions. Choose in favor of what it is that you love." We also say, "What you love and God's will for you are one in the same." It's my experience that when I choose in favor of what brings me the greatest joy, what brings me the greatest happiness, everything else seems to fall into place. If I go in my mind and try to think, Okay what is right and what is wrong, I go absolutely crazy.

It's too big a field in that mind of mine. But when I just drop into what brings me the greatest joy, that's really easy for me, and I keep my attention on those things.

Maharishi Mahesh Yogi said, "Happiness radiates like the fragrance from a flower and draws all good things towards you. Allow your love to nourish yourself as well as others. Do not strain after the needs of life. It is sufficient to be quietly alert and aware of them. In this way life proceeds more effortlessly and naturally. Life is here to enjoy."

This reminds me of a story that perfectly illustrates this point:

A young girl who collected autographs of famous people was at the airport waiting to board her plane when she saw a crowd of people standing around a small man in a white robe. She knew this man had to be someone well known because of the large crowd encircling him. She went up to one of the people standing nearby and asked who the man was. The reply she received was, "That's Maharishi Mahesh Yogi, a great saint from the Himalayas."

The girl excitedly ran up to Maharishi and immediately asked for his autograph. Maharishi took her pen and paper, looked her straight in the eyes, and said, "I will give you something much more important than my autograph." And on the piece of paper he wrote one word: **ENJOY.**

I truly believe that is exactly why we are here on this planet – to enjoy. When we really drop into the things that are truly from our heart, and we start seeing what we enjoy, then life becomes that state of bliss.

All of us have a special gift. All of us are unique. All of us are here to contribute our gifts in our own special way. When we do that, we experience the greatest possible joy and fulfillment in our own lives, and we spread that joy around to everyone we meet.

# Lee Travathan

*"This universe will shape itself around your thoughts; that's the truth.*
*Keep your thoughts clean; keep the weeds out of your garden."*

**Lee Travathan, also known as the Rebel Writer, is a noted inspirational author and speaker, blog writer, workshop teacher, and has hosted and produced TV and radio talk shows. She has been a professional inspirational consultant, mentor and coach to artists, entertainers, and sports figures worldwide in the area of Extraordinary Thinking, Applied Manifestation, and Life Evaluation for over 25 years.**

**Lee is the author of the *Rebel Writer* book series, *The Tender Art of Extraordinary Thinking* and *Ramblings from the Depths*.**

**Her burning passion is to help people get to higher formats of thought in order to improve daily life by understanding the power of beliefs, thoughts, feelings, and actions and create a greater outcome based on the deepest levels of love.**

**Lee teaches people how to become conscious victors, deleting and bypassing the common "victim mentality" of the day. It's all about getting to the place where you understand that you are always better than what you "put up with" in yourself. The higher you reach, the better life gets. You are worth the journey. We all are.**

## Who do you think you are?

I love that as a title. I used to write essays for the local newspapers when I was living in the state of Washington, and I actually wrote an essay with the same title, *Who Do You Think You Are?* When I saw the invitation to participate, I thought to myself, "Now that's going to be a cool title for a book."

It's a hard question to answer because we all have a lot of purposes. But really it does melt down into one, if you really think about it. I've tried to run away from this twice now and, luckily, I have people in my life that were bold enough to confront me and say, "You can't run away from this, it's going to just chase you down and haunt you." They were right. It did. I had to belly up to the bar and just do it on a large scale.

For the last 30 years, I would say my main purpose has been to talk to people and help them really get down deep into the core of their awareness to find out what extraordinary thinking is for them. What part of them is open to that method of thinking? From here, they can seriously just look at what their motivations and options are for behavior.

My main calling, the thing that really lights up my heart and soul, is to be a writer and see that skill open doors for people. I want to see what extraordinary thought is all about. In essence, I want to open the doors to extraordinary thought through practical applications they can easily use every day. The way I write is especially conversational; it's very stream of consciousness, and that disarms readers. I think that the goal of my work is to help people change their minds, if they wish, and realize that it's going to change their lives. It also opens their hearts, which is critical to success in any area of life.

I think the basis of any extraordinary thinking is love, you know, truly walking it, talking it, being it, doing it, trusting it, and realizing that we're born of and to it. We are born to greatness, and the greatest thing we'll ever do is love people and love ourselves to the best of our abilities. More than likely, when this thing is all said and done, and we're at the end of it and everybody's eyes are wide open, we'll all be looking at each other and saying, "Wow, what was your lesson, what was my lesson? I think my mission was to love and allow myself to be loved."

**What event or series of events led to your discovery?**

Mostly, I think it was the way that I was raised. I actually ran away from home when I was fifteen. I had been abandoned by my mother at a much earlier age and was being raised by my father and my grandfather. I loved them, but desperately felt much was missing in my life. If I stayed, it would always be that way, as it had been for many before me. I had to go.

My grandfather was a man who had love dripping out of his pores. He and my father were both circuit-riding preachers and that meant that at any point in time they had four to five churches each. Granted, most of them were little country churches in Missouri that had maybe twenty-two members and they were all cousins, but I had to go there all the same. I followed my dad and grandfather through their journeys. They were both rebels, so I picked that up from them. That's why my books are called *The Rebel Writer* series. They were rebels that colored outside of the lines all their lives and I write and live outside of the lines, too.

My grandfather was like an angel to me. He was the one person that always reminded me that everything is about love, and that we're all more wonderful and more beautiful than we imagine. He taught me that we are all a product of our thoughts; so to make it easy, always think good thoughts. He was there for me when I needed someone. There were other people in my life that were extreme opposites of that. In my family history there has been tremendous turmoil. If I did not have extraordinary thinking and my grandfather's love to count on, I don't know how I would have made it.

It's been a rough ride for some of my siblings and for me, at times. I think it's hard when you're a preacher's kid and granddaughter and you're taught all these things about love, but because you're in so much pain you don't really apply them. My grandfather was the shining light, a true rebel, and when we moved away my dad tried his best to keep everything together, but there was deep and unresolved hurt and such pain running through the entire family from divorce, betrayal, things we all deal with. My mother had abandoned her kids and there were a lot of us. As hard as my family tried to downplay it, that had an effect on our thoughts. Also, we lived in unbelievable poverty when I was growing up, and that can make you feel poor all of your life if you do not get a hand over your thinking.

Even though I saw all that pain, I could always see beyond it. I was constantly in the middle of everything saying, "Can't we all just get along?" Just like Rodney King. The bottom line was, *no;* that just wasn't going to happen. I wanted to focus on what was really important but no one was listening.

In the end, siblings made the choice to hold onto their anger, their pain, their victimhood, and their "I was abandoned" thoughts. They chose to clutch onto all of that with gusto, and I don't think they realized (and maybe they still don't) that it becomes a prayer. That's an affirmation; it's a structure they built a house on. Holding on to such things will define you, your relationships, and how you live. Consequently, they've had truly difficult issues and, for the most part, I haven't had as much because I left all that behind. I'm not sure exactly why I ran away at 15, but it was the single most important thing I ever did thus far. Maybe I just walked very fast to find comfort that I felt was lacking. I made a rebel choice.

I can remember being thirteen and knowing that I was going to leave. No one believed me. I knew there was going to be a time when they'd wake up and say, "Oh wow, where'd she go?" I recall sitting on the steps at my dad's house in a little country town in Missouri on a summer day. My sister had just graduated high school that afternoon and I recall thinking to myself, "When I walk away from all this, I'm really walking away from *all* the negatives, too. I'm going to build a new life. I'm going to become a new person and I'm going to live a new way. If I learn anything from all of this, I'm going to share it, and I'm going to write about it."

I wanted to go to L.A. and work with actors, musicians, writers, and directors and talk to them to learn their ideas. I wanted to seriously communicate with them, find out what their thoughts were, and I did that. I walked away from all the unconstructive stuff to start anew. Later, I tried to heal the family relationships but there just wasn't an opening to do that. Leaving home was my turning point, and I think the biggest lesson was this: you *have* to make a choice. You really can't have it both ways, or serve two masters, as they say. I realized that my mom left because she could not breathe and could not fly. I had done the same thing. Today, it is easy for me to fly out of any dark reality.

I choose not to focus on the negative in my childhood. There have been a few people that have read my books and wanted to make public comment about how sad my childhood was, but I don't allow it. To me, it was such a tremendous gift. It is a treasure and I honor and respect this truth. I could not get seen or heard, of course, but that taught me to find my own voice. Still, I don't ever want to say that bad things happened to me. I really believe that the universe used all of my past for good. When I was twelve years old I was taught that before you go to sleep at night you say your prayers, so I would always kneel down by my bedside and say my prayers. I would say, "Use me as an instrument. I'm not going to ask you to heal all this other stuff, just use me, use me up, use me."

It's been a little tricky in the sense that I have not done the public life as well as I wanted to. I'm a lot better about it now. I'm much more open. Previously, when I reached a peak of "fame," I walked away. I've faded away twice in the last thirty years and took the time MIA reviewing my thoughts, intentions, and lifestyle. During that time of reflection, I've received a lot of support from the celebrity community. Most of my friends are celebrities, which has been very interesting, to say the least. It has ups and downs. I've seen what has happened to them in the fame game and I probably had the feeling that I was going to lose something of myself in the process, as they had.

It was actually my daughter that ultimately said, "Wait a minute Mom, walk your talk here. No one can take anything away from you unless you let them. You know that. So, just go out there and knock that wall down and whatever comes, comes" That's where I've been for quite awhile now. Each day, fame knocks, I answer with a smile, and I'm more at peace with that in my soul.

I estimate that the events that shaped me in my childhood were simple things. I saw what I didn't want to be; the ways I didn't want to live; the things I didn't want to do, and then it was up to me to dig down deep inside and discover how to get past old programs. I had to use all of my experiences for good as a powerful tool instead of turning myself into a victim and believing that I couldn't do any better than what I'd known. I couldn't allow myself to surrender to such dark images. Instead, I surrendered to love. I found out that there was a gift inside of me that had never been opened, so I opened it myself. It is my prayer that many others across the globe use my work to open the gift that they are to the world.

**If you could give advice to those who are still searching for their life's purpose, what would it be?**

My grandmother used to always say, "Where there's a will, there's a way." I really believe that's true. I talk to a lot of people on a daily basis and I hear a flood of can't-itus! It's caused, by saying over and over "I can't, I can't, I can't." I believe that our thoughts are things and they're exceptionally powerful. Our thoughts are our prayers for what we want. Be extremely mindful!

I would also say, "Change your mind, change your world." Where there's certainly a will there's absolutely a way, and there will be a way even if you don't see it right now. As long as you trust that it will be shown to you, you can't miss it. When you come to the table of life prepared to stand in that space and arrive ready, it's going to be shown to you. You will find the way. You'll be led on that path, and your job is to just be open and watching like a hawk. Be exceedingly clear about what you want and what you need, and allow the universe to be in you, for you, through you, as you, and to guide you. Surrender to that. Trust and act accordingly.

This universe will shape itself around your thoughts; that's the truth. Keep your thoughts clean; keep the weeds out of your garden. Don't give in to the naysayers. Don't allow that, because they'll give you a hundred reasons why something shouldn't work. So many of us are born with gifts and deep desires, and if anything is tugging at you in that way, it's a signal and you've got to pay attention to it in earnest.

I tried to walk away from writing, especially rebel writing, but it was just so hard to live with such a decision because the need inside me to write was always burning. I was driven to do it, and particularly to write about extraordinary thinking. A friend, Julian Lennon, has talked about this and what it was like for him when he took a sabbatical from his music for a few years. At the time he walked away from it he was thinking, I'll never go back to it; I'll never do that again. But, in the end, it just hounded him. It burned in his soul and he had to return to it.

I suppose I just want people to know that if they have that deep inner urge, that tug, that pull, that something inside that's very strong, the worst thing you can do is not do it. I'd love people to remember that they were given the passion inside of them for a reason. It was to use it. If you do have to take a break, don't beat yourself up, but don't take too long. Hurry back!

# Patricia Drain

*"You have to understand yourself as well as you possibly can,*
*and know who you are."*

**Patricia Drain is an international author and professional speaker who has over 20 years of experience in the recruiting industry. The *Working Woman Magazine* presented Patricia with the "Most Innovative Business Practice Award." Voted one of the "100 Most Influential People" by the *Phoenix Business Journal*, Patricia is also the past President of the National Association of Women Business Owners (NAWBO) and recipient of NAWBO Business Owner of the Year.**

**Helping thousands around the world discover the secrets of successful interviewing, Patricia authored a book called *Hire Me! Secrets of Job Interviewing*, which has been published in seven different languages. Patricia lectures across the country to groups numbering in the thousands and appears regularly on radio and television.**

**Patricia is the author of numerous books, audio, and videotapes including: *Hire Me! Secrets of Job Interviewing, What Was Your Highlight Today?* and Seven *Secrets For Building A Business That Has Value.* Additionally, she has authored a series of children's books: *I Love Myself, Benjamin the Bumblebee,* and *Melanie the Magnificent.* Her newest book is entitled *What Should I Be When I Grow Up? Now that I'm 40, 50, 60.***

**Read more about Patricia Drain at: www.PatriciaDrain.com**

## Who do you think you are?

So many people are still searching for their answer to that question, and the business that I am in is helping people to find their passion. I found my passion when I was a very young girl, and my passion is helping others be the very best they can be. The mistake I made was that I had to change that later in life to helping others *and* myself to be the best we can be! You see if you don't help yourself along the way, you may start getting resentful toward the people who you're helping.

I thought everybody's passion was the same. I thought everybody wanted to help others be the best they could be, and give them all the information they could give, and I found out that is not a true statement at all. That's why I wrote the book, *What Should I Do When I Grow Up? Now that I'm 40 50 60.* I finally realized that we just keep getting older and asking the same question, now what?

**What event or series of events lead to your discovery?**

Owning an executive recruiting firm, asking and interviewing people, and really understand where they were coming from. I was a school teacher and I would watch these little children light up when they got the "Ah Ha" about their passions or what they wanted to do or be. It was the same in the office. I would ask an adult what they were best at, or what their natural abilities were, what would they really want to do if they didn't have to earn money? Then I kept remembering what a joy it was and how pleasurable it was for me to watch them discover their passion. I've always been the queen of asking the right questions, and in the book I call them purposeful questions.

**If you could give advice to someone who is still searching for their life's purpose, what would it be?**

Well the answer is so obvious to me because it's what I've tried to put together for twenty years while I'm interviewing people. You have to understand yourself as well as you possibly can, and know who you are. The way that you do that is by asking the right kind of questions of yourself. You can even ask living questions (living with the question about yourself for a week) and keep on figuring it out. What you need to do is to find the ingredients to your passion and to the next chapter in your life.

For me there were about seven different points to my ingredients. Once I found those ingredients, as I walked into the first position that I interviewed for, I knew I was at home, and I knew I would be successful because it had all my ingredients.

In my book, I have about one hundred and twenty questions that help people to discover what their passions are. For example, one question is "what was your favorite job that you've ever had, and why?"

People will say things like, "Well, when I was sixteen years old I worked retail, and I didn't get paid anything, but I loved it."

I say, "Oh really...why?"

"Well, everybody left me alone. I was on my own."

You can see that person wants independence. That's one of their ingredients. It's just about asking questions like that, and finding out what the key ingredients are. I came up with a process of how somebody can do that. It's such a good feeling to know that if they ask the right questions, explore their passions, their obstacles, their desires, and natural abilities then they'll find out what is right for them.

# John Gray

*"Keep your heart open, be true to yourself, and continue to follow your heart even when it doesn't look like things are falling into place the way you want them to."*

**John Gray, Ph.D., is the author of 16 best-selling books, including *Men Are from Mars, Women Are from Venus*, the number one best-selling book of the last decade. In the past ten years, over 30 million *Mars and Venus* books have been sold in over 40 languages throughout the world.**

**An expert in the field of communication, Dr. Gray's focus is to help men and women understand, respect, and appreciate their differences in both personal and professional relationships. In his many books, CD's, DVD's, tapes, workshops and seminars, he provides practical tools and insights to effectively manage stress and improve relationships at all stages and ages by creating the brain chemistry of health, happiness, and lasting romance.**

**Dr. Gray has appeared on *Oprah*, *The Today Show*, CBS *Morning Show*, *Good Morning America*, *The View*, *Politically Incorrect*, *Larry King*, and others. He has been profiled in *Newsweek*, *Time*, *Forbes*, *USA Today*, *TV Guide*, *People* and *New Age Journal*, among others.**

**In addition to being a Certified Family Therapist, Dr. Gray is a consulting editor of *The Family Journal*, and a member of the Distinguished Advisory Board of the International Association of Marriage and Family Counselors. In 2001, he received the Smart Marriages Impact Award.**

**John Gray's latest book, *The Mars & Venus Diet & Exercise Solution* (St. Martin's Press 2003), reveals why diet, exercise and communication skills combine to affect the production of healthy brain chemicals and how the need for those chemicals differ between men and women.**

**You can read more about John Gray at: www.marsvenus.com**

## Who do you think you are?

I have a variety of purposes in my life. I'm a father, a husband, and a grandfather. In terms of my interaction with the world, I make a difference by bringing greater awareness to how people can live with greater integrity in congruency with who they truly are as loving human beings.

I'm most famous for my work in personal relationships between men and women. But my whole life has been committed to personal growth and developing my inner potential; so that I could assist others in developing their full potential. I wanted myself and others to be fulfilled in life, to create a life of abundance, a life of love and a life of service. Throughout my life, my primary focus has been in the service of others. My success wasn't a complete surprise. I had always wanted to be successful, but more importantly I wanted to be of service and be successful at that. My notoriety has come through one of my talents, which is to assist men and women in understanding their differences so they can find greater peace and love in their relationships. I truly believe that is a foundation for people to create a more fulfilling life outside their homes as well.

**What event or series of events led you to your discovery?**

I had an epiphany at age nine when I saw the movie *War and Peace*. It was after that movie that I had an experience of expanded awareness of the world being a very divine place with light shining all around me. I knew that I was here for a purpose and that purpose was to contribute to bringing peace into this world. That experience has been forgotten many times, but it is the foundation of who I am and what I hope to achieve throughout my lifetime: to bring greater peace into this world of turmoil, chaos, and hate.        Love is greatly needed, as well as consciousness, awareness of how we consistently create our own problems rather than accessing our potential to solve them. This was reinforced when I went to a lecture on Transcendental Meditation in 1969. At that lecture I heard that meditation was a tool for developing your full potential as well as creating peace in the world. I thought wow, this is really great! It harmonized with a chord in my heart, which wanted me to be all that I could be, to bring peace into the world, and to make a difference.

I began studying under the Maharishi, who founded the Transcendental Meditation Movement. He was a huge influence on me because he was somebody who was actually out there doing it. During the time I worked for him, he developed one of the biggest personal growth organizations at that time. It was international, millions of people were participating in the programs. I was a part of organizing all that as his student and personal assistant.

Over the years, I developed a teacher-training program with him to train teachers of Transcendental Meditation. After nine years of studying with him, I moved on into my own life to find something that I personally had to contribute. I didn't know what that was, but I gradually became aware of how I could apply my talents differently from the way he had and still contribute to the world in a big way. That has been my motivation ever since.

**If you could give advice to people that are still searching for their life's purpose, what would that be?**

Keep your heart open, be true to yourself, and continue to follow your heart even when it doesn't look like things are falling into place the way you want them to. There were a series of events in my life that didn't seem positive, but actually ended up leading me in a positive direction. For example, the nine years I spent with the Maharishi were very fulfilling. Yet during that time I wanted to help my brother, who was bi-polar, through meditation and yoga. I thought that doing meditation and yoga might help, but it didn't. When this didn't help him, I stopped.

I left the TM Movement and moved back to California to study psychology, in an attempt to help my brother in his plight. I was unable to do that successfully before he committed suicide. It did put me on a new path, however, which was to study psychology, and to begin applying psychology. While I was hoping to help my brother, I discovered a talent for counseling couples. I could have never foreseen that I would go from being a celibate yogi (Indian term for monk) to becoming an expert in personal relationships.

You never know what's around the next corner in your life. You just have to keep following what you feel to be true, and what's most important to you, and the universe will support you, but not always in the ways you think it should.

# Mark Thompson

*"Anyone who's even thinking about making a run at a successful career should abandon being advised, in a sense, by other people."*

Mark Thompson is co-author of the international bestseller *Success Built to Last.* He brings to every engagement two decades of experience as a senior executive, board member, management coach, producer, and investor in growing businesses. Mark helps your team *embrace* rapid change, ignite growth as leaders, and engage with influential people who are driving the future of your brand. Our *thought leader* programs inspire deeper relationships with your communities of interest around the world.

As an executive coach and producer of leadership programs, Mark is passionate about unlocking the unique insights and skills of hundreds of remarkable people around the world — from executives, entrepreneurs, nonprofit leaders and billionaires, to the presidents of nations and the leaders of small and large organizations.

Mark's ability to draw out the relevant personal and business stories from thought leader interviews formed the foundation for the book *Success Built to Last,* and also resulted in many audio and video programs including the *Charles Schwab CEO series, Women on Leadership, Seven Sacred Secrets with Maya Angelou,* and the DVD program *Creating a Life that Matters.*

Forbes Magazine included Mark on its list of America's leading venture investors with the "Midas" touch in 2004. He has been an investor and chairman of many technology and media startups. He worked for a dozen years for Charles Schwab, serving in a variety of senior roles, including Chief Communications Officer and, later, as Executive Producer responsible for the customer experience of Schwab.com.

Mark is a venture investor, management advisor and former board member of private and public companies. He served as Chairman of Rioport, Inc., which popularized the MP3 player; he was Chairman of Integration, Inc., a communications semiconductor company; and Chairman of VMAX, which was the exclusive distributor of Micron PCs in China. He has been a speaker at London Business School, Stanford University, U.C. Berkeley, *The Economist* and *Fortune Magazine* conferences, The New York Stock Exchange summits with The Churchill Club and Financial Executives Institute. He served on the Council of The Heartland Circle Thought Leaders Gatherings.

He also created the *Leaders of the New Century* series through his production company, Network Public Broadcasting International, and was a contributor and host for CEO and executive interviews for thought leaders programs by Korn Ferry International and Ernst & Young.

Mark has a passion for education and educational media, particularly for those in need. He volunteers his time and money to independent producers of public broadcasting and to classroom and scholarship programs for elementary and graduate education programs.

**Who do you think you are?**

I think that evolves a lot for people over time, based on life experiences and how we contribute to the lives of others. Right now, I think I'm a guy who cares about improving how people work and how they work with each other. That can take many different forms. I've always thought of myself as the mirror rather than the light. I've discovered how to enable people to contribute to the world in ways they may not have imagined, and to become more effective at what they do and how they work with each other. That's my mission right now. It would be interesting to ask people that question at different times in their lives, and see if they still saying the same thing over a long period of time.

**What event or series of events led to your discovery?**

I grew up around a great deal of scarcity. Early in my life, I found myself on a path that people would consider traditional success. I really wanted to gain business power and make money, because that was never in my family. That was not a possibility for us when I was growing up. I was able to start an early business career, and as I did that and had some early success, I discovered that people who had business success were not any less dysfunctional than I was. They would be suffering in a sense of betrayal of success, where the traditional definition of success was money, fame and power. That's what it actually says in the dictionary, amazingly enough. What people find is that there is usually a betrayal of those values, and that's not really what drives your success in the first place. It's certainly not what gives it meaning or purpose in your life.

I've come to a place in my life where I believe that this is the highest and best use of my time, and I can make a contribution in terms of being able to help you determine what your purpose is. The secret to success is finding meaning, finding what you can contribute to others, and combining those with some core passion, then turning that into action. Those are the ingredients people are looking for. I think people have to find their own sense of success rather than relying on others to define it for them, which is usually the default in people's lives.

I started an early career in the investment business on Wall Street and now I've ended up teaching, writing, and speaking all over the world about how to create success that's built to last.

**If you could give advice to those who are still searching for their life's purpose, what would it be?**

Stop and think how you define success in your life? Personally. Not a politically correct answer and not the answer that you're supposed to give your boss. We did a worldwide success survey with people who have had a big impact in their field for at least twenty years or more. What we found that was universal among all of them was that there are three essential dimensions to the definition of success.

The first, as I stated above, is doing something that really mattered to them. Usually we get sidetracked. For instance, I was talking to Warren Buffet, one of the world's greatest living investors and one of the world's richest people, and he said that people come to him all the time asking him for career advice. They'll say they've found a core business that they want to do, and maybe have an action plan, but the passion is often missing from their plan. They say, "I'll do this because it's the right thing to do for a few years, then I'll get back to doing something that I really love." Then two, three, or five years will pass, and they'll check in again and they'll discover that they're still not doing what they're passionate about. "I'll do that in my next job," they'll say, "Or maybe in my next company or with my next promotion."

Warren said, "Mark, living your life always putting your passion off until later is like saving up sex for old age. It's a really bad idea." What we found is that it's not just something that gives you less enjoyment in your life, it's the one thing that makes the difference between those people who have an average experience in life and those who are able to contribute greatly to a career or profession for a long period of time.

They found some higher purpose, something that really mattered to them, and they care about having an impact on other people. Then they found a way to pull all of that together by creating goals and objectives to accomplish it.

It was all about purpose, passion, and a sense of performance (being able to get things done). I wish I had learned that earlier in life. Anyone who's even thinking about making a run at a successful career should abandon being advised, in a sense, by other people. No one can tell you what matters to you and what your core passion should be. They can help you in the process of putting your goals together or learning how to achieve goals, and that's a really important skill. But those other two pieces were really important to those successful people. The outcome was sometimes money, fame, power or traditional success, but it never really came in a lasting way until they started with something intensely personal that had meaning to them. That is my universal suggestion for getting involved with something that's going to give you a long-term success built to last.

# Rhonda Britten

*"Unless you really have a relationship with fear,*
*unless the fear becomes a good friend and you understand how it operates,*
*fear will make your decisions for you."*

Rhonda Britten - Emmy Award-winner, repeat Oprah guest - is the founder of the Fearless Living Institute, an organization dedicated to giving anyone the tools they need to master their emotional fears, and the author of four national bestsellers including *Fearless Living* which features her groundbreaking work called the Wheel Technology. During her three seasons on the hit daytime reality drama *Starting Over,* Britten was named "America's Favorite Life Coach" and was dubbed *Starting Over's* "Most Valuable Player" by the *New York Times*. She is a globally recognized expert on the subject of fear and fearlessness.

Rhonda has written several national bestsellers based on her principles, including *Fearless Living* (translated into 12 languages), *Fearless Loving,* and *Change Your Life in 30 Days.* Her latest book *Do I Look Fat in This? Get Over Your Body and On With Your Life* alters the way we see, and our relationship to, our body.

A respected life strategist, Britten is both inspired and inspiring with a pin-point ability to see through to the core of the issues at hand and to address them straight on. It is her instinct and intuition, honed over years of coaching private clients, through teleclasses and on her television programs that truly sets her apart. She delivers with spirits and a no nonsense manner, resulting in maximum results. Rhonda is adept at creating dynamic action-oriented exercises designed to compliment her simple yet sophisticated "Wheel of Fear" and "Wheel of Freedom" models upon which her work is based.

Today, Rhonda continues to work as a life coach, and her Fearless Living Institute provides dedicated support, an industry-leading life coach training program, and intensive workshops and presentations for corporations. Her past corporate clients include Southwest Airlines, Blue Shield, Toyota, and Northrop Grumman.

Find out more about Rhonda at: www.RhondaBritten.com

## Who do you think you are? What is your purpose?

I'm here to eradicate the burden of emotional fears. I'm here to support people in understanding how fear operates in their lives, and I'm here to set the world free. I have a particular view of fear that no one else has. I see the world through the eyes of fear of freedom. I see fear as the number one reason the world exists the way it does, in our frustrations and unhappiness. It's the reason that we don't have access to our passions, and the reason we don't have access to our purpose, because we are afraid to see it. When somebody understands how fear operates, they can then begin a relationship with fear that no longer stops them but actually propels them. It's really about creating a relationship with fear that moves somebody to the next place.

**What events or series of events led to your discovery?**

When I was fourteen years old, my father murdered my mother and committed suicide in front of me, and it took me twenty years to recover from that day and what had preceded it. I started going to therapy, doing workshops, reading books, and nothing really helped me get past the barriers that I perceived in front of me. So I started creating my own exercises, basically to save my own life. That is the premise of Fearless Living and the premise of what I teach. Once I understood that I didn't have a list problems, I really only had one challenge and one opportunity (which was to understand and master fear), then my life took off and blossomed. My whole world really began to make sense.

Most people think they have lots of problems and they think they're not good enough. I'm here to support people in embracing their humanity, because fear has stopped us from doing that. I had to learn how to embrace my own humanity to save my own life.

After my third suicide attempt, I was leaving the hospital and I realized that I'm not very good at killing myself. I thought to myself, "If I'm going to stay on this earth, which I wasn't really thrilled about, I had better figure out a better way to do it." I realized that fundamentally I didn't think I was good enough. I think this is the message that most of us receive at some point and buy into, and therefore don't follow our purpose and passion.

The very first exercise I did was to get a calendar and some stars. Do you remember back in kindergarten when you did something right they would give you a star? I decided that every time I did something kind, loving, good, or something that hard for me, I would put a star on the calendar. I wanted to see if there was still something good in me because I had been telling myself that I wasn't good enough for so long. After a month, I had a calendar filled with stars. And that was my turning point. I realized that I was waiting for the world to acknowledge me when I had not even acknowledged myself.

One of my core beliefs is that our willingness to acknowledge ourselves on a daily basis builds our self-confidence and self-esteem giving us the courage to take the risks that we really want to take. When you acknowledge yourself on a daily basis, you now have permission to go to places you never thought were possible. I ask people to acknowledge themselves a minimum of five times a day, and to do what I call stretch, risk, or die. You must acknowledge yourself for something that's uncomfortable, not just for going to the gym if you already do that every day. It doesn't have to be an action; it could be a new thought. Just a new thought is scary for some people. You'll know you're fearless when you're willing to be comfortable being uncomfortable. That's the name of the game! If you are comfortable being uncomfortable, then your feeling of being uncomfortable, which is fear based, no longer stops you.

**If you could give advice to those who are still searching for their life's purpose, what would it be?**

The answer to that question has already been revealed to you and the only reason you can't see it is because fear is covering up your ability to actually access it. Everybody has passion, everybody has a purpose, everybody has a life force within them, and everyone has what I call an essential nature that is attempting to express itself at every turn. You either express that essential nature through freedom, fearlessness, or it gets thwarted by fear. So if you're not living your purpose, if you're not expressing your passion, then you're not self-expressing, you're not accepting your self, and part of that is you're not embracing your humanity. You're caught up in the fear-based mentality of "I'm not good enough" and you're waiting for the world to give you permission.

The bottom line is this: the only thing stopping you is fear. When you start to realize that no one is stopping you, no thing is stopping you, no thought is stopping you, and no behavior is stopping you, it's just fear, then the shame fades away, and the fear moves aside, and you're able to listen to what's waiting to be heard for your ears alone. Fear keeps a bunch of wax in your ears.

Most people aren't doing the work to eradicate fear. What they're doing is trying to find their purpose and passion, but too many people do not have the purpose and passion that's really right for them. They were given to them by somebody else, because they don't understand that fear made the choice for them. Unless you really have a relationship with fear, unless the fear becomes a good friend, and you understand how it operates, fear will make your decisions for you.

# Chris Attwood

*"Your job in this incarnation is to live in joy, and to align your life with what you love most. Doing this provides a very simple yet profoundly powerful method of getting clear on what's most important."*

**Chris Attwood is an expert in the field of personal development. For over 30 years he has studied and explored the field of human consciousness.**

**After rising to become President of Newcomb Government Securities, a secondary dealer in U.S. government securities, Chris retired for ten years. During that time he did extensive research in the field of human consciousness and studied the Vedic literature of India. Today he brings this deep spiritual basis to his workshops and seminars, showing participants how their inner life creates the results they see in their outer life.**

**Chris is an expert in consultative sales and over the past 27 years has been President, Chief Operating Officer, General Manager, or CEO of nine companies with as much as $27 million in annual revenues and over 100 employees. He has sold millions of dollars of consulting, training, and products to companies like Dell Computer, Ford Motor Company, Mellon Bank, Royal Bank of Canada, Sprint, and others.**

**Chris is the co-author of the New York Times bestseller *The Passion Test: the Effortless Path to Discovering Your Destiny*, and co-author of the popular e-book *From Sad to Glad: 7 Steps to Facing Change with Love and Power*.**

**To find out more about Chris and his work, go to: www.thepassiontest.com.**

## Who do you think you are?

What a powerful question. Who I am is the same thing that, in my experience, all of us are: infinite, eternal, unbounded, without limits, without restrictions of any kind. I think the miracle of this is that discovery at my own deepest nature.

It's as if I created this game for myself in which I allowed myself to forget what I've known before. Since I have this infinite potential, I created the forgetfulness to forget who and what I really am, what my real nature is, and created a world in which I have the opportunity to rediscover who I really am. I created within this experience a world that appears to exist, and all the clues along the way are there to guide me along the path.

I created books to teach me, I created teachers, mentors, and masters to give me direction. It's a more and more amazing and miraculous experience as that nature of who I am becomes more and more expressed. I've come to the conclusion that the process never stops and because of being infinite, there is no end.

Some people may say, "Well, who do you think you are? God?" Some would even say harsher things. When I speak in these terms it is not the "I" which has been given the name "Chris Attwood." It's the "I" at the level where God, the Creator, and the creation are no longer separate. I, Chris Attwood, don't think I've created this world with all that's in it. I, that is present everywhere, at all times, and in every moment, has done this creating. That "I" realizes the sense of separation and differences is an illusion I have created in my own infinite nature with my own infinite power.

The "I" who is called "Chris Attwood" seems to have arrived at being okay with everything that is and being okay with every experience that is. Do you know the story of Hansel & Gretel? The kids were carried away by the evil witch and they left breadcrumbs along the way so that they could find their way home.

I've come to realize that the breadcrumbs that each of us has left for ourselves, are the things that we love, the things that we care about, the things that matter most to us. It's no accident that we love the things we love; it's no accident that we care about the things we care about. Those, in fact, are the things that we've created to lead us back to who we really are, to our own true nature. These things help us to rediscover that, and allow them to blossom in their full glory and delight. I've come to realize that the only job that any of us has, is just to live in a state of joy and fulfillment, and to do that in every moment and in every experience that comes up in this apparent life that we are living.

One of the things I love about this body-mind called "Chris Attwood" is this particular personality loves having fun. In fact, *The Passion Test* is all about discovering what matters to one in one's life, what it is that one loves the most, what one cares about the most, and then aligning one's life with that, following those breadcrumbs I spoke of earlier. What I love most is having fun with everything, and it's such an adventure to discover how to have fun with every experience, whatever it may be, even the experiences I have labeled as "bad" in the past, or as not being evolutionary, or as not being helpful.

The path of discovery of who "I" am is the pathless path. One of the interesting paradoxes of life, this apparent world that we've created, is that opposites exist simultaneously all the time. As a result, it's not possible for the intellect to be able to reconcile them. One is the idea that I am infinite, eternal, and unbounded and yet at the same time I experience myself as bounded, limited, and living within the context of a world with apparent rules and natural laws. Yet both things exist simultaneously and the only way for us ultimately to come to a place of peace with who we really are is to be able to let go of the intellect and simply experience both realities simultaneously, as both are expressions of the nature of who "I" am.

## What event or series of events led to your discovery?

For me the path began when I went to University. I went to the University of California, Santa Barbara and lived in a place called Isla Vista, right next to the University. It was a time of great upheaval in America and in the world. The Vietnam War was going on and in Isla Vista there was a big structure in the middle of town, which was the Bank of America building. It had been built like a fortress.

Within a few months of my arrival at the university there was a big outrage for a variety of reasons. Thousands of students went out onto the streets and some of them broke down the door of the Bank of America and burned it to the ground. All night there were people clashing with police and there was a lot of drama.

I was there trying to figure out what was going on and what my part was in it. At one point I thought, "Well what really matters to me, what I'm really committed to, is to making a significant and positive difference in this world and changing the way in which people relate to each other." What I was seeing there was war, a battlefield in the streets of this university town, and I thought there had to be some better way. So I worked very hard and I became part of the resolution. As the Planning Director for the Community Council, I helped to create some great projects.

But I was soon full of stress, overwhelmed by everything, and there was so much responsibility thrust on me at the age of twenty. I didn't know how to handle it. One of my friends told me about this thing called Transcendental Meditation® and suggested that I go hear a lecture about it. He said it was a great way of eliminating stress, so I said, "Okay, that sounds good."

I went and listened to the lecture. They presented the first scientific research studies that had been done on meditation. I decided to learn the TM technique. From the first time I closed my eyes, I noticed there were some very significant differences in my experience. Over the next three days they told us about higher states of consciousness and the ability to go deep within and to experience aspects of reality that maybe had never been activated before.

To be frank, at that time I thought it was all a bunch of bologna. But, I could tell something was happening and so I continued to practice the technique and chose not to worry about anything else. Over the next year I practiced TM regularly, but I was still working sixteen, eighteen, twenty hours a day and was still dedicated to transforming the world.

In the next year some remarkable things happened. I was able to accomplish projects that I never thought I could accomplish before. I was able to get the whole community re-zoned and get students bus rides without charge, or for a low monthly fee. I was able to gather thousands of people for various projects. It was a very dramatic time for me.

As I continued to meditate, I noticed an increasing level of calmness and ease with everything that was going on, even with these very big and seemingly major events. After a while, I stumbled upon the opportunity to get some advanced training, and I ended up becoming a teacher of the Transcendental Meditation® program. After being a TM teacher for a time, I went back out into the world to get a job.

I ended up getting a position as a bookkeeper for $5 per hour at a firm that sold government securities as investments.. I decided I wanted to learn everything about what that company did, and after just nine months on the job, I became President of the company. I got to a point where I realized that as much as I was achieving in the world something in my life was still lacking. It wasn't deeply fulfilling to me, but I continued to meditate through it all.

One day I thought to myself, maybe it's time for me to take some time off. I actually ended up taking ten years off, and I participated in a program of extended meditation. I spent ten years meditating anywhere from four to eight hours a day and I began studying the Vedic literature of India. This ancient literature provided profound insights about who I am, about the nature of life, about the structure of creation, and the structure of life. That was an amazing time.

Coming out of that I quickly re-immersed myself in the world. During my "time off" there was a program of celibacy, so I hadn't been in any relationship at all for ten years. Within a few months I married, and five years later I got a divorce. I went through a series of jobs that my mind told me I could do, and I was able to do reasonably well, but they were not things that I loved to do.

After about eight years, I finally began to rediscover the things I really enjoyed doing. I was able to go back to working in a way that fulfilled me and I enjoyed great success for a while. Then I realized it was time to take a break again, so I went back to the previous program for a year.

After another year of extended TM practice, I was introduced to a woman by the name of Byron Katie and *"The Work."* I was introduced to The Work through my ex-wife Janet, who is now my business partner and co-authored *The Passion Test* with me. Katie created a very simple process of self-investigation she calls "The Work," and doing this simple process I found myself very quickly investigating the truth of concepts and ideas that I had held to be true for a long time. It was through this process of investigation that I came to let go of beliefs that had previously prevented me from being able to really experience and enjoy life.

In the Vedic Literature there is a reference to things that are called Vasanas. It's a Sanskrit term essentially meaning habits, the mental, physical, and emotional habits that we form. The Vedic literature talks about good Vasanas and bad Vasanas. Bad Vasanas may be things like addictions, alcoholism or drug use, the things that don't help us to understand or to realize our own nature.

Good Vasanas are habits that help and support us in coming to realize who we really are. Good Vasanas are things that many of us have heard of or maybe already do, like yoga, breathing exercises, meditation, going to bed at a reasonable hour, or getting up early. The whole field of Ayurveda, the ancient system of health in the Vedic literature, is built upon the concepts of good Vasanas, things that support our health and support our experience of life.

In the Vedic literature there is a statement that good Vasanas are helpful, and are useful along the path to realization of the self with a big 'S.' Yet, in the end, liberation requires letting go even of the good Vasanas. Letting go means letting go of our attachment to them, letting go of our belief that these things are necessary or required for us to live a happy, fulfilled, or joy-filled life, that these things are somehow necessary for us to know who we really are.

That has been the story for me, coming to recognize over and over again this play of consciousness, this play of the mind, and then the process of letting go and letting go and letting go and letting go over and over and over and over again.

**If you could give advice to those who are still searching for their life's purpose, what would it be?**

The first thing I would say is to recognize that it's not an accident that you love the things you love. I said this earlier, but it's such an important point that you love and care about the things you do.

These things are important to you for a reason, and are the things that will allow you to live your purpose in life. These are the things that will allow you to discover who you are and to be able to live your life in joy. Your job in this incarnation is to live in joy, and to align your life with what you love most. Doing this provides a very simple yet profoundly powerful method of getting clear on what's most important.

The second thing I would encourage people to do is to find a means, a technique, a tool, or a mechanism that allows you to transcend the field of duality. As long as the mind remains in that field, and we remain in the field of illusion, we will remain in the field of what is not real. It's only by transcending that field and going beyond that field that we're able to experience who we really are, which is beyond the pairs of opposites. For me that technique has been the Transcendental Meditation® program. It's a very profound process. There are an infinite number of ways that one can transcend the field of duality, to go beyond the experience of separation, the experience of this and that.

The third thing I would say is to investigate the thoughts, which keep you feeling separate. Investigate the thoughts that create suffering or unhappiness in your life. As long as you still find yourself suffering, it means that you're holding on to some belief or concept that is not true for you. The fact is, when we argue with reality we always lose. Investigating our thoughts means investigating what is really true for us. It's amazing that when we ask questions the mind searches and will give us the answers. So it's just really a matter of asking the right questions.

For me The Work of Byron Katie has been a powerful tool for that, because Katie's process of investigation is so simple. It's just four questions and what she calls a turn-around. Those four simple questions can be used to investigate any thought that brings unhappiness - Is it true? Can I absolutely know that it is true? How do I react when I have that thought? Who would I be without that thought?

These questions allow you to go deeply within and get to what's really true, because the nature of who we are is the expression of opposites. Investigate the thoughts that keep you separate because when you investigate these thoughts you'll discover that the opposite of what you believe is as true, or possibly truer, than what you believed.

When you discover that the opposite of what you were telling yourself could also be true, then it opens you up, it creates a bridge of compassion between both those pairs of opposites. When the thoughts that have been causing suffering are in the emotional field, investigation creates a true bridge of compassion that connects us with everything and everyone around us.

The fourth thing is what Janet and I call 'Nature's Guidance System.' Nature's Guidance System is simply that we have created within ourselves the ability to know what the correct direction to take with our life is at every moment. The way we know it is by how we feel.

All of us know what it feels like to feel expanded. At those points we feel full, we feel happy, we feel turned-on, we're loving, kind, compassionate, and generous. Those things are a signal we've created for ourselves to show us that we're on the path of purpose, on the path of discovering our own nature, on the path of discovering the reason that we live in this world and this life to begin with.

We also know what it's like when we feel contracted, when we feel shut down, when we feel the opposite of loving. We feel separated and disconnected and anxious and worried and frustrated and angry and all those things that we generally label as bad feelings, or uncomfortable feelings. Yet those things are no more bad or good than the experience of day and night. When it's daytime outside do we say, "Oh, this is a bad thing, it needs to become night"? Or when it's night out do we say, "Oh, that's a bad thing, it needs to become day"?

No, of course we don't, because we understand that those are just different phases of life. These feelings (what I call expansion and contraction) are neither good nor bad, they're simply messages or signals to us. They're signals of what we are to do in that moment. So, 'Nature's Guidance System' is the realization that sometimes you feel expanded and sometimes you feel contracted and neither is good nor bad. They're simply messages allowing you to know that when you feel it's time to take a break, it's time to rest, or it's time to go ahead, take action and enjoy the fruits of that.

Life is a miracle. It's here for our delight and enjoyment. Whenever there is a time that it doesn't appear that way to us, then we're being guided to go deeper, to step back and reevaluate.

The real miracle of life is that the infinite, unbounded, nature of life means that every single one of us have the ability to experience our own nature as that same infinite, unbounded potential of life and to enjoy the delight of having all possibilities available to us. Wow! How cool is that?

# Christine Hassler

*"A lot of us say that we want to inspire others, but in order to do that, we have to feel something inspirational inside of ourselves first."*

Christine Hassler is a life coach, author, inspirational speaker, and consultant based in Los Angeles. Hassler supports her clients in answering the questions of "who am I, what do I want, and how do I get it" from an authentic place. She brings her experience as a coach, entrepreneur, and businessperson to individuals and corporations to help them manifest both higher productivity and pleasure in and outside the office. Hassler loves to work both sides of her brain, creativity and intellect, and is inspired by connecting with people.

After graduating from Northwestern University, Hassler began her career in Hollywood working through a hodgepodge of low-paying, but resume-building, jobs. She landed at Michael Ovitz's Artist Management Group and became a television literary agent at the age of 25. She was successful, but not passionate about what she was doing.

Her first book, *Twenty-Something/Twenty–Everything* (New World Library 2005), was born out of her own unexpected challenges and experienced and propelled her along a path to becoming a self-investigation and career coach. Her second book *The Twenty-Something Manifesto* (New World Library 2008) stems from her experience coaching and speaking to young adults and describes the developmental phases this decade of life brings. She is also the co-author of *Chicken Soup for the Twenty-Something Soul* (HCI Books, 2008).

As a public speaker and seminar leader, Hassler is passionate about inspiring and motivating audiences to uncover their purpose in life. Christine has recently been featured as a guest on *THE TODAY SHOW,* CNN, as well as various local television and radio shows. Read more about Christine at: www.christinehassler.com

## Who do you think you are?

I think that will be a question that I continue to for answer the rest of my life as I believe self-discovery is an eternal mission. At this point, who I am is really simple; "I am" is me. I've spent so much of my life comparing myself to other people, trying to meet external standards, or chasing expectations to figure out who I am, so it's such a relief to be at this point and say: Who I am is Christine and that's it!

**What event or series of events led to your discovery?**

Disappointment's led me to my discovery. I am not a big risk taker. I like to play it safe, and live life according to a plan. I have always been fairly Type A - the kind of person that makes my bed every day and has a place for everything. But life had a different plan than the one I envisioned for myself.

I had planned to have a great career and I did everything I was supposed to do. I did really well in high school, went to a prestigious university college, built up my resume in college so much I had to type it in seven-point font just to fit it on one page. Then I moved out to L.A. to pursue my dream of working in the entertainment business. I worked my way up to being one of the youngest agents ever. I was a television literary agent representing writers and directors at the age of twenty-five, sitting in my beautiful office in Beverly Hills, with an assistant who sat outside my office, and I hated it. And I hated who I was becoming – stressed out, competitive, irritable, and void of any sense of self.

At that point, the answer to "who do you think you are" would have been, "a bitch." I had a bad attitude and I didn't like that about myself. I hated my job and I didn't know what to do. I realized that trying to make myself feel more confident had perpetuated my whole career path, and the entertainment industry was the adult version of the popular crowd that I was never a part of as a kid. That's why I was drawn to the industry. When I realized that I didn't like what I was doing, I was confronted with the questions "who am I and what do I really want?"

Another humbling experience was getting engaged. Again, I did everything the way I thought you're "supposed" to do it. We dated, lived together, talked about all the topics you're supposed to discuss when you're dating – like religion, family, finances, and so on - and then got engaged. Six months before the wedding my fiancé said, "I'm not marrying you, sorry." Career disappointment and a broken engagement were not major traumas compared to what others have had to endure during life, but they really did shake me, because I didn't expect them. Life wasn't going according to my plan!

I started to realize that who I was trying to become was a version of something I thought I was supposed to be. The result of this was that I wasn't authentic at all. I was just trying to play a role that I had scripted for myself without having enough information about what I really wanted out of my life.

## If you could give advice to those who are still searching for their life's purpose, what would it be?

Once I started to really looking within, instead of externally, for my purpose, I discovered an intense pull to the possibility of all people loving themselves and their lives – but I had to start with me. I had to learn how to like myself and like my life independent of what I was doing or who I was with. Not comparing my life and myself with other people, not trying to live up to some standard, not trying to chase expectations, and knowing that external things could never quench my thirst. I believe that knowing your purpose and true happiness can only be discovered when you not only love yourself and your life but you actually like it too.

The advice I would give anyone who is searching for their purpose is to look in rather than out, look at the life you have and see if you can fall in love with it and yourself in the process. Then see if you can really like it. When you start there, the rest of your life unfolds in a magical way, and it mirrors what you're feeling on the inside. This is the whole principle of the Law of Attraction! If I'm really liking and loving myself and my life, then I attract more of the type of things into my life.

Now, I can't say that I practice this at 100%. I have days where I'm extremely hard on myself and I'm critical, or I look at someone else's life and say, "I want that." Then I realize what I am attracted to about their life is their happiness. So I gently remind myself, "Wait a second, this is your life, you only get one shot at it and you might as well like what you've got because it's much more enjoyable when you do."

I like to think of the word inspire – INspire comes from INside. A lot of us say that we want to inspire others, but in order to do that, we have to feel something inspirational inside of ourselves first. Inspiration and our sense of who we are cannot come from ego, stuff, money, or a really great speech. It's comes from something deeper – a much, much bigger. And the best news is, we all have it inside of ourselves, we just have to commit to rediscovering it and reminding ourselves of who we truly are.

# ARE YOU HERE TO BE A HEALER?

# Curtis Sliwa

*"Give of yourself to those who can least help themselves,*
*and empower them."*

**A bold spirit with a lust for life and amazing energy, Curtis Sliwa is a New Yorker in the truest and best sense of the word. Born and raised in the Canarsie section of Brooklyn, Curtis recognized early on the advantages of growing up in a close-knit community.**

**Curtis spearheads countless public service programs, including food and clothing distribution for the needy and anti-drug speakers bureaus. In 1994, Curtis Sliwa founded** Cyberangels, **the largest online safety and educational program in cyberspace. Sliwa has also authored several books on self-defense and safety, making his vision of community service and fighting crime a reality.**

**Known all over the world as the founder and leader of the *Guardian Angels*, a non-profit, all volunteer, crime fighting organization with 40 chapters throughout the United States and 7 countries overseas, Curtis Sliwa's scope is vast and intensive. His worldwide connections keep him in touch with major breaking news stories across the globe and a few steps ahead of most journalists. However, Sliwa's passion for *"the city that never sleeps"* remains a constant fixation.**

**Featured frequently as a guest lecturer at colleges and universities and making regular appearances on TV news programs, Sliwa's message is one of hope, combined with a healthy dose of common sense.**

**Find out more about Curtis at his *MySpace* site: www.myspace.com/curtissliwa**

## Who do you think you are?

As a youngster, I never perceived that I was here to develop self, to have worldly possessions, or to dedicate myself to improving myself. I was born into an old-style hard-core European Roman Catholic arena in which I was weaned on the fact that poverty and lack of resource would bring you closer God, and that we are all God's children here to serve others, those who can least help themselves.

I realized at a very young age that I was in good physical shape, and had control of my mental faculties. I would always say, "But for the grace of God there could be I," the person without an arm, the person who is feeble, the person who is not in control of their mental or physical capacities, the person who is homeless, the person who is destitute. I always looked at the glass being half full, as opposed to many who would believe that it was half empty.

As I matured and became more educated and worldly, I recognized that armed with some of the human resources that I had been provided with either because of genetics, care, input, understanding, or my parents and extended families desire to mold me that I had a mission to undertake, even though I had no idea what that mission was.

There was a definite natural draw to say that whatever time I would spend in this world would have to be dedicated to improving matters for other people, and not just for self. Growing up in the 60s and 70s, it was clearly a time when young men and young women were venturing out, giving up worldly goods and desires, to try to make a difference in people's lives and to change the world for good. They ended up exasperated; they ended up apathetic and indifferent and becoming immersed into a world of I and me. I think I just blossomed into thinking about us and we. And more importantly, based on that old Roman Catholic worker's tradition of knowing that there will be nine failures for every one success, I knew that this mission, whatever road it would take me on, would be strewn with failures and set-backs and that I'd better start preparing myself. I knew that I'd better get ready.

### What event or series of events led to your discovery?

It was clearly the time that my father spent with me. He was a merchant seaman, so he was away most of the time, but he gave me a global view of things. I wasn't contained in a parochial or insular community. It would have been very easy to become immersed in that, because I was in the ethnic enclave in Brooklyn that consisted of the Jews and Italians. You could become very provincial, as opposed to very open-minded or global. My mom would consistently give of herself as my aunts would also. I was surrounded by females constantly attempting to give, give, and give more, and deriving a great deal of satisfaction and a great deal of fulfillment from that. You could actually see them being almost euphoric every time they would help someone.

St. Francis of Assisi influenced me as well. I saw a movie made about him at a very young age, giving up all worldly desires and resources, and just going on his particular mission. Then I found out about my mission after a series of involvements in all kinds of community service.

I was recycling, when it wasn't at all popular, when you were called a "junkman." There was no such thing as ecology or environmental awareness, no term for recycling, so you were determined to be a junkman if you collected bottles, newspapers or cans to be used to once again. Then there were the community cleanups I organized in my young adult years.

I began to wrestle with the demons of crime and to see the root causes. A society that originally brought us up to believe that we are our brother's keeper could turn and suddenly acquire a malaise of "mind your own business." That's when I decided to fight for what I knew what was right, no matter how many people thought I had the furniture upstairs and rearranged in all the wrong rooms.

I organized it in a very unorthodox way, as a visual presence in red berets, red satin jackets, and white Guardian Angel T-shirts without any weapons, without any special powers or privileges. We just empowered ourselves. The weak, the helpless, those who have always been resigned to sitting on the sidelines being told government will enable you, government will take care of, you're not capable, you're not strong enough, you're not smart enough, you haven't got a college degree, you don't have the mental capacity to control yourself emotionally. I discarded that and said, "From within this resource of humanity can come the answers." It had to do with a respect for one another and coming to the aid of others even if it meant risking your life in the process.

**If you could give advice to those who are still searching for their life's purpose, what would it be?**

There are two types of satisfaction in the world. There's the satisfaction of building and improving your own life, your own self-worth or your own self-esteem. I understand that for a lot of people you really have to do that first before you can go on to the nobler mission, the mission that has a higher calling. To give of yourself to those who can least help themselves, and empower them.

In terms of finding the vehicle, it's got to be something that you're passionate about. Something you eat, breathe, and sleep 24-7-365. Something you're totally obsessed about, where you feel you can make your mark on society, so much so that you become energized. You even take something as important as sleep and begin to think of it as not being necessary, almost to the point of the philosophy that "there will be plenty of time to sleep when you're dead." You've got to scrape the barnacles off your backside, get your rear in gear and get right into it, and suffer all the setbacks so that you can eventually start accruing successes.

I would say that passion, first and foremost, is what people must discover before they're going to be able to find what it truly is that empowers them, fulfills them, and gives them a sense of purpose as to why they're on this plane.

# Alan J. Nuñez

*"Be willing to hear wisdom from the most unlikely places.*
*You just never know where you will find it."*

Dr. Al Nuñez graduated magna cum laude in 1982 from the Los Angeles College of Chiropractic.

Dr. Nuñez has been researching and developing the 3-D chiropractic technique, or 3-DCT, for over twenty years. 3-DCT emphasizes that you can't just treat the back without treating the front! The back muscles are often tight in reaction or in compensation to tight muscles in the chest or deep in the abdomen.

Dr. Nuñez has found that frightening or traumatic events in youth often leave children or young adults with tension in their chest or stomach, which can become chronic or rigid over time. Due to the flexibility inherent in the young spine, these chronically tense muscles can cause distortion or changes in the curvature of the spine. To put it simply: Emotional tension leads to physical tension, physical tension over time leads to rigidity, and rigidity is morbidity, meaning symptoms.

3-DCT is a non-force chiropractic treatment in that there is no *twisting, popping, or cracking* involved in the adjustments of the spine or limbs. Dr. Nuñez found that when the muscles are relaxed or balanced that the bones move quite easily and a gentle thumb thrust is all that is needed to restore motion to the joints.

In addition to 3-DCT Dr. Nuñez has developed a myofascial technique designed to release or break up chronically tense muscles in the body. It is called *Pressure-Plus-Motion* or PPM. PPM works hand-in-hand with 3-DCT to more permanently relax the body and even more importantly it can be taught to the patient! Patients learn how to help themselves so they don't need as many chiropractic adjustments to achieve relief, and their adjustments and pain-relief lasts longer.

Dr. Nuñez is the author of the book, *How To Keep Chiropractors Off Your Back,* which includes all the home pressure-plus-motion exercises.

Find out more at: www.3Dchiro.com or AlanNunez.com

## Who do you think you are?

My philosophy of life affects everything I do. I use the same principles in my home, at work, at my Kiwanis club, and at my church. I think I learned a lot from my father during my childhood. He was an alcoholic, which is a very self-centered viewpoint and leads to a lot of problems, and I would say that I developed those qualities in my youth. I, too, was self-centered.

I'm now what I call *We* centered. I learned the principle of considering "both you *and* me" in the Adult Children of Alcoholics (ACA) 12 step program. The first word in step one is *We, not I.* Now, when I'm making decisions, I consider what's best not just for you, not just for me, but what's best for us. I would say that's my main guiding principle. Whenever I'm interacting with a person or an organization, I don't want to forget your needs, I don't want to forget my needs, I want to consider everybody's needs. Whether I'm dealing with my kids, my patients or my service organizations, this is the main guiding principle that I live by.

I used to give to other people, and I thought I was very generous in giving and loving, but there was always a hook. I was giving, but clearly I wanted something out of it. It wasn't a true gift. I like to ask, "When you give, is it a gift or a payment?" In the past it was a payment, and I had to learn that there are no strings attached when it's a gift. Now when I'm working with my patients, I'm always considering what they want, what I want, and how can we create this relationship in a mutually beneficial way. It's not just about what *I* want anymore.

**What events or series of events led to your discovery?**

Growing up with an alcoholic father included dysfunction, un-predictability, and instability in the home. Because of that environment, I developed a tendency to try and find my own principles and to figure out life by myself. What I developed were the principles that life should be fair, that life should be logical, and that I should always know what to do in every situation, even if I have never been in that situation. Those were my philosophies as I was growing up, and those philosophies basically ruined my life. They were very idealistic principles.

I lived in those principles through my junior college years and then I got married after I got my first job. I was married for five years and then I got a divorce. That divorce kind of drove me to question my principles and question my philosophy. So I started my quest to learn about myself and to see why my philosophy didn't work.

I took some self-help workshops, studied various texts, and eventually ended up in the 12 step program (ACA). It was in that program that I developed the principle that it's not just me, it's not just you, it's us. This is what guides me through my life. While attending the 12-step program I also learned that life gets better, and as I continued to attend my life got better and better.

I met my life-mate in the program. I had to grow spiritually to handle that challenge. After we were married for a while, I realized that I wanted more. I wanted a child. I needed to grow even more to handle a child. I continued a philosophy of continual spiritual evolution. I'm always pushing myself to grow, because I don't know how good life can get. How good can life get? There's a phrase I use, "You don't know how good you can feel until you feel that way!" So I keep on pushing myself. Life is already great, but could it be better? Maybe!

**If you could give advice to those who are still searching for their life's purpose, what would it be?**

Always be a learner. Be willing to learn from others, and don't think that you know it all. Be willing to hear wisdom from the most unlikely places. You just never know where you will find it. In the Old Testament there is a story where God once spoke through the jawbone of a donkey. You just never know where wisdom or truth may come, and you have to be ready. Be ready to hear God speaking at any time. You never know whom God's going to speak through. Develop an attitude of paying attention. Never discount who is talking, because it might be just the message you needed to hear.

# Lisa Rohleder

*"When you're working for people who are really like you,
then you end up working with people who are really like you,
and that's really empowering for everybody."*

**Lisa Rohleder, LAc, is one of the cofounders of Working Class Acupuncture and of the Community Acupuncture Network. She is also the author of *The Remedy: Integrating Acupuncture into American Healthcare*.**

       **Readers who are interested in social entrepreneurship and community acupuncture can get more information from her book and by visiting the Community Acupuncture Network.**
       **Go to: www.communityacupuncturenetwork.org**

**Who do you think you are? What is the purpose of your life?**

I can speak to the vocational purpose of my life; I can't say with any certainty that I know my purpose on a larger level. My vocational purpose is to use acupuncture to educate and for social change in health care, primarily on behalf of working class people.

**What event or series of events led you to your discovery?**

I was one of those kids who always wanted to be a doctor. I grew up in a working class environment, though I didn't figure that out until later. My family was really into advancement through education so I went to a very good college.

       I felt really out of place, but I couldn't pinpoint it as a class issue until later. I probably didn't end up being a doctor because I had an inner dissonance about class. At one point I realized that if I became a doctor I would be in a different class from where I came from, and everybody I was connected to, so I chose acupuncture as a field hoping that it might be different. It took me about 10 years to realize that it wasn't.

       The way health care works in this country, anything complementary or alternative is really only available to people who have a disposable income, and that really bothered me. I wanted to do something about that, so as a result, and with the help of my partner, I came up with an alternate business model for acupuncture that works well for working class people.

We were able to create a thriving business for ourselves, and we began to offer that business model to other people. We had a vision of health care in this country being dramatically different, one where it doesn't have to be divided between the "haves" and "have-nots." There are certain types of health care (and I feel acupuncture is one of them) for which there is no reason everyone shouldn't have equal access.

**If you could give advice to those who are still searching for their life's purpose, what would it be?**

Based on what I've learned, I would say be yourself. Don't try to be somebody else. If you want to help people, think about how you can help people who are like yourself, because solidarity is more powerful than charity. That's definitely one thing I've learned. When you're working for people who are really like you, then you end up working with people who are really like you, and that's really empowering for everybody. It could be easy to get stuck in the helper role, and that isn't really sustainable either for the helper or the helped. If you want to avoid that, look for ways that you can be yourself, give yourself, and be involved in the concerns that are primary for you, as opposed to somebody else's concerns.

# Chanda Zaveri

*"If you start finding out who you are and what you want in life,*
*I think you would find you purpose in life."*

As founder and president of Activor, Ms. Zaveri is the driving force behind all its developments. A molecular biologist, geneticist, and protégé to two time Nobel Laureate Dr. Linus Pauling, Ms. Chanda Zaveri is a leader in the evolution of the biotechnology industry. Her most recent contributions include innovative developments in cosmeceuticals, nutriceuticals, wound-healing technology and cancer chemotherapeutics.

Ms. Zaveri received a Masters degree in Molecular Biology and Genetics from the University of California at Santa Barbara. Subsequent graduate studies were undertaken at California Polytechnic University ("Cal Tech"). After working with a major pharmaceutical corporation in Southern California, Ms. Zaveri chose to pursue her own scientific visions as an entrepreneur. Her subsequent accomplishments have proven her steadfast commitment to scientific integrity and global vision for the application of her research findings.

The respect enjoyed by Ms. Zaveri among her scientific and medical colleagues rightly confirms her status as an innovative and leading personality in the expanding world of biotechnology. Ms. Zaveri has been offered many awards, most notably an honorary doctorate from Harvard University for her discoveries in skin pigment formation. For more than seven years, she has worked diligently to unite her research findings with marketable applications in cosmetics and nutriceuticals. Ms. Zaveri's ongoing goal is to build a company that specializes in peptide chemistry and pharmaceutical innovations

Ms. Zaveri's initial investigation into dermaceuticals started in 1993 with the creation of a biologically active peptide that stimulated collagen synthesis. This technology served as the sole intellectual property asset of Ms. Zaveri's initial corporate endeavor, which began in 1994. After moving onwards in 1998 to create the Activor Corporation, Ms. Zaveri continued her work in dermaceuticals and shifted her focus toward the evolving science of biologically active wound healing products.

**Who do you think you are?**

I am a giver. That's what I think about myself.

**What event or series of events led to your discovery?**

When I was a very young girl, we used to have big birthday parties. I always thought, "What a waste, all of these kids coming to a birthday party." Even as a kid I was already wired for success, and my birthday always came in the winter. In Calcutta, it was really cold in the winter and there were lots of poor people. I asked my grandfather, "Why are there so many poor people?" My grandfather said, "If you're so concerned about them, from now on, we'll take your birthday gift money, buy blankets for these poor people, and give them blankets on your birthday."

Since I was the oldest child, I was more pampered than my siblings. When it came time for my birthday, there were quite a lot of blankets to hand out to the poor people. The driver drove us into the neighborhood and we saw all the people on the street, so we pulled over and gave them all blankets. That night I had the most satisfying feeling inside that I could ever imagine. I realized that although having parties and receiving jewelry was fun, it was certainly not satisfying. I would rather do something for those less fortunate, who have so little. I thought giving would be the most wonderful feeling and the most satisfying to me. And it was.

**If you can give advice to those who are still searching for their life's purpose, what would it be?**

First you have to know yourself. I think most of the time people are trying to find out about what other people are doing, and they don't look at themselves. If you start finding out who you are and what you want in life, I think you would find you purpose. I think that 80% of the time, most people are worried about what he looks like, or what she is doing right or wrong, or if he or she tells lies, or if they'd take money. But they are not looking at what they, themselves, are doing.

In a quiet moment you may think, what do I want to be, what do I want? Even if you wanted to smoke a cigarette, if that's what gives you the most pleasure or calming thoughts, then you should do it. In those calm pleasurable moments I believe you will find your purpose and what you came to this life to do.

# Matthew Loop

*"I think that too many times we render ourselves helpless and without power when we fail to question things, and much of our surroundings."*

**Matthew Loop is a chiropractor, clinical nutritionist, and best-selling author living in Atlanta. He plays a major positive role in transforming many individuals' health, and subsequently their lives, on a daily basis. He has always had his mind in the newest research concerning health and nutrition, and he has found himself constantly educating and clearing up corporate misinformation that's been blindly accepted.**

**His book *Cracking the Cancer Code* became an international best seller and will continue to reach millions and inspire readers to empower themselves with the groundbreaking health information contained within.**

**Dr. Matthew graduated from Logan College of Chiropractic in St. Louis three years ago and he's excited to be back in ATL.**

**Learn more about Dr. Matthew's work at: www.endcancer.net**

### Who do you think you are?

In response to that question, I would like to share a quote by Pierre Teilhard de Chardin. He stated, "We are not human beings having a spiritual experience. We are spiritual beings having a human experience." That's the best way that I could describe who I am because being a chiropractor, nutritionist, author is just the tip of the iceberg. Many times we choose not to see what's underneath, but that's really how I want to live my life.

### What event or series of events led to your discovery?

Being introduced to the holistic healing approach in grad school played a major role in my self-discovery. That's when I really began to look at the mind, the body, and spirit as they relate to the healing of the body and soul. Then, a few years later I was introduced to Bob Proctor's material, and he basically showed me how to harness that universal attractive force in my favor, and I began to live an inspired life.

Now I live the life that I deserve, and I feel that everybody who comes in contact with me is able to feed off that energy. I've made it my purpose and mission in life to help, inspire, and empower others to take control of their health, and subsequently their lives once and for all. At the same time, I'm strongly compelled to help others realize that prosperity and abundance await them financially and in their relationships.

I've heard it said many times that applied knowledge is power, which I truly believe. I think that we live in a society where we are programmed to uncritically accept things. This particular subconscious programming tends to dictate and drive our beliefs, values, attitudes, and actions every single day. I want to help others make those foundational changes that are necessary to live a prosperous life.

**If you could give advice to those who are still searching for their life's purpose, what would it be?**

I would recommend that they study themselves. The more that I study myself; the more I realize how incredible I am. I'm not trying to sound conceited; I have a very healthy respect and a love for myself. I'm just fascinated by the creation of me. I feel that too many times we render ourselves helpless and without power when we fail to question things, and much of our surroundings. I think it's necessary and vital that we consistently reevaluate ourselves, our attitudes, our beliefs, and values in every single area of our life. That's the only way we're going to grow. I feel very strongly that that's the objective of life, to grow. So, I would recommend studying, immersing yourself, and saturating yourself in yourself.

# Sue Morter

*"If we can really operate from this internal guidance,*
*then we are much more likely to create that which*
*is in alignment with the truth of why we came."*

**Dr. Sue Morter is an international speaker, trainer, Bio-Energetic Synchronization Technique (B.E.S.T.) Master Instructor, CEO of multi-doctor wellness center Morter Health Center, co-founder of Morter HealthSystem and co-creator of Dynamic Life Training, one of the world's largest personal and professional development training organizations. Dr. Sue Morter is committed to the mission of "improving the health of mankind worldwide."**

**People around the world have attended her dynamic, energetic, and life-changing seminars about the concepts of Mind/Body Wellness and Intentional Living. A featured presenter for the Tony Robbins seminar group, Dr. Morter was also named to the Transformational Leadership Council (TLC). TLC members include speakers and best-selling authors such as Dr. Janet Attwood (*The Passion Test*), Neale Donald Walsch (*Conversations with God*), Jack Canfield (*Chicken Soup for the Soul*) and others from the movie *The Secret* and *What The Bleep Do We Know?* She is part of a collaborative effort to transform humanity to higher and higher consciousness.**

**Dr. Sue Morter opens hearts, inspires minds, and moves people to action. She and her team, including practitioners around the world, provide strategic information and knowledge that change lives – daily.**

**Learn more about Dr. Morter's work at: www.morterhealthctr.com**

## Who do you think you are?

Who I think I am is who I think we are. I think that we are pure potentiality. We are the choice point as energy beings or spiritual beings in a physical body. We have the capacity to choose anything. Science has shown us, beyond a shadow of a doubt, that what we think is what creates our reality. It certainly creates our experience. Using waveforms as an example, there are waveforms of energy in constant motion in a chaotic manner in every direction, and I think that we are the place where the in wave and the out wave meet. We have the capacity to choose any experience we desire.

We are source energy in the body here to experience ourselves as co-creators. Meaning, if we choose something to be difficult, it's difficult. If we consciously choose something to be a smooth experience, it is. I think that the purpose of our lives and who we are is a synonymous thing. It's really the same conversation.

Oftentimes we have experiences that are difficult or challenging, and then because of the experience, we have the opportunity to define who we are. For example, if something happens to make us feel that we are inadequate in some way, we began to develop a belief that we are inadequate. Then another thing occurs that validates that belief, and we start to look through a lens of inadequacy, constantly looking to validate the truth of that, because the subconscious mind is always collecting this kind of information and recording it.

Whatever the subconscious mind has recorded it wants to validate as true, because its job is to keep us safe. Its job is to keep us from danger, and one of the best ways to keep us safe is to keep us around things that seem familiar. Any validation of a previously established belief reaffirms the familiarity from a vibrational standpoint, from an energetic standpoint; it creates the environment feeling of safety for the subconscious to relax in. Even if it were miserable, it would rather maintain the same rather than step into the unknown.

In the moments where we're defining who we are relative to the experiences that we're having, we have the opportunity to shift, or to step into the front side of the model and say, regardless of our relatives, regardless of our relativity (the experiences we are having), what would we be experiencing if we could have it any way we chose? If I were out on the front side of that, I now have the experience of empowerment. I begin to have the experience of what freedom feels like. Then even in the face of negative circumstances, if I choose to bring forth a different experience from the inside out, I am experiencing my greatest capacity, I am experiencing pure potentiality in the body in human form.

I think we come here, to this dimension, with our consciousness to have that experience. We come to the third dimension where duality exists. We know hot because we know cold, we know joy because we know sadness, and it's in between those polarities that we have the opportunity to move in whatever direction that we choose. We've just never really realized the power that we have on a conscious level en mass. Our culture, our societies do not operate in the full potentiality of that system. The reason we come here with our consciousness and our awareness is so that we can have that experience of choosing. The energy that is emitted in the moment of choice is elating, it's blissful, and it is, I imagine, what we believe heaven, the divine, or abundance to be. It's about choice.

We are pure potentiality taking on human form so that we can experience ourselves as creator (God source energy in the body), with the opportunity to experience what we choose. Just for the feeling of it. Just for the experience.

**What event or series of events led to your discovery?**

I grew up in the environment of natural health care. I grew up in an environment that spoke toward empowerment on an emotional level and intellectual level. It was definitely in the choice arena about what you do with your health, and the basic premise that the body has the ability to heal itself rather than being medicated or surgically altered. There's a reason if the body isn't healing itself, there's a reason for it. We would do ourselves a great favor to be in search of the cause of why the body isn't healing itself, rather than to seek out the next best treatment for the symptoms that result from the fact that the body isn't operating as it was designed and intended.

Growing up in that environment, I knew that there was a natural flow, that there is a grand plan, that all things really are intended to work out. For instance, I've never taken a medication for an ailment. I've never had a cold and gone to the doctor, received an antibiotic and taken it. It's just never happened in my 46 years. I know that the body can heal itself, yet I was riddled with stress, internally and on an emotional level. I was not at peace and I was really struggling to find my own application of that on a personal level, on an emotional basis more than anything, and so I sought out meditation. I sought out a lot of things that our culture would define as aids in that department.

I had some experiences, multidimensional experiences, through meditation that completely shifted my perception of what is real, and who we are. It didn't come easy. I was a perfectionist, and I wanted to learn how to meditate right. I was in a room with 300 other meditators who had been meditating for 30 years. I was constantly doing what I did at the time, which was judge myself, and I assumed that I wasn't doing it right. I practiced, tried it, looked around, made sure I was sitting right and breathing right and doing all these things in a perfectionist kind of way.

I exhausted myself at a particular meditation event to the degree that I couldn't worry about it anymore. I just couldn't think about it anymore. I had asked to help at this event, so I was up all night and all day running around trying to make the event happen correctly. After the third day, my mental capacity was exhausted from only getting an hour of sleep a night. I went into the main ballroom where the event was taking place and I just sat down and decided to chant with everyone else and stop worrying about it. In that process I had a life altering experience, with high frequency light, and it completely changed my version of reality. I experienced myself as a self that was not in the body.

It took me several months, if not years, to integrate that. I'm still integrating all of the implications of that experience. During this process, I experience a stillness that allows me to see that everything happening in my life, without exception, is in service to the unfoldment of my realization that this is the true me. That the temporal circumstances of my daily life, the ups and downs, the successes and the disappointments, are all part of the unfoldment which is offered to us with great grace. It is all pointing us in the direction of a realized notion that we have the capacity to utilize this life experience as a playground of adventure and discovery. When we see every event from that perspective, we are set free.

I see even the most challenging events as the opportunity to grow into remembrance. I don't really know how else to say it, except that it is to allow me to remember that I do have choice in the face of every situation, and when I exercise that choice, I experience myself settled and empowered, so that the degree of freedom far exceeds the challenge. I am no longer in a tunnel, controlled by the circumstances. I can see a much broader explanation of why these things are occurring, and how they are serving my own personal empowerment.

All of the events that have occurred in my life since that meditation experience have been looked at with that perspective. The most beautiful and amazing thing about it is that every single event since then has pointed towards my freedom, towards my empowerment, and it keeps escalating. So much so that even as potentially devastating things occur in my life, I don't see them in that way. I allow myself to feel the experience.

**If you could give advice to those who are still searching for their life's purpose, what would it be?**

I know that this only happens when it can. It can't happen until one comes to the center point within themselves, when they allow themselves to just sit down and be with themselves and completely accept what they are experiencing as valid, and also temporary. If they can allow those two concepts to come together at the same time within their own personal space and in their hearts and minds, then they can experience that magical aspect of being human.

What that boils down to is listening to their gut feelings and the nuances that are trickling up towards their consciousness from their body. Their body is a feedback mechanism that is constantly revealing to them the truth of what's happening. If they can just be present with all of those feelings that are coming up, the ones that are the most eternal or the most True will prevail, and those that are the flickering evidence that we operate in a fear-based manner are only temporary. Those fearful thoughts disappear when we just hold fast to the idea that we are equipped with everything we need. The search is really what keeps us from finding.

I think that it's important to have curiosity and certainly look at this adventure as a grand mystery, but to also realize that we hold the key inside. It's found in the hearts and in the wisdom centers low in our abdomen, and really the mind is supposed to be the servant to those things. Those parts will steer us accordingly to the evidence and information they're receiving from the inside, not the outside. Everything in the external environment is the effect of this. If we can really operate from this internal guidance, then we are much more likely to create a life experience that is in alignment with the Truth of why we came. It will become self-evident, and it won't be because of something from the outside.

# David Phears

*"Seek ye first the kingdom that is already within you
and all the rest shall be added unto you in your experience."*

**A passionate teacher and Spiritual leader, David blends humor and wisdom in presenting his lectures and classes. David has studied many of the worlds religions and settled upon a spiritual belief that includes many philosophies but mostly focuses on practical spiritual tools for everyday living.**

**As the Community Spiritual Leader of a 500 member spiritual community in Huntington Beach, David has a vision that includes making a difference on the planet by how we as human beings treat ourselves, and others who are different from us.**

**David is a seasoned personal success coach and conflict resolution mediator who thrives on finding solutions to everyday challenges in simple, effective and compassionate ways.**

**Co-owner [with his wife Michelle] of PESCO a non-profit educational services company, their vision is to provide support to existing organizations serving challenged communities in the area of training and education. These qualified organizations simply require financial support anchored in awareness, education and commitment to serve at an even greater level than currently possible.**

**You can join David in his adventures by going to: www.davidphears.com**

### Who do you think you are? What is your purpose?

This has changed many times over the years. Today I think that the purpose of my life at this point is to stay as close to unconditional love and compassion as I possibly can remember throughout each day. The purpose of my life is to put myself in the position to be happy and wealthy, so that I can support others in being the same.

### What event or series of events led you to your discovery?

Again, this is an ongoing process. I think anything major that I can look at in my life, as an event that precipitated or was a catalyst for me even caring about who I was, was me recovering from drug addiction. It wasn't just the drugs that I was addicted to. I was addicted to anything that was negative and pretty much destroying what I thought I wasn't. So, I think the big event for me would be putting away drugs, actually changing my lifestyle, and wanting to live.

**If you could give advice to those who are still searching for their life's purpose, what would it be?**

I don't like to give advice. What I can do is express what I've been through, but if someone is actually searching for a long-term solution, and not just something to get through the night, I think my suggestion to them would be to seek and find their spiritual center. Whether that's through a religion or through a journey into nature, or whether that's through a practitioner of spiritual awareness, a church, or a guru. Whatever it takes, find that spiritual connection. Once that connection is made (which is what turned it around for me), that awareness of the spiritual connection that has always been there, my suggestion would be this: seek ye first the kingdom that is already within you and all the rest shall be added unto you in your experience. It is already is there, it's just a matter of awareness.

# David Ross

*"There's a broader spiritual part of you cheering you on moment to moment. It does so through your emotions."*

**David Ross says the darndest things. What he has to say about life purpose is no exception. That's why he has been included in this book.**

**Those who spend time with David often experience profound transformation. He has personally assisted over ten thousand people live healthier and happier lives.**

**David is a health educator with professional backgrounds in psychology, theology, marketing, quality improvement, modern healthcare and holistic healing arts. Having lived such a diverse life, David thinks and teaches uniquely about the subject of life purpose.**

**If you knew David Ross wel, you would know that his chosen purpose for living is to simply celebrate and appreciate life itself. One of the ways he expresses this is by finding joy as an educator and the fields of optimal health and conscious intention (attraction and manifestation).**

**David is co-owner of holistic health schools and spas. He spends much of his time training other health educators and practitioners about how to leverage conscious intention to explore optimal health and life purpose(s) (yes, you can have one purpose!).**

**David's students say that a day spent with David is always a revelation. I trust you will find the same.**

**You may contact David privately at: IamDavidr@hotmail.com**

### Who do you think you are?

Who I am is joy, appreciation, and outrageous possibilities. I choose to spend my treasured time teaching about the message of our emotions and experiencing the joy of living in alignment with them. I listen to my emotions at every possible opportunity. The joy and purpose of my life is, quite literally, allowing myself to experience joy!

I'm here to live joyfully every moment I can. I'm here to follow my bliss. I'm here to feel "good." Paradoxically, I'm also here to fully experience and inquire into the messages hidden in the pain and resistance of life and remember in those moments that joy is still possible—even when it feels as distant as the stars.

**What event or series of events led to your discovery?**

About twenty-five years ago I became quite terrified and depressed when I realized my decision to leave seminary might condemn me to hell. I'm not sure what I was actually most scared of at the time, being rejected by my peers, being rejected by God, or the pain of rejecting myself for renouncing my identity and sense of life calling.

This crisis created a deep yearning to understand who I am and why I'm here—such a deep desire that I now spend much of my life teaching about how to inquire about and live in joyous alignment with our chosen life purpose.

It had become quite clear that I couldn't complete seminary with integrity because the church and I just didn't see eye to eye on the subject of emotions. They tried to suggest that some emotions, like love, were okay to have, while others like anger, were not. I figured that if God had designed the human body with emotions, they must all be important. Not some more than others. In fact, I was quite clear that my emotions were some sort of feedback system for spiritual growth. I thought that since spiritual growth was God's intention for me, I had better let go of my attachment to being a minister. I had better just trust that come Judgment Day, God would understand my decision.

Fast-forward twenty years and I'm listening to a tape my brother was playing by Esther Hicks on the subject of attraction and manifestation. Bear in mind that after leaving seminary, I had spent a good portion of the subsequent 20 years of my life as a counselor and psychiatric social worker continuing to obsess on the nature of emotions. I heard Esther say something quite extraordinary that blew my socks off. It was so deeply aligned with most of what I had learned in the field of psychology and yet so new and revolutionary and simple and obvious that I was rendered stunned and speechless. It was such a powerful revelation, that I can remember exactly where I was the moment I heard it. In fact, it may be the most valuable thing I've ever learned in my life.

What Esther said was this: our emotions are indicators of whether our thoughts are aligned with our desires. The feeling of joy is a physical message letting us know that the thought we just had was aligned with our desires (e.g., a thought of gratitude); when we feel emotional pain, it's a wake up event letting us know that we just had a thought that is not aligned (e.g., a judgment of others or ourselves).

In other words, our emotions simply report to us the content of our most powerful thoughts. They neither tell us what to do, nor if our thoughts are good or bad (something that I used to believe). They don't tell us if our judgment of someone or ourselves is right or wrong either (something I also used to think). They simply awaken us from our obsessively mentally focused lives to tell us to pay attention to the last thought we had so that we may choose to generate more of those thoughts (e.g. of appreciation) or less of them (e.g., negative judgments or painful past or future thinking). That's it. Our emotions are simply an impartial indicator and wake-up call about our thought-desire alignment. Our bodies have been telling us all along that having thoughts of love and appreciation and peace are fundamental to our being and fundamental to our understanding of life, who we are, and why we're here.

Hearing, testing and knowing this truth put me on my current path of discovery.

**If you could give advice to those who are still searching for their life's purpose, what would it be?**

The only satisfying answer to this question will come from the private and silent inquiry of your heart. Who outside of you can tell you how to live in alignment with your uniquely precious and individual needs, desires, and passions? It is you. It is only you. Are you willing to allow yourself to have and relish them?

I have found the writings of Abraham-Hicks, Eckhart Tolle, Marshall Rosenburg, and Byron Katie especially helpful reminders to rely on my own "knowing," live life in the present moment, and notice the messages from my body, rather than from my silly mind chatter.

You are doing so well at this game of life. There's a broader spiritual part of you cheering you on moment to moment. It does so through your emotions. Each time you allow yourself relief from mind-pain, find a moment of stillness, or a way to appreciate your world a little bit more, you connect with that broader dimension of you and fulfill your magnificent purpose.

And remember, all your answers are here, right now, rather than in an imaginary future. They have always been here waiting for you to feel and welcome them. Now is a good time for you to tune into the messages of your emotions.

# Terry Cole-Whittaker

*"It's a real training of the self to keep the consciousness spiritualized and in relationship to God and seeing God presence in everybody and everywhere."*

"If you have ever been in the presence of someone who is motivation, enthusiasm, and inspiration personified, then you know what it is like to be in the audience of Dr. Terry Cole-Whittaker. Her vitality and enthusiasm are contagious and her wisdom produces extraordinary results."

World-renowned, inspiring and motivating speaker, teacher, best-selling author, television producer, business consultant, & counselor to the "stars," Terry Cole-Whittaker is a catalyst for Wealth, Happiness, Health, and Enlightenment.

Terry Cole-Whittaker has remained the single most influential trailblazer of her time. Those who have been touched and inspired by Dr. Terry's lectures, seminars, books, and television programs reads like a *Who's Who* of global leaders, movie, stage, and television stars, best selling authors, motivational speakers, spiritual leaders, musicians, artists, politicians, educators, psychologists, government, and business leaders.

She was the executive producer and spokesperson of an Emmy Winning six-year international weekly television ministry that reached millions and continues to make a positive impact on countless lives.

Her five best selling books highlight the body of her work: *What You Think of Me is None of My Business*, a classic pioneering book on co-dependency; Number One on the New York Times Best seller list *How To Have More in a Have Not World; The Inner Path From Where You are To Where You Want To Be; Love and Power in a World Without Limits;* and her newest book, *Dare to Be Great.*

Learn more at: www.terrycolewhittaker.com

**Who do you think you are?**

I'm a servant of God.

## What event or series of events led you to your discovery?

It's by the grace of God that that comes. We can think that there's a series of events that led to this, but cause and effect only takes place in the material world. In the spiritual world, there is not cause and effect, so there's no event that actually brings God realization. It is a gift of God that comes, and we do our best by whatever work we do on ourselves to attain enlightenment and become our true and divine god-like selves. And this works in our favor.

I first got on the spiritual path in this lifetime, at around seventeen years old, through prayer. I think if there's really any type of event that helps people to attain God-realization, self-realization, to recognize who they are and their relationship with God and how life works it's through prayer. God is in the heart of every living being (Mother-Father God). So, everybody is always in close contact with the divine witness and the divine guide. I would say, whatever anybody wants, whatever it is spiritually or materially, you go to the source and sincerely do your prayers, as this is always has worked for me.

## If you could give advice to those who are still searching for their life's purpose, what would it be?

Pray and ask for what you want and at the same time really have an open mind, because what will happen is this: prayer is always answered but sometimes we turn our back to it because we don't want to learn anymore, or we don't want to hear anymore, or we're really fixated on our beliefs or our past conditioning. That's what I have found is the biggest stumbling block, because people have a concept of who they are but the concept of who they are may not be who they are. They have a concept of how life works, which may have nothing at all to do with how life works.

I would say that when they ask and pray to really have an open mind. Then when knowledge comes to them, before they eliminate it, really meditate on that and ask for guidance. I would also recommend that people study the teachings of Jesus. I like the four gospels: Matthew, Mark, Luke and John. I'd also recommend they read the Bahavagita, which is a very powerful book on the distinction between the self and the body and our purpose and mission in life. In these teachings, which are usually somewhere in the teachings of the great religions of the world, there are the principles of life. When they understand these things they can learn to apply them, and the basic thing is that we're here to become a supreme human being, and a supreme being is already living in the kingdom of God.

People can contact me on my website, or whatever teacher they feel guided to, and they'll be in the right place at the right time. Right where a person is, they can have it all. It's really about love and flowing in love all the time. What we tend to do is get caught up in all the problems, focus on the problems and fear the future or lament the past. All of that is destructive. It's a real training of the self to keep the consciousness spiritualized and in relationship to God, and seeing God presence in everybody and everywhere. We can have as much love flow through us as we are willing to.

# Lawrence Edward Carter Sr.

*"Just doing what you enjoy doing, what makes you happy, what fulfills you is one way of discovering your purpose, your destiny."*

**Lawrence Edward Carter Sr., Ph.D. is the first dean of the Martin Luther King Jr. International Chapel, a tenured Professor of Religion, and College Curator at Morehouse College since 1979. He is formerly an instructor at the Morehouse School of Medicine in the Master of Public Health Program. For 45 years, Dr. Carter has studied and worked in fourteen American universities, colleges, and professional schools; spoken at more than 80 different colleges, universities, and seminaries; received over 500 speaking engagements from eighteen denominations; and traveled to 35 foreign countries. He has made over 60 radio and television appearances.**

      **Currently, Dr. Carter teaches Psychology of Religion, Religion and Ethics, and The Life and Thought of Mohandas K. Gandhi and Martin Luther King Jr. at Morehouse College. He has also taught "Introduction to Spirituality and Health" at the Morehouse School of Medicine.**

## Who do you think you are?

Vocationally, I think of myself as a servant, who is here in order to fill in some major gaps in the staff at Morehouse College, and to help people not forget the life and work of Martin Luther King Jr., Mahatma Gandhi, Daisaku Ikeda and Prince El Hassan bin Al Talal. It is in the spirit of these great world teachers that I am here to bring peace and harmony by nonviolent means. Helping others develop their potential to the fullest and to express everything that is in them is the essence and fulfillment of what I've been doing professionally for nearly 40 years.

      I write hundreds of references for people to get into the highest ranked graduate schools and jobs as well as raise money for scholarships. By helping people with their personal, developmental, and experiential crises to become free from doctrines and outdated world-views, the frontiers of ignorance are pushed back and transformation picks up speed. In order to leave the world more beautiful than I found it, I find myself picking up trash everywhere to keep mother earth from being trashed, and though in certain conflicts I'm often on the side of the underdog. I am always oriented towards being a prince of peace.

**What event or series of events led you to your discovery?**

It happened around the age of 15 when my pastor insisted that I be part of the Prince of Peace Speech Contest. I had never competed in any kind of contest like that. I had to choose a speech from a collection of speeches about peace, memorize it, and deliver it. In the process I learned a lot about the atomic bomb, its cost, and the damage it could do to people and property. It was eye-opening to realize what money used to build the bomb could pay for in a peace-oriented society. I was shocked and could not imagine that anyone would ever drop an atomic bomb.

After learning of Hiroshima, the place where the bomb was dropped in 1945 and the nuclear classroom of the world, I, along with several of my students, visited Hiroshima and was devastated. If the American people could see what the atomic bomb did to Hiroshima, I believe they would become socially active today, and not radioactive tomorrow and they would not be in favor of war as enthusiastically as they now are.

Also when I was 15, I discovered the *Life Magazine* coffee table book on the great religions of the world. I asked my mother to buy it for me for Christmas. It was at that age that I discovered different ways of being religious and started believing that every religion had its own brand of wisdom; that the wisdoms of all faiths, including Christianity, were similar and held a common wealth. I thoroughly bought into the ideas of Matthew Fox's book *One River, Many Wells*. For quite a while, I had been looking for a pattern that united people across all boundaries in order to bring about global peace.

Now I am in academia using the liberal arts to inspire and educate global citizens and ambassadors of peace. I have always been a reconciler trying to negotiate understanding when there was conflict between individuals and institutions. I was born on September 23rd, 1941 on Walnut Street in Dawson, Georgia at 5:30 p.m. which classifies me on the zodiac cusp, as a Libra, symbolized by the scales of justice. I've always tried to bring balance.

**If you could give advice to those who are still searching for their life's purpose, what would it be?**

Keep reading, taking adventures in travel and eating not as a tourist but as a pilgrim. Keep exploring and learning how to listen to your own inner voice, because when you are "still" the Universe reveals its secrets in your daily experiences. We discover our purpose and reason for being in our activism; a vision then comes to us of our place as planetary citizens. We are pulled by our passion for such a long time, we fail to realize that we are living out the definition of our names.

For instance, my name, Lawrence Edward Carter, three British names: Lawrence means "poetic prophet," Edward means "the guardian of the treasures," and a Carter is the person who carts things around…like a coolie who pulls passengers through a city in the Orient. I am the poetic prophet who is guarding the treasures and who carts souls into heaven, an awareness that heaven is within you as ever-expanding good.

Just doing what you enjoy doing, what makes you happy, what fulfills you is one way of discovering your purpose. Your destiny, I believe, is written in the meaning of your name. It is engraved in your heart and it will not pass away until you fulfill it. I believe I'm fulfilling my destiny here at Morehouse College, helping thousands of young men, particularly those interested in the ministry.

When I was about fifteen I promised that I would send hundreds of young men and women into the Christian ministry and it has happened. I have sent hundreds to seminaries, schools of divinity, and schools of theology, many of whom have graduated with their Ph.D.s from the leading research universities, some of whom studied abroad. This will be my legacy to Morehouse College. These young people will be the future drum majors of justice and peace, helping us grow up into democracy's crown.

# ARE YOU HERE TO BE A TEACHER?

# Phyllis Davis

*"Instead of trying to move forward with new beliefs,
why not dismantle the ones you've got and live belief free."*

**Phyllis Davis is a Master Certified Coach, President of Executive Mentoring and Coaching, Inc. and Founder and Director of *American Business Etiquette Trainers Association*. Phyllis is recognized as a leading authority on corporate etiquette in American business. Having taught corporate etiquette in American business to companies, groups, associations, and individuals since 1975, her expertise is well documented.**

**Phyllis also finds time as an author, workshop leader, corporate trainer, keynote speaker, radio personality, business owner, and Etiquette Coach. She is author of her best selling book, *E2: Using the Power of Ethics and Etiquette in American Business* (Entrepreneur Press/Media/ Magazine, May 2003)**

**Phyllis has been featured on CNN *Headline News*, *Good Morning New York*, *Bloomberg Radio* and in the *Wall Street Journal*, *USA Today*, and many more publications.**

### Who do you think you are?

I've had the same mission statement for thirty years. It is to create civility in a troubled world. I work with individuals and companies talking to people about their purpose, creating higher levels of communication, and breaking down the differences in gender, religion, ethnicity, sexual orientation, and age. I'm trying to bring one-hundred-and-forty cultures together in this country, and four generations, and it's no small task. I want us all to see ourselves as one organic system that creates civility in the world.

### What events or series of events led to your discovery?

There's a famous question posed by Oprah: what do you know for sure? What I know for sure is that there is no certainty. Any time that we have a choice it creates suffering. It's been the awareness of the importance for discerning truth that has been my discovery. Not that I have a belief system, because I don't. The amorphous challenge of just being present in life is enough for me.

What led me to that was this: I wrote a book, and the book came out at the time when the United States military went into Afghanistan. I did a twenty city national media tour. I didn't get all the press I wanted because there was nothing on but war news. ABC, NBC, CBS, FOX...everything was war news. When I came back I spoke with a woman who I knew and trusted and respected, and I asked what I should do.

She looked at me and she said, "Phyllis, let it fail."

I said, "What you talking about? I spent the last two years of my life trying to create success on this project."

"Let it fail," she repeated. "The only thing that can bring you peace is to let it fail, and then watch what happens."

I went home, rested, and decided that I would go on with my life and see what happened. The book has done well, and that was three or four years ago. I try to use that philosophy in everything I do now. Just wear life like a loose garment, and do the best I can on projects. It's not about making them fail, don't get me wrong. I can't control the outcome, all I can control is what I did. I wrote the book, and I did the best I could.

If I don't invest my soul in all my projects, then I can't get hurt. I've had more success in the last four years than I ever had in my life, and a lot of it is because of that. I know this sounds counterintuitive to someone in business that wants to be a success. But just try it.

**If you could give advice to those who are still searching for their life's purpose, what would it be?**

I'm a philosopher. In the last few years, I've begun to study philosophy. Not in lieu of pursuing my ultimate purpose and career goals, or by looking at the spiritual or the health sides of my life. But to truly explore philosophy and find out what's true instead of searching outside for the right answers.

Just choose some philosophy to learn how to deconstruct your ideas and beliefs that you hold so dearly, because they pass, and all of a sudden one year you may discover you don't like licorice any more. It's true! A lot of the beliefs we've had since childhood, like that this country is safe and would never have war, or that I can have all the ice cream I want. We need to readdress some of the principles in life that have been our guiding light.

Instead of trying to move forward with new beliefs, why not dismantle the ones you've got and live belief free? Believe in nothing but the present and the principles that guide our moral structure. Experiment with freedom and see where that leads you instead of trying to search for answers, which is what we do. That's what Western culture does, it looks for answers and solutions and experts to give them to us. But really, truly look within and find out how you can dismantle all of your beliefs and truly experience freedom and joy from that.

# Jennifer McLean

*"The pitcher is you, and the pitcher needs to be full*
*in order for you to give of yourself."*

Jennifer has trained in three disciplines of healing: CranialSacral, Polarity, and Reiki Therapies, as well as sound healing. She has been practicing these modalities of healing in private sessions with individuals for 15 years. She is also a marketer and has written a book called, *The Credibility Factor.*

Jennifer's dichotomous experience as a healer and marketing professional afforded her unique insights into the multiple models people use to manage their worlds. This coupled with her lifetime exploration into spiritual challenges and opportunities, and her training as a healer, gave her the tools to write *The Big Book of You* and create the mini-movies that accompany the book. Endorsed by Jack Canfield, Gary Renard, Joe Vitale, Peggy McColl and more, *The Big Book of You* was released in February of 2008.

Jennifer also contributed a chapter in Joe Vitale's best-selling book, *The Key*, with over 500,000 copies sold, in which she was featured as a contributing healer. Her contribution included techniques for clearing old, unwanted beliefs, and thoughts that get stuck in the body as emotional blockages that limit expression and human potential.

You can reach Jennifer at: jennifer@healingrelease.com www.healingrelease.com

## Who do you think you are?

There are a lot of things I think I am. I am a being of light. I am a soul searching for the truth of God in every moment. I am a creative expression of the Divine that infuses my world with evidence of who I am in every moment. I create reflections of my being and project them into my surroundings, which then reflect back to me all that I am and all that I am not. I am committed to my own growth and to the growth of those I interact with. I focus my attention on nurturing our unique human potential, and creating forgiveness, financial abundance, and joy along the way. What others see as obstacles, I see as opportunities. I share my light, without hesitation. I am a creative being, and I also believe that I am part of this one mind, that is all actually ONE integrated comprehensive whole.

Recently, I had a moment of clarity around our oneness. I was turning a street corner in my car, and at that same moment a man fell off of his bicycle. It was a moment of violence, and it was kind of sudden and shocking as those things can be. Although the man wasn't hurt, he was definitely shaken up, but he got up and dusted himself off and rode away. Here is what was curious to me…I know I am a creative being, and I know that I co-create the things that I experience in my life. In that moment I wondered, "Did I make this guy fall?"

I wanted to explore this a little bit further, so I pulled the car over and I took a look inside myself. What I saw inside of my mind was violence; it was kind of like this part of my limbic brain that appreciated violence. And as I looked deeper, I witnessed the larger scale violence in the world and this notion that we are all one. I saw that the same energy of violence within me is also projected outside of myself. I felt this deep level of oneness with the group agreement regarding violence, and again I saw myself as part of that.

I knew intellectually that, by my thoughts, I actually have a hand in creating the violence that's in the world. I realized more clearly in the moment that what comes into my radar, within my purview, is an even more personal creation. As I looked within, I could see the energy within me, that can be creative, *and* the belief system within me, that can create violent incidents in the outside world. In that moment as I looked inside, I actually saw what my projected violence might look like, and it was shown to me kind of like a painting.

What I saw was a little string of my belief in violence. I saw this string coming out of me and attaching to the war in Iraq. That was my piece of the manifestation of violence. Then I saw other strings from all over the world attaching to war. The image was kind of like a Seurat painting in which all the individual dots together form a picture. And I realized that all the strings of our beliefs together, in aggregate, create reality. Whatever our belief system is inside can create itself externally. So, did I make him fall? Not exactly, yet I was a witness to it, so I could explore my feelings of violence and, in turn, share this with you. In fact, you are now part of this creative process. You might even ask… did I create this?

So, who do I think I am? I believe that I am a creative being that is a piece of this whole puzzle, and I create the wonders that are in my world and the challenges that are in my world as well. I also recognize that this creative being that is me can construct and unravel my own life. I can create the violence that's in front of me and I can unravel it too. When I unravel my own violence within myself, then, it disrupts and disengages the "strings of belief" or the "dots" of violence that are around me found manifest in the world. That's when I feel that we're all one. When I am unraveling my piece, then it inherently shifts the infrastructure and the aggregated belief systems. This gives all of us the opportunity to shift and change.

**What event or series of events led to your discovery?**

I started my spiritual path at twenty-three, just after I graduated from college. In fact, it was Shirley McClain (God bless her) and a TV Special I watched, based on her first book on spirituality, *Out On a Limb*. I read every book in its entire bibliography and that started me on my spiritual path.

The next incident was the Harmonic Convergence in 1987. I didn't know what it was, but my friends dragged me to it. I was young and naive, and there was this event that was in the middle of the night and it sounded like fun and an adventure. In that moment, I felt something shift inside of me. It was like a flutter, an opening. So I continued to explore.

A pivotal time came several years later. I had several regularly occurring weekly migraine headaches that I found out were a result of Temporalmandibular Joint Disorder (TMJ). I basically had a headache for about three years. I was waiting in a doctor's office considering going in for surgery when a pamphlet fell off the table, literally onto my lap. I looked at the pamphlet, and it was from an orthodontist who specialized in TMJ. So I thought, well, before I go into surgery, I better check this guy out.

It turned out that the doctor and his wife worked as a team. She performed cranial sacral therapy, and he did applied kinesiology with a mouth splint. He would put a splint in my mouth, then muscle test me to see if the splint was in the right place. That was after she had done cranial sacral work with me to correct some of the problems with the cranial system. Within six weeks I was completely cured from the migraines.

Cranial sacral therapy got me into the healing arts, and I dove in head-first. I trained in several different disciplines of healing: polarity therapy, cranial sacral therapy, sound therapies, and Reiki. That was a huge part of my discovery, working with myself using those techniques.

Working with others using those healing techniques has allowed me to make all kinds of unique discoveries, including other aspects of who I am. I don't think I would have been able to go as deep within myself, and seen the truths about myself, if I hadn't explored these healing techniques with others.

More recently, I've been working with Joe Vitale and using a technique called Ho'oponopono. Joe talked about it is his book, *Zero Limits*. It's been a real important technique in the newest progressions of my life. Of course *The Secret* was what inspired me to find Joe, and many aspects of the law of attraction are a foundational philosophy for me. I think *The Secret* has helped bring me to a deeper level of understanding. Joe's work and the other healing modalities I have learned have allowed me to sustain it and move me through any blocks that come up.

I believe that when you make big requests of the universe, when you have big dreams, and make them known, and ask fervently with visualization and feeling, whatever is not in alignment with those dreams will come up for viewing, airing, acknowledging, thanking and, ultimately, releasing. Joe's work and the law of attraction are two fantastic practices that have really allowed me to find my current level of bliss.

**If you could give advice to those who are still searching for their life's purpose, what would it be?**

There are a few things I'd like to share from my book, *The Big Book of You*. One is called the "consistency theory." Most people are extremely consistent with their behavior, and there's good and bad in that. People who are not on a spiritual path are usually quite consistent in their behaviors. What that means is they typically respond in a very predictable manner. If you're about to tell them something, for example, and you anticipate that they're going to respond in a certain way, they probably will.

At some point, it becomes *your* responsibility to find a new tactic with that person. If you say something to your mother, and she responds in the exact same way that she has for the last 45 years, you have a number of choices to alter the pattern—you can either not tell her at all, or you can choose a different way to be with her reaction. Find a way to respond to her, rather than react in the same predictable manner yourself. That simple choice helps a lot of people. Once they know that this other person is going to react exactly how they always have, they can take responsibility and ask themselves, "How can *I* respond differently now?"

This usually changes the dynamics of an otherwise predictable outcome. It opens up all kinds of other possibilities within the relationship.

My other advice is, "don't compromise your true self." People often feel challenged by this one initially because most of us were taught that life is all about compromise. My theory is that the moment you compromise that which you know to be true deep within you, the next emotion is resentment. If you can find a way to look at a situation so that you do *not* feel compromised, and you don't feel that resentment, then you've changed it by changing your perception of it, not by compromising yourself.

Let me give you an example of this. Let's say there's a couple, and the man and woman have completely different tastes in music. The man loves hard rock, and the woman absolutely adores folk music. They go to each other's concerts, and one time, the man turns to his wife and says, "You know, I really hate folk music. I don't like it. I don't like the people. I just don't like anything about it. I'm not going to compromise anymore. I'm not going to go to these anymore."

Well, she keeps on going to his rock concerts and he's stopped going to her concerts. So one day he asks her, "Why are you still going to my rock concerts?" She says it's because she absolutely loves being with him when he's in his joy, and he is truly in his joy when he's at a rock concert. He thinks about this for awhile, and he thinks, Well, maybe I could try that at a folk concert. So, he goes with her to her next folk concert with this new perception. He goes thinking, I just want to watch her having fun and appreciate her having fun. And at this particular event, he has a really good time.

He is having a good time because his perception has shifted. He's moved from a point of "I am being affected by something I don't like" to "I am now in charge and looking at this a different way. As a result I am no longer compromising." He is then being true to a deeper desire in him for her to be happy, so there is no reason to feel resentment. I fully believe that if you are feeling compromised, either find a different way to see the situation and be with it, or don't do it at all. Resentment is destructive and serves no one unless you learn something from it.

Finally, and ultimately, what I discovered is that you are the "brass ring." Whatever you're seeking isn't somewhere "out there" outside of yourself…it's already within you. Once you discover, acknowledge, know, feel, and truly understand that you are the gift that you are seeking, all the other troubles of the world will fall away.

# Norma Milanovich

*"Partner with God, at all times, and to then go within*
*to find all the answers, for the "Universe is within."*

Born in the upper Midwest, Dr. Norma Milanovich's foundation is built upon solid values and rooted in high standards of living, a deep love for education, and a desire to succeed and contribute to the world.

Norma obtained her Master's and Doctoral degrees from the University of Houston, and went on to serve on Advisory Boards for Ohio State University and Southwestern Indian Polytechnic Institute. She also represented Senator Binghamin's office on the Japanese Youth For Understanding Program for five years. For eight years, she held a top-secret clearance for the Department of Energy and was a lead instructor in training their security and police force personnel in Job-Task Analysis. She also spent twenty years in academia as an Assistant Professor of Education.

She has trained personnel for many large US corporations, the Navajo Nation, Sandia National Laboratories, Los Alamos National Laboratories, and Government Offices in areas such as needs assessment, team building, job task analysis, sexual harassment in the workplace, and effective communication, making her a leading and desired trainer all over the US.

For the last 20 years, Norma has served as a beacon for those seeking self-empowerment, and for thousands who also feel called to serve the world. She is a channel for the Ascended Masters and has brought through thousands of messages that have served to assist in humanity's evolution, and that have guided hundreds in their quests toward world peace. Norma's communications with Beings outside of the third-dimensional existence, and her extraordinary communication and motivational skills, allow her to convey information that these Beings have for humankind today.

Norma has visited almost 100 countries, and every continent on the planet, often guiding groups of Light workers to sacred sites to perform mediations, activations, and ceremonies that strengthen and repair the electromagnetic gridlines of planet Earth, serve to heal serious rifts in time and space, and allow individuals to become more self-realized through the process of soul retrieval.

Norma has been invited to speak at the United Nations seven times, most recently in September of 2004. She conducts workshops on various self-empowerment topics all over the world, is passionate about educating people about the power of Feng Shui, and is the author of three books, which remain some of the best sellers with the leading spiritual book distribution company in the United States.

Contact Norma by going to: www.athenalctr.com

# Who do you think you are?

My soul is an infinite spark of Light and is an integral part of the Great Mystery – and I am my soul. My strength comes from my connection to the Great Mystery. Everything I think, perceive, feel, or experience contributes to the illumination of who I AM. Therefore, I AM the Light of this world, come to Earth to serve my fellow brothers and sisters.

My journey is my life, my mission, and my joy, and the purpose for my journey is to learn to conquer fear and control my mental and emotional bodies. I came into this world alone, and I am destined to depart from this world in the same way. Therefore, I must learn to be self-reliant in partnership with my Creator, for I have learned that God and I are a majority.

What feeds my soul is the Light of who I AM, and eternal gratitude. I AM that I AM.

## What events or series of events lead to your discovery?

When I turned 40, almost over night, I experienced a spiritual awakening. Suddenly the veil was lifted and I had total recall of ancient knowledge and wisdom that I had not learned in this lifetime. My Higher Self quickly reclaimed skills and abilities, lying dormant in my soul for centuries, and I used these gifts to embark upon a journey of self-discovery and enlightenment.

I am a person who searches for the root cause or the root meaning of all things in life. What rides on the surface no longer interests me for I know that superficial knowledge and understandings are but temporal solutions to the deeper, more meaningful and theoretical questions that define the meaning of life.

## If you could give advice to those who are still searching for their life's purpose, what would it be?

I would tell them to partner with God, at all times, and to then go within to find all the answers, for the "Universe is within." Secondly, I would encourage them to channel gratitude for everything they experience and witness in life. Finally, each must learn to think positively at all times, and, in so doing, should use this approach to find the deeper meaning of all the experiences in life. Challenges present themselves as opportunities to learn how to evolve and embrace change. Positive thinking helps the person look at the world from a higher perspective, and open the mind to embrace new ideas and concepts in life.

# Liz & Ric Thompson

*"My advice would be to explore, to play, to see what's really out there, and most importantly, what resonates with you?"*

**Ric and Liz Thompson are successful business owners, personal development consultants and co-founders of the top online magazine, *Healthy Wealthy nWise*. They are both committed to helping people realize that wealth-building and healthy living are truly interconnected and to providing tools people need to build successful lives.**

**"A business can't operate without the holistic nature of life," says Ric. "Success in business is about balance. The financial aspects need the human aspects, even the spiritual aspects, to create a fully integrated paradigm."**

**"Everyone defines success differently," says Liz. "That's one reason why Ric and I started *Healthy Wealthy nWise*. We wanted to introduce readers to a wide range of successful people that anyone could use as mentors or guides, and not limit their exposure to just one person's idea of what success means."**

***Healthy Wealthy nWise*** **was developed to help readers learn that they can be healthy, wealthy *and* spiritual—all at once, and to provide a safe place for people to explore their potential. In the virtual pages of this magazine, Ric and Liz seek to inspire, motivate, educate, and help people find their balance in the world.**

**Ric and Liz are successful because they help improve people's lives. "Success is everywhere and in everyone, says Liz. "The more we share our passion and fulfillment with others, the more we create it in our own lives."**

**Ric adds, "*Healthy Wealthy nWise* is a journey of discovery for Liz and me. And we've invited a few hundred thousand of our closest friends along for the ride!"**

**Find out more at: www.healthywealthynwise.com**

# Liz Thompson

### Who do you think you are?

I wouldn't give a title to myself. It's not really a *who* I am. It's more related to what my purpose is, and that is to help people empower themselves, to help them discover that power within and own it and use it to make their lives better.

## What event or series of events led to your discovery?

As I look back over the types of businesses I've started and the things that I've done, I realize there was a common theme. Regardless of how remote it seemed, each one had to do with helping people discover something in themselves, that inner sense that they can do something more!

For example, my first business was in the gift industry. I started a gift basket business. In that business I think I screwed everything up that you could possibly screw up. After doing that for a while, I finally put my foot down and decided I was going to figure out how to make it work. The problem was, once I figured out how to make it work it wasn't fun anymore. So I sold the business and put together a book that taught other people in the industry how to create this type of business and to make it work. Most people in the industry didn't know how to run a business. They were doing it because they thought it was fun. Since they didn't know how to make their business work, they were losing a lot of money and pretty much making their lives miserable. I saw a way that I could help people understand how to make their business work, and that was the second business I started.

From there is just kind of cascaded as we went through successive businesses. At one point I taught college courses on business etiquette. How silly is it that business etiquette can be considered empowering people? I didn't teach it from the angle of this is what you have to do, this is what you don't have to do. It was more like, these are the rules of society and you want to know them so you can choose how to play the game. It was all about letting people understand what impressions they were giving, and how other people were perceiving them, so that they could choose to do more of it or less of it and understand where they were going.

*Healthy Wealthy nWise* is all about that. We're starting a new project now specifically geared toward businesses and small entrepreneurs, to help empower the small entrepreneur to become successful. And so it continues.

## If you could give advice to those who are still searching for their life's purpose, what would it be?

In a course that I've written called *The Science of Creating Your Dreams*, there's an exercise that everybody has to do. It deals specifically with that voice in your head that tells you that you can't do something, or says, "Who do you think you are? What are you doing? You can't do that!" Most people think the exercise is really funny. Here's what happens. I have everyone get out a piece of duct tape and put the duct tape on that voice. You don't want to put it in your hair because that doesn't work very well, but you can put it on your computer or someplace where you can see it. Every time that voice pops up and says something negative about you, you can look at the duct tape and say, "Sorry you have duct tape over your mouth, I can't hear you!"

Once that little voice shuts up, sit quietly, go deep, and really look at that one big goal, that wish that you had, that purpose that scares the living crap out of you and makes butterflies dance around in your stomach because you think it's way too big. When you get that feeling in your stomach, then you know you're getting close to what your real purpose is.

So, the first step is to get that voice that says that you can't do certain things to shut up. The second step is there to assist you in exploring what excites you. It helps you to discover what gets you going, what gets you jazzed, what gets you out of bed in the morning. This is how people can start to find their purpose.

# Ric Thompson

### Who do you think you are?

I'm a guy who likes to stretch the limits of what's possible. Not only from a personal level, but also the general concept of stretching the limits.

### What event or series of events led to your discovery?

The path I took helped me to form that definition. It all started for me as a child. I was never one to go along with the status quo. My life was about being rebellious, trying to find my own way in life, and really doing things outside the norm. It was definitely a factor of rebellion against authority.

Over the years, this quality of mine has grown into tackling larger and larger challenges, whether it was college, becoming an entrepreneur, or refusing to succumb to the typical ordinary mundane nine-to-five job environment. Personally, I like to start a business, see where I can go with it, and see how far I can stretch things. Not accepting the status quo has been my path all along. For me, it's fun to explore what the limits *seem* to be, because to me there aren't any limits. It's just a matter of figuring out how to stretch it farther and farther.

**If you could give advice to those who are still searching for their life's purpose, what would it be?**

My advice would be to explore, play, and see what's out there. Most importantly what resonates with you? What makes your eyes light up? What makes you feel on fire? What are your experiences? What are your skills? Find out what those things are, then explore and stretch your own limits and see what else is out there for you.

# Sharla Jacobs

*"Keep asking Spirit, who am I, what am I here for, what is my purpose?*
*Continue to ask Spirit, because it's a never-ending inquiry."*

**Award Winning 6 Figure Success Coaches Jesse Koren and Sharla Jacobs teach Holistic Practitioners, Coaches and Heart-based Consultants How to Earn 6 Figures in Their Business. They are the co-founders of Rejuvenate™Training, the home of the *Rejuvenate Your Practice 2 Day Intensive.***

**In the last three years Rejuvenate™Training's workshops and training programs have helped over 1,000 Conscious Business Owners increase their business success. Jesse and Sharla are the authors of seven information products and eight training programs. They teach business owners how to serve more people by creating cd sets and leading lucrative seminars. And they teach business owners the skill of sales, marketing, and delegation, so that they can double, triple, and even quadruple their income.**

**Find out more about Jesse and Sharla by visiting: www.RejuvenateYourPractice.com**

## Who do you think you are?

I spent three months in total silence in a Zen Monastery, hoping to find out the answer to that question. But the answer keeps changing…

The best answer I can give you is that I am a channel for whatever Divine Spirit asks of me. Instead of trying to impose my own will, I often ask Spirit, "What is it you want to use my life for?" And the answers I get shape who I become…even when the answers I get from Spirit don't make sense right away.

About six years ago, I was in acupuncture school and I got a message that I was supposed to teach holistic practitioners how to be successful in business. That didn't make ANY sense to me because I hadn't even built my own practice yet. But the message was crystal clear and it stayed with me.

Today, my husband Jesse and I, teach holistic practitioners, coaches and entrepreneurs how to make a 6-figure income in their business, while staying true to their core values.

Our mission is to be a leader in the planetary movement to shift business from a competitive model based on scarcity to a cooperative model based on unlimited abundance.

So, who I am is a powerful business woman who is sourced by Spirit. I am also newly married to my amazing husband, Jesse Koren

## What event or series of events led to your discovery?

When I registered for acupuncture school, I was confident that since acupuncture was a "booming field" I would have no problem making a living at it. After three years and a grueling board exam, I was excited to finally make the difference I had been dreaming about for three years. I expected masses of people to flock to me. But was I wrong…

What I discovered was that I still had a lot of healing to do in the realm of receiving money for my services and feeling good enough about myself. It wasn't until I really put myself out there in the world to try to get clients that I discovered how painful it was to want to serve people so badly but to not know how to reach them.

It didn't take long to realize that I was $80,000 in debt from acupuncture school, and instead of decreasing, my debt was growing. After a few months, I canceled my gym membership and was on the verge of giving up organic food because I "couldn't afford it."

I was confused because I knew I was divinely guided to help people, I just didn't know how to get clients. I was totally scared and thinking "who's going to pay me for what I do when I can't even handle my own life?"

But if I've learned one thing it's this: whatever problems I've had, there are people out there who have had the same problem and overcome it. The key is to find those people and learn from them.

A friend, who is a coach and mentor to new coaches told me that if I worked with him that I would triple my income in three months. At the time this meant going from $20,000 to $60,000 a year. The only catch was that I had to do the homework.

I didn't know what the homework was going to be, and I didn't have the money to hire him. But when I checked in with Spirit I knew that I had to hire this coach to help me.

So, I borrowed the money from Jesse, and signed up for coaching. When I found out what the homework entailed, I almost fell off my seat. My homework was to have twenty business conversations per day, five days a week.

But, there are no accidents in the world. Because of the sheer number of conversations I had during those three months, I started to become very clear about what works and what doesn't work in "sales conversations" with a potential client.

It was during those three months that I "downloaded" the HeartSelling model that we now teach. While I was in Acupuncture School, I had studied the five elements of Chinese Medicine: Fire, Earth, Metal, Water, and Wood. According to this system, we're all made up of the five elements and when one of these elements is out of balance, your health will suffer.

It dawned on me that the same was true for a sales conversation. If any one of the five elements was missing in a HeartSelling conversation, the person would usually decline my services. But when all five elements were present, my potential client often said "Yes."

It was like I had received a treasure map to share with the world. As you can probably imagine, I tripled my practice in three months just as my coach promised.

When other practitioners, coaches, and friends saw how quickly my practice filled up, they started asking me how I was doing it. They were so excited by what I was sharing that Jesse and I created the *Rejuvenate Your Practice 2 Day Intensive* and the *Rejuvenate Your Practice with HeartSelling CD Set.*

We just kept asking Spirit and (our clients) how we could serve more fully…and each time we asked, we were given the next steps.

Now we have nine programs in a rapidly growing company. And we couldn't be happier.

**If you could give advice to those who are still searching for their life's purpose, what would it be?**

The first thing is I would encourage you to do transformational work. Reading this book is a great way to get the principles we're all sharing on a mental level. It is also important that you get them on an experiential level. You can work one-on-one with a holistic practitioner or coach, or you can attend live workshops and seminars.

And as you're doing this work, keep asking Spirit, "Who am I? What am I here for? What is my purpose?" Continue to ask Spirit these questions, because it's a never-ending inquiry.

The second thing is I would encourage you to get a mentor. A mentor is a special person who has done what you want to do and who has qualities that you'd like to grow in yourself.

I see a lot of entrepreneurs who are trying to reinvent the wheel or worse, taking advice from people who are less successful than they are. Sometimes a mentor will show up, but they get scared, and they say "No" instead of saying "Yes." My advice is to have the faith and say "Yes" to working with a mentor. And by saying "Yes" to your mentor, you're saying "Yes" to what's possible in yourself.

# Jesse Koren

*"Ask yourself: 'What does Spirit want to use my life for today?'
Allow a new answer to arise every time you ask."*

**Award Winning 6 Figure Success Coaches Jesse Koren and Sharla Jacobs teach Holistic Practitioners, Coaches and Heart-based Consultants How to Earn 6 Figures in Their Business. They are the co-founders of Rejuvenate™ Training, the home of the** *Rejuvenate Your Practice 2 Day Intensive.*

**In the last three years Rejuvenate™ Training's workshops and training programs have helped over 1,000 Conscious Business Owners increase their business success. Jesse and Sharla are the authors of seven information products and eight training programs. They teach business owners how to serve more people by creating cd sets and leading lucrative seminars. And they teach business owners the skill of sales, marketing, and delegation, so that they can double, triple, and even quadruple their income.**

**Find out more about Jesse and Sharla by visiting: www.RejuvenateYourPractice.com**

## Who do you think you are?

When I was first growing up my Spirit was very bright and I believed anything was possible. But when I was eleven years old, I had a dream to play on the Chicago Sting, our pro soccer team. My next door neighbor said, "Did you know that there are millions of other boys all over Chicago who want to play for the Sting, many who are way better than you? He laughed at me, punched me in the stomach, and said, "Who do you think you are?" So I gave up on that dream and put myself in a small, tight box of limitations.

But my Spirit is HUGE, bigger than ANY box I've built for myself. When I was sixteen years old, my dad introduced me to Wayne Dyer, who helped me break out of my first box. I keep breaking out of boxes, to find another box, a bigger box, containing who I am. And each time I find a bigger box, I discover a new piece of myself.

And so I'm constantly reinventing myself, discovering more and more pieces of who I am. My Spirit keeps brightening, and even though

I haven't put all the pieces together yet, I know that I'm an Uncontainably Bright, Powerful, Divine Being.

**What events or series of events led to your discovery?**

After listening to the Wayne Dyer tapes, my whole life started to open up. I'd love to share three key events that quickened my awakening.

The first event began the semester before I graduated from college when everyone was asking "what are you going to do after college?" When I told them I was going to travel, it didn't go over so well. You just graduated from one of the most prestigious Universities in the United States and instead of getting a prestigious job, you're going to WHAT??? TRAVEL??? FOR TWO YEARS??? Who do you think you are?

But it turned out to be the best decision I ever made. I made $10,000 stretch the span of two years, by riding Greyhound buses and living at a dozen intentional communities throughout the United States.

While I was traveling, I filled a journal every month, trying to figure out who I was. Instead, I discovered over and over who I wasn't.

I stayed at several yoga centers, and discovered that although I loved yoga, I was not cut out to live the life of a yogi. I lived in an artistic community, and realized that although I loved art, I was not cut out to be an artist. And on and on...

At each community I peeled off a layer of who I thought I was (or should be.) I finally reached the point where I learned a lot about who I was and wasn't, but I was driving myself crazy with all the inner work.

The second event was when one of my mentors Moe Ross, asked me a question that completely changed my life. Questions have the power to do that. (Which is why this book is so powerful.)

The question Moe asked me was: "what will you regret, if you don't do it in the next seven years?" In that moment, the answer came to me, even though I was scared to act on it. My heart's calling was to work with teenagers as a wilderness therapy counselor.

I sent out 50 letters to Wilderness Therapy Camps all over the country, hoping that none of them would respond.

When I took the job as a Wilderness Therapy Counselor in North Carolina, I agreed to be responsible for ten teenage boys, seventeen hours a day, five days a week, for two years. All the boys chose to come to this camp to avoid doing time at Juvenile Hall.

I was their authority figure, and at any given time there were usually several boys yelling and swearing at me. To make matters worse, we lived outside in tents and my hands were numb and my nose dripped for the entire winter. I wanted to quit almost every day. But, when I discovered that nine of the ten boys in my group didn't live with their parents because their parents were either in jail, dead, or had left them to their grandparents I vowed that I wasn't going to be the person to break their trust and leave again.

So, I fulfilled my two-year commitment and discovered that who I am is a man who loves to serve. At the same time, something else had woken up in me. I was no longer willing to spend my waking hours getting yelled at while I froze my butt off and made less than five dollars an hour.

I made a pact with Spirit: "I'm happy to serve. But you've got to meet me halfway. I need to be served as well."

This discovery sparked the third event. I moved to Santa Cruz to become a life coach and workshop leader. I tried everything I could to get clients and workshop participants, but even though my rates were much higher than at the Wilderness Therapy Camp, I couldn't get enough people to work with me to pay the bills.

So, I got a j-o-b working at a nonprofit organization, pretending like I was making a difference. nine months later, I was stuffing cookies down my throat in the back room of the office, when I realized that not serving people deeply was killing me. I watched my wife Sharla hire a coach and triple her practice in three months. So, filled with newfound inspiration I hired my own coach and went for my dreams again.

Using the system of HeartSelling™ Sharla had downloaded; we took our company, Rejuvenate Training, from 0 to 6-figures in our first year. People started wondering how we grew our business so quickly. By sharing our answers and continually asking: "Spirit, what do you want to use my life for today?" our business has exploded over the last three years.

We now teach holistic practitioners, coaches, and entrepreneurs how to make a six-figure income in their business without sacrificing their core values. We stay passionate about it, because we believe that the world will be a better place when the people with big hearts have bank accounts that match the size of their hearts.

**If you could give advice to those who are still searching for their life's purpose, what would it be?**

There are two parts to my advice: The first part is to ask yourself every morning: "Spirit, what do you want to use my life for today?" Allow a new answer to arise every time you ask.

What you'll find is that your answer will often come as a way to serve. Especially when you're feeling great, you'll naturally want to help other people feel the joy and abundance that you're feeling.

The second part is the guidance we give all of our clients. You see our clients are holistic practitioners, coaches and entrepreneurs who naturally want to serve. The mistake they often make is the one I made when I worked at camp. They let their desire to serve other people overtake them and keep them from including themselves in the service.

The best way to burn yourself out is to serve everyone but yourself. Giving is no more spiritual than receiving and depriving yourself of your birthright of abundance, love, and support is the best way to shortchange others of it.

So, here's the second question to ask: "What do I need to receive today in order to serve fully?" By asking these two questions, you will be amazed by how quickly you become the leader you've been waiting for.

# Alex Mandossian

*"If I tell someone something, they will forget. If I show someone something, they may remember. But, if I involve someone in something, then they will learn."*

**Since 1991, Alex Mandossian has generated over $233 million in sales and profits for his clients and partners via "electronic marketing" media such as TV Infomercials, online catalogs, 24-hour recorded messages, voice/fax broadcasting, Teleseminars, Webinars, Podcasts and Internet Marketing.**

**Alex has personally consulted Dale Carnegie Training, NYU, 1ShoppingCart Corp., Mutuals.com, Pinnacle Care, Strategic Coach, Trim Spa and many others.**

**He has hosted teleseminars with many of the world's top thought leaders such as Mark Victor Hansen, Jack Canfield, Stephen Covey, Les Brown, David Allen, Vic Conant, Brian Tracy, David Bach, Harvey Mackay, Robert Cialdini, Harv Eker, Bobbi De Porter, Michael Masterson, Joe Vitale, Gay and Katie Hendricks, Bob Proctor, and many others.**

**He is the CEO of Heritage House Publishing, Inc. – a boutique electronic marketing and publishing company that "repurposes" written and spoken educational content for worldwide distribution. He is also the founder of the Electronic Marketing Institute.**

**He has trained over 8,300 teleseminar students since 2002 and claims that practically any entrepreneur can transform their annual income into a weekly income once they apply his principle-centered electronic marketing strategies. Alex's 2001 annual income became an hourly income by 2006 and he has tripled his days off.**

**He lives in the San Francisco Bay Area with his wife, Aimee, and two children, Gabriel and Breanna, and enjoys over 90 "Free Days" each year.**

## Who do you think you are?

I am a trainer and teacher who inspires and leads others to discover their own unique ability so that they'll increase and accelerate their personal productivity, in their personal life and in their professional life. Sometimes I'm a mentor, other times I'm a trainer, other times I'm a teacher, but most of the time I'm a student. By becoming both student and teacher, I accelerate my own learning and accelerate my productivity so that I can get more done in less time.

## What event or series of events led to your discovery?

I learned all about training on a park bench, after I'd lost a quarter of a million dollars in a business venture. It was my first business venture after getting out of college. The park was Macarthur Park in Los Angeles, California.

Eighteen months before, I'd started this new venture. It was a frozen yogurt and bakery store, which turned into a devastating loss. It was not just a loss of resources, because ninety percent of the quarter million dollars wasn't even mine, it was money that was handed to me through relatives and grandparents, and money that was gifted to me by my parents. I had a lot of guilt surrounding this, and I wanted to learn how to never have that happen to me again.

On the way home from Long Beach, California I took the long way, and I went to Macarthur Park. I wish I could say it was a brutally cold winter, but it wasn't. It was summer and sunny outside. It was very comfortable. I was sitting right across the street from a hotel owned by one of my father's friends. I figured if it got too uncomfortable, I could at least go up to the hotel and sleep there.

While I was on that park bench, I was watching a heavy-set woman who was there in the park. She put a dime into a bird birdseed machine. She turned the knob, and the birdseed came out. Her goal was to get the pigeons that were at the park to feed from her hand. So, I was just watching this from the park bench. There was someone else on the park bench, too. We thought about what to call this woman, and she became The Pigeon Lady.

What was interesting was how she went about having her first beak-to-hand experience. The first pigeon that walked up to her – you know how pigeons walk – it bobbed up to her and put its beak into the palm of her hand. It had that level of trust, and all the other pigeons followed the one pigeon that started it. I considered it a dance – she was dancing with them to get them to that level of trust. Once the trust was initiated, they would always come back.

How she did it was she started walking gently and quietly and casually – non-invasively – towards the pigeons. There was a whole flock of pigeons bobbing along on the concrete there by the park. She'd walk towards them and they'd walk away, and so she'd turn around and she'd show them the birdseed. It looked like they knew that she had birdseed, so they would walk towards her when she had turned around. She turned around again and walked towards them, and the pigeons walked away. She turned around to walk away from them, they walked towards her.

The distance between her and the flock became narrower and narrower in that dance she was doing. If she walked too quickly, it would startle them, and some would fly away. If she walked away without showing them the birdseed, they didn't walk towards her.

It took the better part of an hour until she turned around and one of the pigeons, probably and adolescent who didn't have too much fear, walked up to the palm of her hand, actually genuflected on one knee – I remember it like it was yesterday – and fed from the palm of her hand.

At that moment, I thought that was the miracle. At that moment, I didn't feel very highly about myself, my self-esteem was very low, so anything was a miracle. I was so embarrassed at what had happened with the business, so ashamed of losing all this money, and I felt like I didn't have a friend in the world, so this woman was kind of my virtual friend. I don't know if she even knew I existed. She had all these friends, these pigeons, and when the first pigeon came up to feed from her hand, I thought the miracle was that all the rest of the pigeons came up and started doing the same thing. They landed on her shoulder. They landed on her head. They were all over her!

That wasn't the miracle, though. The miracle was that the next day she didn't have to go through the dance. They remembered her, and just went straight up to her and fed from her hand. They wanted birdseed, and she didn't have to go through the dance. That trust was initiated. From that point on – and I was there a couple of days – she didn't have to go through the ritual. That's been a central metaphor for my life and for my training business, and that's how I teach people.

Interestingly enough, there was this young kid who was there in the park, maybe age five or six, and he got a coin from his mom, did the same thing with the bird seed, and wanted the same result as the woman. But because he didn't know how to dance with the pigeons, because he didn't have the patience or the vigilance to dance, it didn't work for him. He'd run towards the pigeons, startle them, and they'd fly away. He'd walk away from the pigeons without showing the birdseed to them, so they wouldn't follow him. Finally, he got frustrated and just threw the birdseed at all the pigeons, and never had that beak-to-hand relationship.

If he had watched what the lady did and had the patience she had, he would have had the same experience. On one side, no patience, no dancing, and no beak-to-hand relationship, and on the other side you have this woman who knew what to do, went through the process for the better part of an hour. I stayed at the park about a week, and I saw her at least two or three days, and these pigeons would just flock to her! They wouldn't flock to anyone else; they'd flock to her because they trusted her.

I wondered how in my own life I could do this same thing. I needed to go through the dance. I didn't go through that dance with the business that failed. I was like that young kid, without patience. I just ran at the business, not knowing a thing about it, and then lost a ton of money – most of it not mine – and created this five-year hole in my life. I never claimed bankruptcy, but it took me a long time to pay it back. After many failed attempts at starting a business, I eventually got on my feet in 1994, which was five years later.

That specific incident inspired me to become who I am today. I define myself as the result I get in communicating with others, in teaching and training them how to learn about their unique abilities, and how to teach and train others to do the same. I'm a trainer's trainer, and I utilize the teleseminar method to teach thousands of people every year. Currently I have eleven thousand students, and that probably will double in a couple of years. And I always remember the Pigeon Lady at Macarthur Park in the summer of 1989.

**If you could give advice to those who are still searching for their life's purpose, what would it be?**

It would be to observe the lessons, like I did. I was told what to do, but I didn't do it. I was told to research and to dance with my business partners, and I didn't do that, I just jumped right in. I was told to be vigilant with my research and to make sure it was a good deal, and I didn't do that. I learned through observation.

Many people are told what to do, but unless you demonstrate to them through case studies, like how they teach at Harvard, they don't get it. You must demonstrate – not just articulate what to do and how to do it, and why it's so important. Like Jim Rohn says, "The bigger the why, the easier the how." The how is not enough, you have to have a big enough why.

I would advise others to observe the things around them, like I did with the Pigeon Lady. Give meaning to those things as metaphors for life. Depending on what they stand for, they will attract incidents like that to learn from, so they can demonstrate, not just articulate their greatness to others. Then you've not only seen it, but also actually lived it.

If I tell someone something they will forget. If I show someone something they may remember. But, if I involve someone in something, then they will learn. My goal is to involve people and have them experience. I believe that experience is the most convincing thing that anyone can do. So, first observation, then experience what you learn through observation. When you begin to live this way you'll love teaching others, and the Teacher you become will love it even more.

# Terry Tillman

*"There's a light inside of you and basically you're just connecting with it…
I have found that when I do this my life really works well."*

Terry Tillman has led personal growth, effectiveness, motivation, and leadership seminars for over 100,000 people since 1977. His work has taken him to 40 cities and 26 countries. Recently he has been pioneering experiential education seminars for large groups of 2,000 to 15,000 participants.

His simple uncompromising philosophy of the limitless abundance available in life, and his quest to experience purpose, love, and peace has led him into a variety of environments.

From the time he started his first business manufacturing track hurdles at the age of 15 to his current work designing workshops on the leading edge of the human potential movement, Terry has had many adventures. He has been on television, records, and on international tours as a singer, banjo player, and original member of the New Christy Minstrels folk group.

After graduating from Stanford University with a degree in Economics, he founded a real estate development, construction, and sales company. He became a member of the Million Dollar Sales Club his first year in 1966 (Back when $1,000,000 meant something). He has been a part owner and Director of a network of television stations, a satellite cable business, and a video production company.

Terry holds a private pilot's license, has been a white water rafting guide, a ski instructor, and a marathon runner. Terry now travels six to ten months each year, conducting leadership seminars. He presents and designs seminars, trains seminar leaders, and assists people to produce results, discover their value, and realize their dreams.

Read more about Terry by visiting: www.227company.com

## Who do you think you are?

This is a good question, and one I ask business people when I'm working with them, though I ask, "Who are you?" rather than who do you 'think'. There's a distinction. I asked them who they are and why they are there. I had been asking this question of myself for years and years and I found the answer eventually.

I revisited the town I grew up in about 10 years ago, and I saw a childhood friend that I hadn't seen since we were kids. We were reminiscing about old times and the things we had done together, and at one point he said, "Do you remember when we were lying out on the front lawn looking at the stars, and I was talking about trading bubble gum cards, and you looked over at me and said 'Hey Jack, did you ever wonder why we're here?' We were probably like six years old." I did not remember asking him that, but that would've been like me to do so, because I was in pursuit of the answer to that question for many years.

I am a scout. I remember the moment I realized that. I could write books on what that means, but the bottom line is that's it. My job is to go out and explore and have experiences and gather information and bring it back to people and offer it. I say, here's a direct sense, here's how to get from here to there, and it may not be the way, but it's a way, and I offer it to you. As long as I'm doing that, I'm doing pretty well in my life and making a contribution. 30 years later, people still find my offering to be of value. So that's what I do. And it's a contribution to the expression of who I am.

**What events or series of events led to your discovery?**

I used to live in Phoenix in 1972, and when I lived there I would go up to Sedona, Arizona. At the time, Sedona was only about three thousand people, today it's about fifty thousand or so. There was this little artist community in the red rock country. It was very beautiful.

On my way to Sedona off on the right hand side up on a rock was this building. To me it looked like it grew right out of the rock and there was nothing else around. I said what the heck is that? I turned off the road and drove in the direction of where it was. There was a parking lot right below and a walkway that went right up to the building, which was a church. I walked in and nobody was there. It was completely empty. There was a Bible open on the podium.

I wandered around this beautiful place, and I read a plaque that said an artist, not an architect, designed it. I took some pictures, and I sat there quietly by myself in some form of contemplation and introspection and had a great experience. I was blown away by the place. I was curious. I was like, what is this place, who did it, why did they do it, how did they do it, what's it for and who comes here? That was in 1972, and I went along on my way and I forgot about it.

Flash forward to 1978, and I'm with my friends and we have a free day. We'd all been working hard and traveling and I thought we should just have a good time and maybe drive up to the Grand Canyon. I said, "You know, I used to live here. Let's go to Oak Creek in Sedona. It's a cool little community, and it's on the way to the Grand Canyon. We can take adetour."

As we are driving up to Sedona I suddenly remembered this church, and I got really excited and I said, "Hey, let me show you something really cool." I saw the church, drove into the parking lot and parked the car. I ran up the ramp, because I was so excited and I was almost all the way up to the church before the rest of the guys were barely even out of the car.

The moment I turned around and looked back at the car was like a "burning bush" experience for me. It was like this energy came over me and I actually heard a voice. I didn't know if it was my voice or not, but it was speaking in the first person and it said, "I am a scout." It didn't say "you" are a scout. It said "I" am a scout. I had this flood of energy and tears and this moment of clarity.

That's who I am. I knew what it meant, and that's what I've been doing ever since. I go out and explore, I have experiences, I have a great curiosity, and I follow that, and then I find something, I find some kind of spiritual truth or what I call a life principle. Then I bring it back and I offer it to people, and the way I offer it to them is I give them an experience. I might tell them the information, but it's better if they can have the experience of discovering it themselves. That's how I found it.

I went to school and was a good student. I was president of the honor society, class vice-president, a quarterback on the football team, I got into Stanford, got out of school, started six businesses, made money, did the thing I thought I was supposed to do: got married. I built my own house, did the American dream kind of thing, and with all that success I was actually miserable. I was killing myself. I had an ulcer, I was smoking two packs of cigarettes a day, drinking 12 cups of coffee a day, sleeping two hours a night. I had insomnia, but I was living the way I was taught to live. That's what I thought life was, you know, you go out and make money, build and business and collect things. And at some point I got so miserable that I just had to find something else. I got far enough off course that I eventually chose to wake up.

Then I took a Lifespring training. I had never done any of that Self-help, Human Potential stuff. I was a businessman who didn't do those things. I took it in another city. The guy who enrolled me had been asking me for nine months. Thank God he was persistent. I just kept telling him I was too busy and not interested.

Finally, the company sent the president to Eugene, Oregon and he invited me out to dinner. That flattered me, so I went. I had a nice time and then they offered me a scholarship to the training. I had no consideration of the cost, but just the fact that they offered it appealed to my ego again. So, I took the training in another town, I didn't want any of my business associates to know I was having difficulty inside (that wouldn't match the image I thought was expected of me). I had a pretty good experience.

I took a second training because my wife signed up for it. In that training I had unexplainable experiences. I experienced altered consciousness, I was seeing through solid things, I found a missing person, I found my heart again, I found energy I didn't know was there, it was amazing.

I started volunteering for the company and I helped create the first training they did in Eugene, Oregon. I helped put 60 people in that training in about a month (I don't know if that's what got their attention). I was assisting in a training and the trainer came back and handed me an envelope and said, "Here, use these and go down and talk to Handley."

I said, "Who's Handley?"

He said, "Handley is the president of Lifespring."

"Why would I want to talk to the president?"

"Talk to him about working for us," he said.

"Why would I want to work for you? I own six businesses. I don't have enough time for those and they are bigger than your business."

But in the back of my mind I was thinking, "this is a lot more valuable than what I'm doing. This is serving, this is peace, this is love, this is how to have a better life, this is everything they were trying to teach in church but didn't".

So I flew to San Francisco, and ended up working for Lifespring. Three months later, I closed my businesses, moved to Seattle, Washington and within a week I was in front of the room doing trainings, and I'm still doing it.

**If you could give advice to those who are still searching for their life's purpose, what would it be?**

It's simple, but not necessarily easy. It's the eternal advice that has been used for millenniums. Follow your heart. Be true to yourself. Follow your bliss. But that's not easy because it requires great courage. It requires risk. It requires what I call faith steps, stepping into the unknown with zero guarantees and no certainty. It only works if you do it 100%, completely detached, and all along you have to learn life lessons. Surrender, acceptance, detachment, cooperation, enthusiasm, letting go, focus, and all of that is learned in the process. At some point, with a little awareness, it shows up.

Everybody has a purpose and it's uniquely theirs. On a grander level every human has the same purpose, but it has a unique expression in each person. I say, "I am a scout." That's how I identify mine. Someone else may say, "I'm an explorer." Someone else may say, "I am a teacher." Someone else may say, "I'm here to learn loving relationships, I'm here to share something." But how do you find out what yours is?

It's not an analytical process, it's not a mental process at all. It's an awareness process. If you try to figure it out mentally or analyze it, you won't find it. It's uncovering it, where you just know it. The easiest way I know how to do it, or to lead someone to it, or to support them to it, is to have them make a list of all the times in their life when they experienced great joy, clarity, pure loving, wonderful enthusiasm, peak moments, memorable moments in their life that were genuinely positive. It could be a peace, it could be a loving, it could be a victory, enthusiasm, it could be when you were acknowledged, it could be the birth of a child, whatever is there. It could be an A you got in a class, a test you passed, a swim meet you won, a book you wrote, something where the experience inside was full of great joy and happiness and ease. I think everybody's got some of those.

Once they have their list, I can see the thread that runs through the list and that's their purpose. Then all you need to do is identify it in your own words. You need to do it quietly and just allow it to happen. If it doesn't show up really fast, then I'd put it aside and come back to it later. It isn't something you try to figure out and analyze and puzzle over, you just get it. There's a light inside of you and basically you're just connecting with it. And this is a mechanism through which people can connect with it again, to uncover it and bring it to life. Once you've got it, do your best to make your choices on purpose. I have found that when I do this my life really works well.

# Steve Keough

*"Find in your life that one thing that you love, then do it.*
*Look for an edge. What way can you do the thing you love to do,*
*in a way that others aren't doing it?"*

**Steve Keough is a well-established life coach and business coach. He's a masters certified coach, which means that he's logged in over 20,000 hours of coaching. Steve has an MBA in business, and has been a business coach for many successful companies.**

**Steve founded a company called Business Coach Alliance. This company has offices in Boston, Dallas, and Los Angeles and employs business coaches all over the country. Steve is also the executive director of SuccessTracs, a division of Peak Potentials. One of the seminars that Peak Potentials provides is called Life Directions. This seminar actually birthed the idea of SuccessTracs. Life Directions helps you to find your "Big Dream and your Desires" and SuccessTracs will assist you in following through and changing these dreams and desires into your reality.**

**Find out more about Steve Keough, SuccessTracs, and Peak Potentials at: www.PeakPotentials.com**

## Who do you think you are?

I think I am a naturally gifted leader with a lot of talents. I'm a believer. God has given me many gifts, particularly with regards to the human condition. I've been told I'm a great motivator and fairly innovative with my ideas. By and large, I'm a person who's in service to others and it comes across in the form of coaching, which I've been doing now for about fifteen years.

At the core, who I really am as a person is someone with three very important values. The first one is courage, and I'm not sure yet whether it's courage in a brave way or courage in a dumb way to do things in a way that others won't do. I haven't really figured that out just yet. The second is freedom. In other words, I have the ability to do what I would like to do, which is to make a difference to people. The third piece is to be independent. And while these two are very similar, the independence means that I'm able to do it my way. Not necessarily in an arrogant way, but in an effective way. I get to choose what I get to do and how I do it, so I can feel the 100% satisfaction of my efforts. And that pretty much sums up in my mind who I am.

## What event or series of events led you to your discovery?

One thing I noticed early on, somewhere between five and seven years old, is that I didn't want to be like my brothers and sisters or like my parents. I'm not exactly sure where that came from, but it has served me in my life, because most of the rest of my family are blue-collar workers. Not that there's anything wrong with that. Being a white-collar worker was just important to me, not so much for the white-collar work, but that I wouldn't be doing blue-collar work.

So there was something ingrained in me there, and about eight years ago I was running a business, and the business was doing fair at best. I wasn't sure what I should do next. I went on the Internet to see if there was something that could help me. I actually typed up the word "consultant" on a search, and what came back was a number of consultants. At the very top of the list was a company called ABC Consulting.

When I called the firm and talked to the principle owner, he said, "You don't need consulting you need business coaching." This was the first I ever heard of coaching. I hired him for a period of about a year-and-a-half with the thought of bolstering up a failing business. I ended up selling it for a million dollars.

I had no intention to sell it when I first talked to him. I was determined to just fix what was broken. Through the process of working with this coach, he expanded my horizons to even be able to think about selling it, and since then I've been financially free and able to do what I want to do, which plays into my two core values of freedom and independence.

After working with him, I thought, "Wow this business coaching is really cool." So after I sold the business, I went back to him and he trained me how to do it. I've been coaching people in one capacity or another ever since. As I did business coaching, more and more things kept coming up about psychology to the point where I was fascinated by it. It would just stop me in my tracks when I watched human behavior or saw shows where people were acting in certain ways, or read a text that talked about human behavior. I've been fascinated with human behaviors for the last ten or twelve years of my life.

**If you could give advice to those who are still searching for their life's purpose, what would it be?**

The first thing I would recommend is to create a vision for your life. Many times the words "mission" and "vision" get interchanged, so I'll define my definition of vision. For me a vision is a dream that never ends. In other words, even as we're speaking babies are being born left and right, so my job will never really end. There will always be people for me to help be the best human beings they can be.

Second, find something you're passionate about. Find in your life that one thing that you love. Then do it. Look for an edge. What way can you do the thing you love to do, in a way that others aren't doing it.

These two pieces will work in tandem for every female I've come in contact with, but for guys it seems to be mushy, so they need a little bit more guidance. For the guys, if finding your passion, vision, or edge doesn't work, I would look inside and ask yourself what the three core principles that drive your life are. Remember for me I said courage, freedom, and independence.

The three core values will not likely change in a person. From there they can go out into the world and ask, "What are the kinds of things I could do? What kind of career? What kind of vision or missions in my life fall into these three core principles? How do I align myself with those kinds of things, based on the fact that I know myself so well and that these things have to be in everything that I do?" After you find the answers to those questions, it's just about making some intelligent choices. That would be the greatest piece of advice I think I could give anybody at this time.

# Keith Leon

*"Everything you need to know is already within you.*
*You are the answer you have been searching for."*

**Entrepreneur, family man and full-time student of life, Keith Leon, is co-owner of Successful Communications, Inc., a consulting and training company. With his wife Maura, Keith has co-authored the best-selling book, *The Seven Steps to Successful Relationships.* Acclaimed by best-selling authors, John Gray and Terry Cole-Whittaker.**

**With eighteen years of personal growth and development under his belt, Keith is both skilled and passionate about helping others to discover their own passions and talents, and achieve their dreams. As a professional life coach and relationship coach, a developer and facilitator of transformational seminars, and a gifted professional singer and songwriter, Keith is a recognized expert at building relationships that work.**

**Keith is also a regular poster at www.HuffingtonPost.com and a member of the *Agape Spiritual Center*, the *Agape International Choir*, and the all-male singing group *The Feeling Tones*. He is happily married and the father of an eighteen-year-old son named Timar.**

**You can get helpful relationship tips, hear Keith sing, and even shop for unique gifts by visiting his website at: www.Relationship-Masters.com**

## Who do you think you are?

I choose to answer this question in a few different ways. I am a trainer, a singer, an author and a relationship expert on the surface. These are the skills that I have developed in order to express my true purpose, which is: I am a loving, trusting, worthy man, expressing what's in my heart and sharing my joy. I am also here to touch the lives of all those who I come in contact with in a positive way, and to pass on the things I have learned to those who are willing to listen.

## What event or series of events led to your discovery?

I spent many years searching for my answer to the questions: "Who am I?" and "What is my purpose?"  During those years I did an extensive outer search. I visited every church I could find, looking for somthing or someone to *show me the way* to the answers I was seeking. I wished that I could sit down in front of people that I considered to be successful and ask them questions about life purpose and their discovery. Years later, after receiving my own answers, I discovered that I often wondered about those who were still searching for theirs.

At one critical time during my inquiry I found myself a single father who had just ended a thirteen year marriage. I had no idea who I was. Because I had met my now ex-wife at such an early age, I only knew who I was with her. I found myself with a big empty hole and I had no idea how to fill it.

After spending much wasted time actively trying to figure it all out in my head, I decided that I needed to go within and listen for my answers. Fortunately, I had learned from a church how to quiet my mental noise, ask questions, and receive answers from my inner guidance. So, the pain I was feeling and the confidence I had gained in listening to my inner voice motivated me to spend the next year meditating on the question, "Who Am I?"

From that came the questions: "What is my purpose?" and "Why am I here?" I would ask these questions one at a time, and I refused to do anything else (except to go to work, or to deal with immediate family issues) until I received my answers. I spent each waking moment waiting in the silence for answers to just "drop in." After many months of eager anticipation, the answers started to present themselves to me!

1. "Who am I?" I asked. I heard, "You are a child of infinite spirit. You are pure energy. You are actually living proof that God exists. You are a wonderful way that joy, love, happiness, melody, truth and compassion are happening on this planet you call home."
2. "What is my purpose?" I asked. I heard,"To teach and inspire the masses to know that they are perfect just the way they are. The gifts you have been given are innate; it is your purpose to share them. Keep them not inside of you, but let these feelings, stories and sounds OUT, and those who are ready will hear what they need to hear and be moved by them."
3. "Why am I here?" I asked. I then heard, "You are here to touch the lives of each person you come in contact with. You are here to remember all that you have forgotten. You are here to *love and be loved*, and to learn to *just be* in each moment."

I asked my inner voice, "But how am I to teach and inspire the masses, as a singer and songwriter?" "Yes." the voice said. "What about as an author, a teacher or as a preacher?" Again, I heard, "Yes." "Wait, which one? I asked." All I heard was silence. "Which one," I asked again and again. There was still no answer to my question. I soon came to the realization that the answer to this question would be revealed either *to me* or *through me* at another other time. I had received the answers I needed to hear regarding my purpose already. This came with grace. It wasn't until I started trying to figure out the *how* that my clarity started to cloud up on me. I decided not to focus on the *how*, but to allow my inner knowing or instincts to point me in the right direction.

I soon decided to start dating again, and consciously using the Law of Attraction, I found my perfect mate. She shared with me this same sense of life purpose, and out of that came our unified vision to make a difference in the world in the field of relationships. We both agreed that until someone becomes completely okay within themselves, there is no room to add someone else into their life. Until one is able to love themselves full out, they will end up using their relationships to fill that empty unloved space within them.

It is our belief that once we tap into the love inside of us, and become comfortable in our own skin, *then* the fun of finding a life mate begins. I would suggest that this is the perfect time to go within and let inner guidance reveal your next steps toward creating your perfect relationship. We're talking about the type of relationship that *adds* to your already great life. One that is built on a foundation of, *we are both good enough just the way we are, so there's nothing for me to change or fix about you.*

**If you could give advice to those who are still searching for their answers to these questions, what would it be?**

There is no one who can answer these questions for you better than your inner guidance system. I've heard this inner guidance system called by many different names. I've heard it called God, instinct, the still small voice, Holy Ghost and many other names. You can call it what ever you like, I just know it's there for me when I am willing to sit and listen.

Sometimes people ask me how is it that I hear voices in my head, and I say, "it's easier than you think." Let me explain:

Start by sitting down, turn off the noise of the world and your random passing thoughts, and just listen. Listen to your breath at first, until you hear only your breath. If thoughts come in, let them pass through as quickly as they come and go back to your breath. Once you get to where all you hear is your breath, you work on turning the sound of your breath off too. There is a lot revealed in the space between two breaths when you are tuned in and listening.

Sometimes this *voice* shows up as an inner knowing. You just all of a sudden become crystal clear on something you were wondering about before. You may hear a voice literally. I think the bottom line is to know and remember that you have every answer to every question within you. The question really is, are you willing to slow it down enough to listen?

I think mentors are great. I've used them myself, but only as a sounding board. I take what they say and I go to my "inner mentor" to see if it agrees. I choose *external* mentors for specific purposes. I have mentors for guidance about reaching financial goals. I have a handful who guide me spiritually. The mentors I trust the most and who have given me the most support are those mentors who lovingly and unceasingly remind me that there is no more powerful guidance than that which comes through my *inner* guidance.

We as human beings seek incessantly, thinking that there is so much we need to learn. Most of us have allowed ourselves to become *human doings*, not *human beings*! Plus, with all the external noise and activity in our lives, it's easy to forget how to use our innate ability to tune in to the guidance available through our thoughts and feelings. Until we stop, slow down, turn off the television set, the stereo, the video games, or the opinions of our friends, co-workers or mates, we're unable to hear the wisdom that is within each of us. It is ALL inside of you. I urge you to consider that perhaps we already know everything and just need to stop and listen, in order to remember.

Everything you need to know is already within you. *You* are the answer you have been searching for. Stop, ask and listen. Stop, ask and listen. Then, stop, ask and listen again. And why not start this process *right now*?

*Upon the day that I was born, I opened up my mouth*

*To joyfully express what my existence was about.*

*I raised my arms, I clapped my hands, I tilted back my head,*

*I blinked my eyes, I looked around, and this is what I said:*

*"Hello my little planet Earth, I've come to bring you love*

*Which — for your information — I've got an abundance of.*

*My question, though, is when and where and which way do I bring it?*

*Do I speak it, write it, guide you through it, dance or sing it?"*

*And when I asked this question, Spirit lovingly replied,*

*"You'll know just how to share it when you know just what's inside."*

*"I do know," I responded, "it's my love and I've got tons!"*

*"Then bring it forth, sweet child, and don't forget to have some fun!"*

*So on that day that I was born, I opened up my heart*

*And learned my first great lesson: How to get there is to start.*

Written by: Maura Leon